May 22, 1996

For Mom —
Here's to good books
and good-looking men!

Much love,
Rebecca

CARY GRANT

Other books by Warren G. Harris

GABLE & LOMBARD

THE OTHER MARILYN:
A BIOGRAPHY OF MARILYN MILLER

CARY GRANT

A Touch of Elegance

WARREN G. HARRIS

Doubleday
NEW YORK
1987

C 1

Library of Congress Cataloging in Publication Data
Harris, Warren G.
Cary Grant a touch of elegance.
Filmography: p. 273.
Includes index.
1. Grant, Cary, 1904–1986. 2. Moving-picture
actors and actresses—United States—Biography.
I. Title.
PN2287.G675H37   1987   791.43′028′0924 [B] 87-8901
ISBN 0-385-24285-9

For Georgina Hale,
"Too Marvelous for Words"

Contents

CARY GRANT

Prologue

Even Cary Grant had to die sometime, but in Davenport, Iowa? In Beverly Hills, New York or London maybe, but not in a remote Mississippi River town in the corn belt of America.

The white-haired octogenarian arrived in Davenport with his thirty-six-year-old wife, Barbara, on November 28, 1986, to give a stage presentation billed as *A Conversation with Cary Grant*, in conjunction with the city's "Festival of Trees" celebration. The long retired actor had been traveling around the country making appearances for charitable causes on and off since 1983.

The day after checking into the Blackhawk Hotel, the Grants were taken on a morning tour of Davenport's main points of interest, including the extensive Grant Wood collection at the municipal art gallery and the historic campus of Palmer College of Chiropractic, which has turned out the majority of chiropractors in the United States. The couple's guide, local businessman Doug Miller, said later that Grant was in "wonderful spirits."

In the afternoon, Grant and his wife went to the Adler Theatre to arrange the technical details of that evening's program: film clips from the star's movies, followed by a question-and-answer session with the audience. During the run-through, event coordinator Lois Jecklin chatted briefly with the visitor from Hollywood.

"I asked him why a man as wealthy as he kept doing one-man

shows in towns like Davenport," Jecklin recalled. "Of course, I was grateful he'd accepted the invitation. Still, I was curious about his reason. He told me, 'I want my wife to see this country. I want Barbara to get to know every fascinating corner of the United States. Touring with her at my side is the best way I can think of managing that.' "

Grant said that he generally needed between two and a half to three hours to respond to all of the audience's questions. "It must have been a strain," Jecklin said. "He looked chipper and in good spirits when he arrived in Davenport the evening before. But he could not make it through the rehearsal.

"He took great care with every detail, telling the projectionist exactly when to come in with movie clips and checking that microphones would be placed throughout the audience exactly where he wanted. It got to be too much, and he sank into a chair."

Grant complained that he wasn't feeling well. Leaning on his wife for support, he walked offstage and into a dressing room. Asked if he wanted a doctor, he said no.

Grant stayed in his dressing room for an hour, hoping that he would feel well enough to go on with the show. But instead he grew worse and was taken back to his suite at the Blackhawk Hotel. At seven o'clock, Barbara Grant called the theatre and said that her husband was too ill to appear. The performance was canceled.

According to Doug Miller, who accompanied the couple to the hotel, Grant kept refusing medical treatment. Finally, Miller took it upon himself to call in his own doctor, Duane Manlove.

"I got there about eight o'clock," Dr. Manlove said. "Grant was weak, complaining of dizziness and a headache, and had been vomiting. His wife and Doug weren't sure what was wrong with him, but they were pale with worry. I examined him, asked him about his health history and called for a cardiologist—Dr. James Gilson. I realized he was having a stroke. Grant's blood pressure was extremely high—my reading was 210 over 130."

Neither Dr. Manlove nor Barbara Grant could convince Grant to go to the hospital. "He was insisting that the hospital was a waste of time," Manlove said.

"By about eight-fifteen he was beginning to have a lot of pain, but he was still coherent. He was talking about going back to Los Angeles and maybe seeing a doctor there. But I knew that was impossible.

"He didn't have that much time left to live. The stroke was getting worse. In only fifteen minutes he had deteriorated rapidly. It was terrible watching him die and not being able to help. But he wouldn't let us."

Around eight forty-five, the cardiologist, Dr. Gilson, arrived and also tried to persuade Grant to go to the hospital. But Grant told him: "Leave me alone. I don't need doctors. I just need rest."

Finally, the doctors took matters into their own hands and called for an ambulance. A few minutes later, a paramedic team from St. Luke's Hospital arrived.

"We found Cary Grant lying on a bed—without shoes, wearing slacks, a shirt and jacket," said paramedic Bart Lund. "He was conscious, and despite his age hardly looked as though he was ill. He told us: 'I'm feeling a little pain in the chest. But I don't think it's anything. I don't want to make a big fuss.' Then he reached for his wife's hand. She let a smile mask her concern as she said, 'It's going to be all right.' "

Barbara Grant leaned over and kissed her husband gently on the face as the paramedics followed their standing orders and started hooking up life-support equipment.

"Grant was put on a heart monitor, given intravenous medication and administered oxygen," Bart Lund said. "Once or twice during this operation, he reached out for his wife's hand and squeezed it gently. He even briefly held the hands of my partner and myself, to let us know he was aware of what was going on and the procedures that were being taken."

The paramedics lifted Grant onto a mobile stretcher and took him downstairs to the ambulance via the hotel's service elevator. En route to the hospital, "Grant kept calling his wife's name: 'Barbara . . . Barbara . . .' and held out his hand for her," Bart Lund recalled. "As we turned into the driveway leading to the hospital's emergency room, the ambulance went over a slight bump. Grant turned to me and said, 'That was a little rocky. It felt funny.' "

The ambulance pulled into St. Luke's emergency bay around nine-fifteen. "As we took Grant out," Lund said, "he murmured to his wife, 'I love you, Barbara . . . don't worry.' And they squeezed hands."

The hospital staff took over from there and rushed Grant to

the intensive care unit. A CAT scan revealed that he'd suffered a massive stroke. At 11:22 P.M., Cary Grant was pronounced dead.

According to one of the nurses: "Barbara Grant was in a waiting room adjacent to intensive care. When the doctors came out and told her, she turned white and tears began falling from her eyes. She was visibly trembling. But then she pulled herself together and went to make the necessary phone calls."

Practically every obituary written about Cary Grant described him as handsome, dapper, debonair, charming, jaunty, ageless, dashing, blithe, witty, stylish and incomparable. But in trying to separate the real Cary Grant from the romantic illusion created by his seventy-two movie roles, one discovers a very different man, a sensitive and vulnerable person who spent the majority of his eighty-two years searching for love and fulfillment. Whether by chance or by fate, the search started and ended in two river cities, the other being 4,500 miles from Davenport, Iowa on the banks of the Avon in his native England.

1

Bristol Boy

Everyone called him Archie, but he was christened in the Anglican faith as Archibald Alexander Leach. He was born on January 18, 1904, in Bristol, England, at that time the seventh-largest city and third-ranking seaport in the kingdom. Who would have dreamed that the only surviving child of impoverished parents would grow up to become Bristol's most famous native son or its leading export next to cream sherry?

It was the third year of thirteen that comprised England's Edwardian Age, the golden lull before the maelstrom of 1914. With lots of money in circulation, it was a period of extravagance and gluttony for those who could afford it. Unhappily, at least a third of the British population couldn't. In the words of a popular music hall song of the time:

> The rich get richer every day;
> Monopolizing all life's joys.
> While the poor the piper have to pay.
> French cooks and tailors for the great,
> For the small, hard fare and oft no shoes,
> And hundreds forced to emigrate.

Archie's parents, Elias and Elsie Leach, weren't destitute, but they could barely manage on Elias's meager earnings as a presser at Todd's Clothing Factory. They resided about two miles from the city center in a rented two-story house that looked identical to the ones attached to it on either side. Built of stone and heated solely by a few small fireplaces, it was freezing in winter and bone-chillingly damp the rest of the time.

Except for cases of serious illness, hospitals were places to be avoided because of all the germs in the air, or so the public thought in that unenlightened era. Like most children, Archie Leach was delivered at home in his parents' bedroom. The uncomplicated birth caused more than the usual rejoicing. Several years earlier, the couple's only other child, also a boy, had died of convulsions at the age of two months.

Such incidents were all too common. Disease and ill health accounted for one of England's worst problems and made no class distinctions. One out of every four infants died before reaching his or her first birthday.

But the harsh reality gave no comfort to Elsie Leach. She had nursed the sick baby until she collapsed from exhaustion and was put to bed. Had she not been asleep in another room when her son reached his final crisis, she could have saved his life, or so she believed. Her sense of guilt haunted her for the rest of her life.

Delicately built, with black hair and olive skin, the former Elsie Kingdon was in her early twenties when Archie was born. As the only girl among five children, she grew up to be spoiled and rather domineering. She tended to be emotionally unstable and was probably manic-depressive, although the term wasn't widely used then.

When her four brothers emigrated to Canada, Elsie stayed behind to care for their elderly parents. Her situation as the equivalent of an unpaid servant quickly stirred a longing to be off on her own. Marriage was one of the few escape routes for a "respectable" single woman who didn't have the inclination or education to become a teacher, nurse or governess. Working in a factory, shop or office was considered too undignified for a girl of the lower middle class.

Since Elias Leach was an ordinary laborer, he seemed an odd choice for Elsie's husband. Of course, there might not have been any other candidates at the time, but a more likely explanation is that she truly loved him. He was a real ladies' man, tall and handsome, with a luxuriant mustache and a captivating sense of humor. All that Elias Leach seemed to need to become successful was a determined wife behind him. Elsie Leach believed that she could easily fill that role.

But it didn't turn out that way after they were married. Rather stolid in his outlook, Elias resented Elsie's constant nagging that he should try to better himself. She also objected to his heavy drinking. Bristol, being the center of the wine trade, had more than its share of bars and pubs. Elias stopped off at too many in his travels between home and factory.

The death of the couple's first child added to the dissension. Elsie became depressed and withdrawn. Finally, the family doctor advised the couple to have another baby to compensate for their loss.

Archie Leach would grow up to be tall and handsome like his father, and with his mother's swarthy coloring and cleft chin. The bonny-faced, healthy baby restored Elsie's zest for living and for a while, peace and harmony reigned in the Leach household.

Elsie kept Archie in long curls and baby dresses much longer than other children. Perhaps she was compensating for being deprived of the experience of raising her firstborn, but for a time, Archie wasn't sure whether he was a boy or a girl. Confusion over his sexual identity still was a problem when he entered LSD therapy more than half a century later.

It didn't take long for Archie to become aware that his mother and father were miserable together. Since a growing child had to be fed and clothed, the lack of sufficient money became a constant cause of quarreling between his parents. Elias was no match for Elsie's sharper tongue. After a while, he gave up trying to defend himself. He started drinking heavily again, usually in the company of women who were more convivial than his wife.

Cary Grant's fabled miserliness undoubtedly originated during that early period of his life. The most noticeable economic realities of his experience were his father's inability to earn a decent living and his mother's unwillingness to accept that fact. Little Archie learned that money is very important. It would be absolutely unthinkable to waste it or spend it foolishly. Archie Leach and Cary Grant never did.

Elsie Leach became determined to make sure that her son didn't end up like his father. She enrolled him in school when he was four and a half years old, although five was the usual age for

admission. Convinced that Archie was smarter than average, she
made the headmaster believe it as well.

Bishop Road Junior School just happened to have a few empty
places, so Archie started classes immediately. Timid and frightened at first, he proved adept at the alphabet, drawing and clay
modeling. But he failed miserably at arithmetic and was too shy
even to talk to the little girl with whom he shared a desk.

Somehow or other, Elsie Leach also managed to save enough
money to send Archie for piano lessons. She wanted him to be a
cultured young gentleman. He wore a crisp linen Eton collar on
weekends and a celluloid one on school days. He learned to speak
only when spoken to, to keep himself clean at all times and *never* to
ask his parents for money.

In return for helping his mother with the shopping, fetching
coal for the fires and emptying the waste bins, Archie received a
weekly allowance of sixpence. A fine of tuppence was deducted for
serious breaches of etiquette like spilling food on the fancy table-
cloth that was reserved for Sunday dinner and special occasions.

In 1911, when Archie was seven years old, war broke out
between Italy and Turkey. While England was not directly involved, a jittery government accelerated its armament activities. As
a consequence, Elias got a higher-paying job in Southampton,
eighty miles from Bristol, in a factory that made army uniforms.
Since the position seemed temporary, it was decided that his family
would not accompany him.

Both of Archie's parents welcomed the separation. For his
father, it meant being free to pursue the ladies with less chance of
getting caught. For Elsie Leach, it brought a sense of financial
security for the first time since her marriage. She and Archie
moved to a larger house in a better district of Bristol. To offset the
increase in rent, she sublet rooms to two nieces who had just
started working as secretaries, a new profession for women.

During a school holiday, Elsie sent Archie to visit his father in
Southampton, a rare treat for the boy because traveling by train
was still a luxury for all but the well off. Archie found Elias Leach
greatly altered, not only happier and younger in spirit, but also
foppishly attired, which the boy thought would greatly upset his
ultraconservative mother.

Archie didn't know that the reason for his father's metamorphosis was that he'd fallen deeply in love with another woman. Elias Leach kept that part of his life secret from his son.

After six months, Elias Leach lost the Southampton job and had to return to Bristol. Even on a larger salary, he couldn't afford to maintain two residences, let alone a second family, which his clandestine love affair was threatening to become. Luckily, with so many people going into war-related industries, his former presser's job in Bristol was still vacant.

Although they were back living under the same roof again, Archie's parents were just as miserable as before. If Elias Leach came home at all, it was mainly to eat and sleep. He would retire right after the evening meal to avoid confrontations with his wife. Archie saw what was happening, but felt helpless to do anything about the situation.

Archie was growing fast, but it wasn't until he was nine that he got his first pair of long pants. Elsie made them herself, but Archie was ashamed to be seen wearing them. Sewn from the cheapest grade of material, they fitted improperly and didn't compare to the store-bought pants worn by his friends.

"The long hours of my mother's labor and love went unappreciated," Cary Grant remembered. "How sad that we can't know what we know until we know it. I wonder if the appearance of my name on so many best-dressed lists is a consequence of the boyish shame from wearing those handmade flannel trousers."

Also in his ninth year, Archie Leach fell in love for the first time, with the pleasingly plump daughter of the local butcher. No words ever passed between them, but Archie would walk blocks out of his way just to stroll past her house and watch her playing with her dolls in the front garden. One day, as Archie turned around for one last glance at her, he crashed into a lamp post and nearly cracked his skull. Staggering to the curbside to recover from the shock, he was sure that he'd made a total fool of himself in his beloved's eyes. He could never get up enough courage to pass that way again.

At school, Archie received only average grades but was quite popular with his classmates. Whenever they played football, he was the only one who volunteered for goalkeeper, the most hazardous and punishing of all the positions. But for Archie, a well-saved goal was worth a few bruises and skinned knees.

"I learned the deep satisfaction derived from receiving the

adulation of my fellow little man," Cary Grant said. "Perhaps it began the process that resulted in my search for it ever afterwards."

At his mother's insistence, Archie was studying for a scholarship examination that could win him entry to a better school. Homework occupied much of his spare time, but he continued taking piano lessons as well. Although he was left-handed, he had difficulty playing the bass notes, and he wasn't helped any by an irascible teacher who rapped him across the knuckles with a ruler whenever he made a mistake.

Even Elsie had to admit that her son would never become a concert virtuoso, but she envisaged plenty of other opportunities for him. Why in Bristol alone, there were new "picture palaces" opening all the time, each employing a pianist and sometimes a full orchestra to play along with the films.

Archie was just a few years younger than the newly emerging motion picture industry. Developing from storefront "penny gaffs," the British equivalent of the American nickelodeons, England's first authentic cinema was built in 1901. It was the cheapest and most accessible form of entertainment yet devised. For the lower classes especially, it acted like a narcotic, providing an instant if only temporary release from their dreary lives. Archie Leach became addicted at an early age, probably six or seven judging from his later memories of that period.

Every Saturday, Archie and friends flocked to the little neighborhood cinema and plunked down tuppence each for a raucous afternoon free from parental supervision, which was an attraction in itself. The noisy whistling, cheering and hissing, punctuated by outbursts of hand-to-hand combat over the relative merits of certain actors and actresses, was the highpoint of Archie's week. His particular favorites were Chester Conklin, Ford Sterling, Fatty Arbuckle, Mack Swain, John Bunny, Flora Finch, "Bronco Billy" Anderson, Mabel Normand and, somewhat later, Charlie Chaplin.

Archie's parents sometimes took him to one of the bigger cinemas, but it was typical of their troubled relationship that it was always separately, never as a family. Elsie Leach preferred the ritzy, perfumed atmosphere of the Claire Street Picture House, where tea and dainty refreshments were served during the intermissions and the main attraction was usually a heart-stirring romance or tear-jerking melodrama.

Elias Leach took Archie to the larger and cheaper Metropole, where men were permitted to smoke and women usually stayed away. Despite the bad ventilation, hard seats and bare floors, the theatre was Archie's favorite, partly because those visits were just about the only times when he felt any real intimacy with his father. Although Elias never had much money to spend, he always insisted on stopping on the way to buy Archie a piece of fruit or some peppermint drops. A birthday or exceptionally good behavior could mean a piece of Bristol-made chocolate, reputed to be the best in the world.

With feature-length films still a novelty, a typical bill at the Metropole consisted of several action thrillers of one or two reels each. Since they were silent, it didn't matter that some were produced in Europe rather than England or America. Archie and his father loved them all, especially a brand-new form known as serials. In the week between episodes, Archie found it hard to concentrate on his homework while he tried to figure out how the hero or heroine would escape from their latest seemingly hopeless predicament.

Coming home from school one day, Archie tumbled into a real-life situation that would have more twists and turns than anything shown at the Metropole. It might have been titled "What Happened to Elsie Leach?" His mother was gone—vanished without a trace.

2

Stagestruck

Cary Grant never made any public disclosures about his mother's disappearance until 1959, when he was well advanced in LSD therapy. Clearly, it was only then, some forty-five years later, that he could come to terms with what was probably the most traumatic experience of his life.

Archie Leach was ten years old when it happened. The outbreak of World War I was imminent, and the fear and uncertainty connected with it undoubtedly made the situation worse. In any case, Elsie Leach was nowhere to be found when her son returned home from school that day. His cousins the lodgers, who were the only ones in the house at the time, told Archie that his mother had gone to a seaside resort.

"It seemed rather unusual, but I accepted it as one of those peculiarly unaccountable things that grown-ups are apt to do," Cary Grant recalled. "However, the weeks went by and when Mother did not return, it gradually dawned on me that perhaps she was not coming back at all. My father seemed to be in correspondence with her, and always told me that she sent her love, which, of course, I always asked to have returned.

"There was a void in my life, a sadness of spirit that affected each daily activity with which I occupied myself in order to overcome it. But there was no further explanation of Mother's absence, and I gradually got accustomed to the fact that she was not home each time I came home—nor, it transpired, was she expected to come home."

Decades passed before Cary Grant discovered that his mother had been only a few miles away in Fishponds, a rustic district at the end of one of Bristol's main tramlines. She was a patient in the rather cruelly named County Home for Mental Defectives. But just why Elsie Leach landed in the local lunatic asylum may never be explained until the next century. British law prohibits the unsealing of psychiatric case records until a hundred years after the patient's death.

According to Cary Grant, his mother had had a nervous breakdown, caused, he believed, by marital disharmony and suppressed grief over her firstborn's tragic death more than a decade earlier. "It was her way of rejecting society and rejecting my father," Grant said.

While that explanation is plausible, a second might be that Elsie Leach hadn't had a nervous breakdown at all. She may have been put out of the way because she was becoming too much of a nuisance in her husband's life, and in his affair with another woman.

Basic to whichever theory one wants to believe is a fact that Cary Grant tried to conceal all his life; namely, that at the time of Elsie's disappearance, Elias Leach had a mistress and they were expecting a child. In view of all the unhappiness that Elsie Leach already had experienced in her marriage, it is conceivable that the shock of her husband's indiscretion would be jolting enough to push her over the edge into madness or at least a nervous breakdown.

But if that is what occurred, how did it happen without Archie noticing? Surely an alert, intelligent ten-year-old would have detected such a dramatic personality change coming over the person nearest and dearest to him. That Archie was stunned and completely baffled by Elsie's disappearance supports the notion that she was institutionalized for a different reason. Furthermore, one of her relatives later revealed that she wrote beautifully composed and coherent letters begging to be released, which would hardly have been possible for an insane woman to do.

Although it now seems like a situation out of a Gothic novel, the mental institutions of that time were often used as dumping grounds for people who didn't belong there. So little was known about psychological illnesses, their diagnosis and treatment that not only was it fairly easy to get people committed, but it also almost guaranteed that they would spend the rest of their lives there. The traditional means of controlling rebellious or troublesome patients in those basically custodial institutions were like those used in prisons—solitary confinement and/or mechanical restraint.

While we can only speculate on the reasons for Elsie Leach's confinement, one thing is certain: it lasted for more than twenty years. That her release came as a result of Elias Leach's death is getting ahead of the story, but it is important to know because it again suggests that her husband might well have been her jailer. Divorce was both socially unacceptable and financially impossible. But while Elsie was locked away, Elias Leach was free to pursue a common-law marriage with his mistress and their baby son.

Meanwhile, what was to become of Archie Leach? There was no way that he could understand or be compensated for his mother's disappearance. In a sense, it was even worse than if she had died, because there was not only a feeling of loss but also of mystery and frustration. Archie thought his mother had abandoned him without just cause, and his hostility toward her would eventually be directed at all women.

Cary Grant later cited Elsie's disappearance as one of the reasons for his bad marriage record. "I was making the mistake of thinking that each of my wives was my mother, that there would never be a replacement once she left," he said. "I had even found myself being attracted to people who looked like my mother—she had olive skin, for instance. Of course, at the same time I was getting a person with her emotional makeup, too, and I didn't need that."

Since Archie wasn't supposed to know about Elias Leach's other family, he couldn't very well be taken to live with them. Instead, he and his father moved in with Elias's mother, who had a house nearer to town. That saved Elias an extra expense in his double life and also provided someone to look after Archie while his father was occupied elsewhere, which was most of the time. But Grandmother Leach had other responsibilities as well, so more often than not Archie was left to fend for himself.

Archie was studying harder than ever for the scholarship exam that Elsie Leach had urged upon him. If he believed that winning it might help to bring his mother back, he was mistaken. But he did pass the test and was accepted to Fairfield Secondary School, starting in September 1915.

Awarded what was known as a "free place," Archie still had to pay for his books, uniforms and other necessities. Any dreams that he had of going on to the university quickly faded. He doubted that he'd be able to get through Fairfield on the little money that his father gave him.

It's hard to imagine even a young Cary Grant as "scruffy" or "poorly dressed," but that's how many of his former Fairfield classmates and teachers remembered Archie Leach. Undoubtedly, it was the lack of both money and a mother's tender loving care that were responsible for his tattered clothes and ink-smudged face and hands.

In his first winter at Fairfield, it did nothing for Archie's general appearance when he slipped and fell on the ice-covered playground, losing a front tooth. Nature gradually narrowed the gaping space, however, and only the most observant moviegoers ever noticed that Cary Grant had only one front tooth where there should have been two.

Unconsciously seeking the attention he didn't get at home, Archie started to acquire a reputation as a prankster and "naughty boy." With that new gap in his front teeth, he learned to squirt a stream of water five or six feet, usually at his fellow students, who were not amused. A crack marksman with a slingshot as well, he could create pandemonium in a class by projecting a few paper pellets at carefully chosen targets.

Archie had joined the Boy Scouts, which, in those wartime years, also made him a Junior Air Warden. Since Bristol was a main seaport, it was under constant threat of a German plane or zeppelin attack. In the event of a raid, Archie was supposed to extinguish all the gas-lit street lamps in his designated territory. He dutifully kept his uniform ready in a chair next to the bed at night, but the emergency never came. In the second World War, however, Bristol was not so lucky, and suffered some of the most devastating bombings in all of England.

At the end of his first year of secondary school, when Archie was twelve, he volunteered for summer work wherever his Boy Scout training could be used for the war effort. It was 1916. The United States had not yet entered the war and British youths of sixteen were being drafted into the country's rapidly dwindling forces.

Archie's patriotism was exceeded only by his need to get away from Bristol for a while. "I was so often alone and unhappy at home that I welcomed any occupation that promised activity," Cary Grant said.

He was assigned to working as a messenger and general helper on the military docks at Southampton, which were heavily guarded and sealed off from public access. For two months, he watched thousands of boys not much older than himself sail away into the night toward France. Some had already lost an arm or leg in combat but were going back for a second time. Some would be drowned when their ships were sunk before ever reaching the battlefront.

"If I was on gangplank duty, I sadly noted the quick moment of apprehension cross each face, the first premonition of danger, as I issued every soldier a life belt and accompanied it with a few cheerful words of instruction to hide my feelings," Grant remembered.

Apart from his regular duties, Archie also ran errands and mailed letters for the soldiers. It was a point of honor among the Scouts not to take cash gratuities, but if a soldier offered a military button or badge, Archie would accept and display it proudly on his belt along with similar trophies. Sometimes he received free tea and cakes in the canteen, a treat for a poor boy at any time but especially welcome when civilian food supplies were strictly rationed.

Although it was tinged with tragedy, that exciting summer in Southampton filled Archie with wanderlust. Back in Bristol, he began to haunt the waterfront, where schooners and steamships sailed right up the Avon River into the center of the city. On weekends, Archie sat for hours watching the ships come and go, imagining himself another Jim Hawkins, whose fictional voyage to Treasure Island had also started in Bristol.

Archie's fantasies didn't help his concentration at school, especially in mathematics and Latin, which he never liked anyway. His favorite subjects were geography, history, art and science. Surprisingly, it was the latter that started Archie Leach toward a show business career.

Fascinated by electricity and the way it was revolutionizing everyday life, Archie became friendly with an electrician who assisted with experiments in the science lab. A jovial man with six children of his own, he responded paternally to Archie's eagerness to learn and invited him to inspect a new switchboard system he'd installed at the Hippodrome, Bristol's top vaudeville theatre.

"The Saturday matinee was in full swing when I arrived backstage," Cary Grant remembered. "I suddenly found my inarticulate self in a dazzling land of smiling, jostling people wearing and not wearing all sorts of costumes and doing all sorts of clever things. And that's when I *knew!* What other life could there *be* but that of an actor? They happily traveled and toured. They were classless, cheerful and carefree. They gaily laughed, lived and loved."

But if it was to be an actor's life, how was the lanky thirteen-year-old supposed to begin? He hadn't a clue, so he started hanging around the Hippodrome and the rival Empire at every opportunity. Soon he made enough friends to be permitted to assist the technicians who worked the limelights from tiny, rather precarious perches high up at each side of the stage.

Although he wasn't getting paid, Archie was deliriously happy in his newly discovered world of make-believe. People liked him, he had a place to go, and he saw all the shows for nothing. Then he had to go and spoil it all by disrupting a performance of The Great Devant, the most popular magician of the day.

While helping an electrician, Archie became enraptured by one of Devant's spectacular tricks and carelessly allowed the spotlight to wander to parts of the stage better left in darkness. Suddenly there was a blinding flash as the beam reflected off mirrors that were supposed to be hidden from the audience's perception. Needless to say, David Devant appeared less than great that night, and Archie Leach was no longer welcome at the Empire's stage door.

Fortunately there was still the Hippodrome. Running errands and carrying messages, Archie tried to get to know everyone and anyone who'd tolerate his eager inquisitiveness. He was starting to spout the actor's vernacular: "Don't milk your bows," "Pick up your cue," "Never walk on the other fellow's lines." "Playing to the gods" meant projecting to the last rows of the highest balcony. "At liberty" was an upbeat euphemism for unemployed.

But Archie's expanded vocabulary still left him a long way

from becoming a performer. After all, what sort of talent did he have to offer? He could recite a few poems that every schoolboy knew, mimic his father bellowing a music-hall ditty and play the piano loudly but not well. It could never be said that Archie Leach was "star material." But he did have two qualities that can be just as important as talent or expertise—a boundless determination to succeed and a shrewd, analytical mind.

How else could Archie have grasped the potential in a tidbit of backstage gossip about a troupe of knockabout comedians that was run by a man named Bob Pender? As he was constantly losing his young performers to the wartime draft, Pender was reported to be in desperate need of replacements. Archie decided to apply, figuring that with the manpower shortage, Pender couldn't afford to be too particular.

The fact that he was only thirteen, a year too young to get a work permit, didn't concern Archie, who was tall and mature-looking for his age. When he wrote to Bob Pender, he sent a photograph and neglected to mention how old he was. The letter itself, supposedly written by Elias Leach, was a forgery. Archie had struggled with it for hours, imitating his father's handwriting and signature.

Although it seemed like an eternity to a deceitful boy who had to monitor every mail delivery to make sure that Pender's reply didn't reach his father, the letter came in a matter of days. Elias Leach was instructed to send his promising-looking son to be interviewed in Norwich, where the troupe was appearing. Luckily, Pender removed the one obstacle to Archie's trip by enclosing the much needed train fare.

Archie had never felt such inner turmoil. In his room that night, he neither slept nor rested, finally sneaking out of the house in the middle of the night and walking through miles of deserted streets to the station to catch an early-morning train. He tried to avoid thinking about what would happen when his father and the school authorities discovered that he was missing.

When Archie arrived at the theatre in Norwich, the Pender troupe was rehearsing. Pender, a stocky, robust man in his early forties, had had an illustrious past as a clown in spectacles at London's Drury Lane Theatre. Margaret Pender, his wife and co-director, was former ballet mistress at the Folies Bergère in Paris.

Archie took a liking to them immediately, although he suspected that they were on to his game.

After Archie had passed various gymnastic tests, the Penders hired him as an apprentice, subject to his father's approval. He was given a simple handwritten contract stipulating that he would receive meals and lodging plus ten shillings a week pocket money. Archie could hardly believe it. To become a performer, he would have paid *them*.

Accommodation was found for Archie in the same theatrical boardinghouse where the Penders and the rest of the troupe were staying. The next morning, on the bare theatre stage, he began lessons in tumbling and acrobatic dances.

As the novice in a highly trained group of young athletes, Archie felt—and looked—clumsy and inept. "My progress suffered from the disparity," Cary Grant said. "But slowly and often too painfully, I showed improvement and began to feel the pride and confidence born of accomplishment. I was resigned to the fact that it would be some time before I was considered proficient enough to actually join the others in front of an audience."

Inevitably, Archie received a rude awakening from his dream. Ten days later, when the troupe had moved on to Ipswich, Elias Leach turned up to claim his runaway son. The Penders had written to him to verify Archie's vow that he had his parents' consent.

Pleased with Archie's progress, Bob Pender wanted to keep him in the troupe, but Elias Leach refused. First of all, the law had to be considered: with or without his father's permission, Archie was too young to work. Second, Elias Leach felt the boy should complete his education. Leach disapproved of a show-business career, and he wanted Archie to go into the Civil Service, as the majority of Fairfield School graduates did.

Archie returned to Bristol without even once performing in public, a fact that he carefully concealed from his classmates. For several weeks, he kept them goggle-eyed and open-mouthed as he demonstrated cartwheels, handsprings and nip-ups and told exaggerated tales of life on the wicked stage.

As soon as his captive audience lost interest in the "star" in their midst, Archie's high spirits evaporated. Remembering the excitement of learning new skills and making new friends, plus the wonderful feeling of being part of a family again caused him to be more miserable and lonely than he had ever been before.

It didn't take him long to figure out a solution to his dilemma. As Archie saw it, there were two main obstacles to overcome before he could rejoin the Pender troupe—his age and his father's insistence that he finish his schooling. In the first case, time and patience were all that Archie needed. He would be fourteen, the legal working age, on his next birthday in January 1918.

Changing Elias Leach's attitude would be more difficult, but Archie started by trying to get himself thrown out of Fairfield Secondary School.

"Although I regret the recollection, I did my unlevel best to flunk at everything," Cary Grant said. With the exception of gym classes, which kept him in shape for acrobatics, he confessed to "exasperating every professor who had the misfortune to come into contact with me."

The offense that finally brought deliverance was a stealthy visit to a forbidden zone—the girls' lavatory. "No one was around," Grant remembered. "I kept watch at the end of the corridor while another boy of equal curiosity went in to see what it looked like in there. And then, just as it came my turn to explore the inner sanctum, I was suddenly and shrilly nabbed by a powerful female who must have been the hockey teacher at least."

While his friend dashed to freedom, Archie was escorted to the headmaster's office for sentencing. The next day, in the school assembly after the morning prayer, Archibald Alexander Leach heard his name called.

"I was marched up the steps onto the dais and taken to stand next to the headmaster," he remembered. "Through a trance-like mixture of emotions, I hazily heard such words as 'inattentive,' 'irresponsible,' 'incorrigible' and 'discredit to the school.' I suddenly realized that I was being publicly expelled."

It was March 1918, not quite two months after Archie's fourteenth birthday. His plans were proceeding close to schedule, but the confrontation with Elias Leach was less dramatic than he had expected.

"Though he must have been very disappointed in me, my father did not reproach me," Grant said. "He quietly accepted the inevitability of the news. We discussed my needs and happiness and future, until he seemed reconciled to the uselessness of hindering my purpose further."

More than likely, Elias Leach also was happy to be relieved of the responsibility for his son. He couldn't afford to send him to another school (Archie had a scholarship at Fairfield) and the boy was only an extra burden in Leach's complex marital situation.

Three days later, Archie was back with the Pender troupe. And three months after that, he was performing with them at the Bristol Empire, where he had once disgraced himself by disrupting the Great Devant's magic act.

With Elias Leach and many former classmates in the opening-night audience, Archie gave a performance that made up in exuberance for what it lacked in experience. Afterward, he walked his father home and they held hands part of the way. "We hardly spoke, but I felt so proud of his pleasure and so much pleasure in his pride," Grant said.

Touring the English provinces with the Penders, Archie mastered the art of pantomime. No dialogue was used in the act. In addition to dancing, tumbling and stilt-walking, Archie was coached in the ways of conveying a mood or meaning without words. He learned how to establish silent contact with an audience, to effect an emotional response like laughter or tears immediately and precisely.

Unquestionably, Cary Grant's later success as a comedian was due to what he learned from the Penders. Physical coordination and timing are the most important elements of comedy. The Penders' act was a roughneck affair in which the scenery was always collapsing and the performers ran around whacking each other's backsides with bed slats. In essence, Cary Grant borrowed the baggy-pants comic's slow burns and double takes. It was the same kind of clowning, but done with more sophisticated overtones.

Archie quickly adapted to living dormitory style with the other boys in the troupe. They followed a strict routine of morning exercise and rehearsal, plus two or three performances daily.

His formal education was over. If he had any spare time, he went to the cinema or read "penny dreadfuls" and show-business magazines. Coming across a photograph of the Broadway stage star Florence Reed, he developed a teenage crush and wrote her a letter requesting an autograph. He also asked her whether emigrating to America would improve his chances of becoming successful in the theatre.

Much to Archie's astonishment, Florence Reed eventually replied with a photograph inscribed with a line from her latest play:

" 'Tain't *where* you are makes things happen, but *what* you are."
Archie Leach made it one of his guiding principles, and Cary Grant
always quoted it whenever young people asked him for professional advice.

On November 11, 1918, the day that Armistice was signed, the
Pender troupe was appearing in Preston, Lancashire. After playing
to a nearly empty theatre that evening, Archie and the other boys
walked around the town center. The streets were filled with people, but few of them were in a joyful, celebratory mood.

"As in every other town in England, so many of Preston's
families had lost someone close to them that the finish of the war
was hardly an occasion for revelry but rather for reverie," Cary
Grant observed. "Their only consolation was that there was never,
never again going to be another war. No. Never."

Some former members of the troupe did return safely from
the war, enabling Bob Pender to form two complete units by
Christmas, the season for the fairy-tale musical spectacles known
in England as pantomimes, even though they're far from mute.
Archie was assigned to the lesser of the two groups, spending a
wretched holiday working in arctic temperatures at a theatre built
on an amusement pier that jutted into Colwyn Bay, Wales.

Archie was part of a chorus line of ten outlandishly costumed
stilt-walkers, arranged in height from smallest to tallest. Their
heads were completely encased in huge papier-mâché masks,
Archie's suggesting Mother Hubbard with a white bonnet. His
long wooden stilts were hidden by a voluminous calico dress with
frilled collar and cuffs. The sight of the fantastic contingent of
giants cavorting about the stage with amazing precision and grace
never failed to win an ovation from the predominantly family audiences.

When the eight-week pantomime season ended, it was back to
the standard variety tours. Archie looked forward to London bookings the most, because he was more likely to be working on a bill
with famous headline artists, which gave him the chance to study
them close up from the wings.

"I grew to respect the diligence, application and long experience it took to acquire such expert timing and unaffected confidence, the amount of effort that resulted in such effortlessness,"
Cary Grant said. "I strove to make everything I did at least *appear*

relaxed. Perhaps by relaxing outwardly I could relax inwardly. Sometimes I even began to enjoy myself on the stage."

Business was booming for the troupe, and Archie found his weekly pocket money raised to a full pound (about five dollars). He had more places to spend it now, for peace had opened the way for work outside England.

In 1919–20, Archie traveled with the Penders to many of the major cities of Europe and the Middle East, and as far away as Russia and China. It was an incredible experience for anyone, but especially for a boy who had been daydreaming about it just a few years earlier.

3

Archie in America

In July 1920, Archie Leach started an ocean voyage toward the most wonderful destination of all—America, the fabled land of opportunity. As if that weren't excitement enough for a sixteen-year-old, the passenger list of the SS *Olympic* included the King and Queen of the movies, Douglas Fairbanks and Mary Pickford, who were returning from a six-week European honeymoon that had generated more headlines than any event since the Armistice.

Archie's inclusion in such elite company was a proof of his talent and also showed how indispensable he had become to the Pender troupe. There were twelve boys, but provision for only eight in the contract that Bob Pender had signed with Charles Dillingham, a New York theatrical impresario. Competition was murderous as Pender put each boy through rigorous tests, but Archie was one of the first to be selected.

As the *Olympic* steamed out of the English Channel into the Atlantic, Archie discovered that the crossing wasn't going to be a pleasure cruise. For the next seven days, the Pender troupe was kept busy exercising and rehearsing in the fresh sea air or in the ship's gymnasium. There was little time to spy on "Doug and Mary," though gossip had it that they were sticking to their stateroom as much as possible to avoid autograph hunters.

Early one morning, however, when the decks were still fairly clear of passengers, Douglas Fairbanks suddenly appeared. A superb athlete who performed all of his own stunts in films, he couldn't resist joining in while the Pender boys limbered up. The ship's photographer happened along and took a picture of the group. Standing beside Fairbanks, Archie tried shyly but unsuccessfully to express his admiration.

It was inevitable that Archie's first meeting with a movie star would prove an important influence on the future Cary Grant. Fortunately, the meeting was with Douglas Fairbanks and not Wallace Beery. Grant always attributed his maintenance of a perpetual suntan to that first glimpse of Fairbanks's deeply bronzed complexion. He was too young and naïve then to even suspect that Fairbanks actually applied it from a bottle!

But more important, Douglas Fairbanks's charm and affability were always evident in the Cary Grant persona. Fairbanks was "a gentleman in the true sense of the word. A gentle man. Only a strong man can be gentle," Grant once said.

At daybreak on July 28, Archie spotted the Statue of Liberty and the skyline of Manhattan coming into view. With the other Pender boys, he'd stayed up all night for fear of missing it. Of course, they'd seen it all before in photographs, but even at firsthand it seemed unreal. Archie had to pinch himself to make sure that it wasn't another daydream.

Someone in the crowd at the rail pointed to the Gothic tower of the Woolworth Building and said it was the tallest building in the world. Archie nodded in agreement because it dwarfed all the other skyscrapers in sight. But if anyone had told him that one day he would marry the granddaughter of the multimillionaire who had built it, he would have thought them loony.

While waiting in a long queue for customs inspection, Archie observed that there were definite advantages to being famous. "Doug and Mary" were whisked through and steered to a welcoming delegation headed by boxing champion Jack Dempsey, who brought along two busloads of celebrity well-wishers from the Friars Club. Thirty-five thousand ordinary mortals were massed outside the terminal. Archie had never before heard such cheering and hysterics as the most famous couple in the world drove away in an open limousine decked with American flags.

Eleven days later, on August 8, 1920, Archie Leach made his American stage debut in Charles Dillingham's *Good Times,* but it must have been extremely difficult to spot him, given the circumstances. He was appearing with the Penders in the world's largest theatre, the 5,697-seat Hippodrome, which occupied an entire block in the shadow of the Sixth Avenue El between Forty-third and Forty-fourth Streets. His co-workers numbered 1,332 people: 82 principals, 204 chorus, 180 ballet, 94 specialty artists and clowns (Archie among them), 12 equestrians, 44 animal handlers, 42 orchestra, 412 stage crew, 193 house staff, and 69 swimmers and divers who "disappeared" into a 960,000-gallon tank of water in the grand finale!

The sixth in an annual series of Dillingham super-spectacles, *Good Times* paid tribute to the innocent fantasies of childhood. In the second of three hour-long acts, the Pender troupe did a specialty number set in a toy shop.

As the critic for *Variety* described it: "Starting with a midget and winding up with a stilted figure some twelve feet tall, they marched on and lined up abreast in 'pair of stairs' formation for comedy business. When the tallest dropped his hat, the distance was so far to the ground that he dared not stoop to pick it up. The smallest one grabbed the hat, however, and passed it along until it again reached its exalted position. They were given a very warm reception by the audience."

Good Times received excellent reviews, many calling it the best production since the Hippodrome opened in 1905. With tickets for the twelve weekly performances priced reasonably from fifty cents to two dollars, a long run seemed certain. Archie unpacked his trunk down to the last piece of tattered underwear and settled in for what he hoped would be a new and happier existence.

Still very much chaperoned by Mr. and Mrs. Pender, the entire troupe was living in a hotel for "theatricals" on Forty-sixth Street just off Eighth Avenue, within easy walking distance of the Hippodrome. Across the hallway from the Penders, Archie and the other boys shared a long, narrow railroad flat with its own bathroom, a luxury they'd never enjoyed in England.

Each boy had rotating household responsibilities. Depending on what day of the week it was, Archie kept accounts, made the beds, shopped, cooked, cleaned, washed, ironed and mended for himself and the others. Thanks to his Boy Scout training, Archie excelled in the kitchen. Beef stew was his specialty, or more likely the extent of his repertoire, since he prepared it whenever his weekly turn as chef came around.

With the Hippodrome dark on Sundays, Archie was free to

explore New York from the Battery to the Bronx Zoo. He could ride anywhere on the subway for a nickel, even to Coney Island and back if he stayed on the train when it turned around. His favorite trip was to take an open-top double-decker bus that went up Fifth Avenue and across to Riverside Drive, a route inhabited mainly by the wealthy. He loved to imagine himself living in one of the countless mansions and majestic apartment buildings along the way.

Archie had become addicted to American ice cream, which unlike its British counterpart, came in a seemingly infinite variety of flavors and colors. During his Sunday rambles, he always stopped for several ice cream sodas plus a mammoth concoction called a banana split, which was unknown in England.

There were no Sunday movies in England either, but in New York Archie could take in as many as he could afford on his day off. Within a few blocks of the hotel, all the latest films were on display, though he gravitated toward those with his favorite comedians and action stars. They were the ones Archie tried to learn from: Charlie Chaplin, Buster Keaton, Wallace Reid, Douglas Fairbanks, Louise Fazenda, Harold Lloyd, Pearl White, Gene Pollar, Buck Jones, George Walsh, Tom Mix, Zasu Pitts, Mabel Normand.

By the time Archie arrived in America, he had had some sexual education, if not any actual experience. Recalling his early years in Bristol, Cary Grant said: "I first found out about the birds and the bees listening to a youthful slouch under the corner street lamp. Something about the young man's smirkingly patronizing manner while doling out the details made me doubt his veracity. I later found his information to be correct, but it was many years before I had the courage to put it to a test. It turned out to be a workable and pleasurable theory."

Backstage at the Hippodrome, Archie fell in love for the first time since his ill-fated romance with the butcher's daughter in Bristol. Again it turned out to be a matter of timorous worship from afar. She was a blond, blue-eyed ballet dancer whom Cary Grant later identified as Gladys Kincaid, although no one by that name is listed in the *Good Times* program credits.

"She didn't seem unmindful of my distant infatuation," Grant said, "but somehow neither of us ever managed to improve the relationship. Still her presence inspired me to better work whenever she was watching, and I became extraordinarily reliant upon her smiles of approbation." At Christmas, Archie bought Gladys a matching sweater-and-scarf set at Macy's, then lost courage and sent it to her anonymously.

Good Times ran for nine months, giving 455 performances before closing at the end of April, 1921. Capitalizing on their success at the Hippodrome, Bob Pender was able to book the troupe on a tour of the B. F. Keith vaudeville circuit, hitting most of the major cities east of the Mississippi River.

Cary Grant was a rabid baseball fan. His love for the sport dated back to that first American vaudeville tour, when the Pender troupe frequently found themselves riding the same trains and staying at the same hotels as the New York Giants. The ballplayers went to see their shows and the Pender boys turned themselves into a cheering section at Giant games. To show his appreciation, the Giants' owner gave Archie and the others gold season passes to the Polo Grounds, the team's home stadium.

The tour of Keith's circuit was scheduled to wind up back in New York at the Palace Theatre, the most important vaudeville showcase in the world. But Archie almost didn't make it. While the Penders were appearing in Rochester, New York, he contracted rheumatic fever. He was ordered to stay in bed for six weeks, so as not to risk permanent damage to his heart.

Bob Pender gave Archie money to pay for his lodging and meals until he was well enough to rejoin the troupe. He spent a lonely convalescence brightened only by visits from a kindhearted actress named Jean Adair, who was staying in the same boarding-house and kept him supplied with candy, fruit and the latest show-business news.

Archie had plenty of time to think about his future. He'd become enchanted by America and wasn't looking forward to returning to England. Both countries were going through a postwar recession, but in England unemployment was reported to be far worse. What chance did he have there?

But in America, Archie had never stopped working. Health permitting, he would soon have played both the Hippodrome and the Palace, two theatres that symbolized the best that a performer could achieve. It seemed a good omen for the future.

Also, Archie no longer felt any strong family ties to England. His father had never answered his letters and postcards. And his mother—well, she didn't bear thinking about. Her disappearance seemed a mystery never to be solved.

Fully rested and fortified with a box lunch from his landlady, Archie took the train to New York to rejoin the troupe for the Palace opening. By that time, Bob Pender had no further American bookings and was getting ready to sail back to England. Two of the members decided to remain behind. Archie needed no persuading to do likewise.

Bob Pender gave them all the price of a one-way passage home in case they should change their minds. Archie treated it as a bonus and banked it for a rainy day, confident that he would be able to find work on his own in no time flat.

Intent on putting together a solo act, Archie rented a furnished room for $3.50 a week in Hell's Kitchen, west of the theatre district. For a total of seventy cents daily, he could get three plain but satisfying meals at Ye Eatte Shoppe, at Forty-fourth Street and Eighth Avenue. His biggest expense was clothing, but he found a couple of stylish suits and basic haberdashery by scouring the secondhand shops.

It was the summer of 1922. If theatres were air-conditioned at all, it was by fans and not by refrigeration. Many were closed or coasting along with their current shows until autumn. Work was scarce, especially for an eighteen-year-old who had never spoken a line of dialogue on stage. "To do so became my ambition, my highest hurdle, my greatest fear," Cary Grant said.

Hoping to make connections, Archie sat in the lounge of the National Vaudeville Artists Club or stood on the corner of Broadway and Forty-seventh Street, where show people traditionally gathered in the shadow of the Palace Theatre to gossip and exchange information about jobs.

For Archie, none materialized. He was forced to dip into the money that Bob Pender had given him for return passage to England. Fortunately, being tall, good-looking and the owner of a dark suit kept him from going hungry. In his job-hunting rounds, he sometimes received last-minute invitations to fill a vacant place at a private dinner party or business banquet that was being held somewhere around town.

On one such evening, Archie was introduced to George Tilyou, Jr., whose family ran the world-famous Steeplechase Park at Coney Island. With his mind always attuned to the possibility of a job, Archie talked Tilyou into hiring him as a walking advertisement for the gigantic indoor-outdoor amusement center.

For five dollars a day, Archie would roam the boardwalk and streets of Coney Island on stilts, done up as a giant version of the Steeplechase doormen in a bright green jacket with red trim and matching jockey cap. Archie had to supply the stilts and the long, tubelike black trousers that concealed them, which some friends in the Hippodrome workshop made for him at cost.

After his first weekend on the job, Archie demanded ten dollars a day for Saturdays, Sundays and holidays. The huge crowds during those peak times increased the chances that some mischief-maker would try to topple him from his perch. He needed the extra five dollars a day to pay for bandages, liniment and occasional medical treatment.

The job had one fringe benefit. By standing in front of certain food stands and restaurants, Archie could quickly attract a crowd. The grateful owners would pay him off with all the free hot dogs, hamburgers, french fries, corn on the cob and frozen custard he could eat.

Although the Coney Island season was still in full swing, Archie quit when he was hired for Charles Dillingham's latest revue at the Hippodrome. This one was called *Better Times*, not only to imply that it was superior to *Good Times*, but also to signalize the end of the postwar recession and the start of a boom period. Appropriately enough, it opened during the 1922 Labor Day weekend.

Hardly a celebrity, Archie Leach was at least becoming a somebody. For the first time, he saw his name in the Hippodrome program (the Pender troupe was always listed as just that, without identifying the members).

In *Better Times*, Archie did stilt-walking in two scenes with Marceline, the famous clown. He also donned female drag as a "Joyful Girl" in the fantasy number "The Land of Mystery," which featured special effects of ghosts and witches flying around the stage and auditorium. In the spectacle "At the Grand Opera Ball," he played an energetic but silent *Meistersinger*.

Archie's appearances were not important enough for the drama critics to mention him in their reviews. But *Better Times* itself was well received, with Heywood Broun calling it "the sort of show which Ziegfeld and Barnum might have been expected to put on if they had happened to be partners." Archie foresaw months of steady employment and started concentrating on his first serious love affair.

His new romantic interest was a show girl in *Better Times*, who obviously must have been quite beautiful, since she was able to meet producer Charles Dillingham's high standards. This time, Archie not only worked up enough courage to talk to her, but actually started taking her out on dates after the performance.

Late one night, they attended a party given by another member of the cast. Prohibition was the law of the land, but everything from smuggled Canadian whiskey to bathtub gin and hard cider was being served.

Archie had a low tolerance for alcohol and was sticking to the hard cider, which he believed was the least likely to cause him distress. But in no time at all, he was laid to rest in a spare bedroom, where, thanks to some well-meaning friends, he was soon joined by his sweetheart.

As Cary Grant quaintly described it: "We awakened to find ourselves falteringly, fumblingly and quite unsatisfactorily attempting to ascertain whether those blessed birds and bees knew what they were doing. Up to that time, it was my closest contact with wine and women. I cannot add it was an occasion for song."

The romance eventually cooled when Archie got tired of taking his girlfriend home every night to her family in some remote part of Brooklyn. After several round-trip subway rides that returned him to Manhattan at daybreak, he decided that his sleep was more important.

While *Better Times* ran for 409 performances, it suffered a huge financial loss as a result of production costs that were triple that of *Good Times.* Archie had the dubious distinction of appearing in the last of the great Hippodrome spectacles. They could not continue without drastically raising admission prices beyond the reach of the mass audience.

On closing night in April 1923, Charles Dillingham assembled the company of more than a thousand to sadly announce that there would never be another chance for them to work together at the Hippodrome. The theatre was to be demolished and replaced by a hotel. But plans do change, and a scaled-down Hippodrome lasted another sixteen years under various policies of musical comedy, vaudeville, and movies. It was briefly a jai alai palace before being razed in 1939.

After *Better Times* closed, it was back on the road again as Archie and some friends broke in a new Pender-style act in small towns in New England, New York and Pennsylvania. A booker for the Pantages circuit liked it enough to sign them for a long tour to California and back, with a swing into Canada as well.

Since Archie and crew were only a low-paid supporting act, on their travels they were confined to seedy rooming houses, greasy-spoon cafés and cheap day coaches on trains. If they were lucky, some of their more successful friends helped them out. Whenever they were appearing in the same town with Eddie Foy's performing family, they could always count on the younger Foys' treating them to an enormous hotel meal by charging it to Papa's account without telling him.

In Los Angeles, Archie took advantage of a long-standing invitation from Douglas Fairbanks to the Pender troupe to visit him if they ever got to California. Archie couldn't have received a better introduction to the world of moviemaking, for Fairbanks was in the midst of filming his magical spectacle *The Thief of Bagdad.* Although Archie was an accomplished acrobat by now, he knew that no one, least of all himself, could ever match the leaping, running and tumbling that he watched Douglas Fairbanks do that day.

Archie was equally impressed by his first glimpse of Hollywood, with its palm trees, orange groves and what was then smogless sunshine.

Decades later, Cary Grant said: "I didn't know I would make my home there one day. And yet, I *did* know. There is some deep prophetic awareness within each of us. I can't remember consciously daring to hope I would be successful at anything. Yet at the same time, I knew I would be. I believe that all of us, with a clear knowledge of the past and present, and an estimation of the consequences of every action we intend taking in the future, can foretell the paths of our lives. Certainly we ourselves create those paths."

But in 1923, Hollywood, or more precisely, Los Angeles, was just another one-week stand for a struggling nineteen-year-old vaudevillian who lived out of a wardrobe trunk. The tour continued through the spring, when Archie and his friends decided to disband and go their separate ways. Without a strong leader and manager like Bob Pender, they couldn't cope with the grueling

routine and were constantly quarreling and blaming each other for
their problems and mistakes.

With what little money he'd managed to save, Archie returned
to New York and took a room at the National Vaudeville Artists
Club while he looked for work. His goal now was anything that
would give him a chance to speak lines, preferably funny ones. His
personal experience told him that if he stuck to acrobatics, he
might find steady employment but would never become a head-
liner.

Soon Archie was teaming up with other young hopefuls who
were as inexperienced as he was but just as eager to learn. At the
union minimum scale of $62.50 for a duo, they could get weekend
bookings at suburban theatres that stressed quantity over quality
by offering three or four "live" acts in addition to a feature movie
(silent, of course).

Over the next few years, Archie Leach played practically every
small town in America, usually as the straight man in comedy acts.
"I learned to time laughs," Cary Grant said. "When to talk or to
not talk into an audience's laughter. When to wait or to not wait for
the laugh. When to move or to not move on a laugh."

If he was working and could afford it, Archie lived in cheap
Broadway hotels and rooming houses. When he was broke, he
spent the night on park benches or in the empty offices of friends.

For a few weeks, Archie was part of Parker, Rand & Leach,
"two boys and a girl with a skit idea that gets nowhere," according
to *Variety*. Archie quit and was replaced by another young hopeful
named James Cagney, who stayed with the act until it expired in
the boondocks.

Archie joined Jack Janistar, a popular comedian of the time, in
a vaudeville sketch called "The Woman Pays." Archie's role was
supposed to be that of "the handsomest man in the world." Until
he came to audition, agent Jean Dalrymple had interviewed nothing but "Rudolph Valentino types," whom she considered too
unctuous for the part.

"Suddenly this gorgeous young man came in and I said,
'That's the one I want,'" Jean Dalrymple recalled. "My partners
almost talked me out of it. They said that Archie's voice didn't
project well, that his English accent made him even more difficult
to understand and that he had 'rubber legs,' a term for actors who
sort of wobbled instead of walked."

Archie also worked with comedian Don Barclay, whom he had first met back in England when the rotund, apple-cheeked American appeared on a bill with the Pender troupe. Since coming to America, Archie often sought Barclay's advice and sometimes ended up working as his straight man.

A frequent collaboration was a spoof of mental telepathy acts called "Professor Knowall," with Archie in the title role and Don Barclay as his assistant in the audience. Barclay would place his hand on a young woman's shoulder and defy Archie to guess her name. The patter went something like this: "This girl is an upper and lower, professor!"

"Bertha!"

"And here is one, not deaf but dumb!"

"Dora!"

"No, dumber than that!"

"Belle!"

"Right you are, professor . . . Good people, I call your attention to the fact that we use no signs, no codes." Although such cornball material was one of the things that eventually killed vaudeville, a public still untouched by radio, talking pictures or television loved it.

Besides Don Barclay, Archie had two other close friends in New York whom he could always turn to in time of need. That both of them were homosexuals may or may not have entered into the relationships, but they were devoted to the handsome twenty-year-old fledgling performer.

The first was Lester Sweyd, a remarkable character even for the Broadway show world. Ten years older than Archie, Sweyd had been a child performer, specializing in female impersonations under the name of "Fonzo, the Boy Wonder in Skirts." As if that weren't enough to make a reputation, Sweyd also claimed to be the heir to the Canadian territory of Labrador. Constantly fighting his case in court, he never won anything but publicity, which probably was his main goal anyway.

By the time that Archie met him, Sweyd had become a playbroker and talent agent, just the sort of well-connected friend that an aspiring actor could use. After Sweyd saw Archie in a vaudeville skit, he tried to persuade Samuel Goldwyn to sign him to a movie contract, but the producer wasn't interested. Meanwhile, Archie was welcome to share Sweyd's apartment whenever he was between jobs.

Archie's second gay chum was John Kelly, an Australian who originally came to America for the same reason, to get on the stage. Seven years older than Archie but physically unimposing, Kelly had to depend on his exceptional talent as an artist to support himself. He painted murals in nightclubs and illustrated title cards for silent movies. Adopting the name of Orry-Kelly, he later became one of Hollywood's foremost costume designers.

For about a year, Archie and John Kelly lived together in a one-room studio apartment in Greenwich Village. To help pay the rent and grocery bills, they developed a profitable side business that took advantage of both their talents.

Kelly made hand-painted neckties and Archie hawked them on street corners. He could get a dollar for them in Union Square and two dollars in posher uptown areas. It was a true test of an actor's abilities. If sales were lagging, Archie knew that he was giving an inadequate performance.

But the middle 1920s were hard times. On many an early morning, Archie rushed to Sixth Avenue to join the throngs outside the employment agencies, waiting hopefully for any temporary job that would tide him over.

Archie worked as a messenger and clerked in haberdashery shops. Sometimes he got out his stilts and stomped around Broadway and Herald Square, advertising department-store sales or the opening of a new chop suey parlor. Eventually he saved enough money for steerage passage back to England, where he wormed his way into the Nightingale Players, a minor repertory company, so that he could learn the rudiments of acting.

For two years, Archie toured the English hinterland with the Nightingale group, playing any part that they threw at him and giving it his all. One role required singing. Squeezing enough out of his salary to take a few vocal lessons, he was astonished when the teacher told him that his baritone voice was definitely worth cultivating. Pretty soon he was playing small parts in touring productions of musicals like *No, No, Nanette* and *The Arcadians*.

It was during that period that Archie Leach unconsciously laid the foundation for the eventual Cary Grant as he started emulating some of the leading British stage stars of the time. In the polished and debonair category, Archie idolized the mature Gerald DuMaurier and A. E. Matthews, as well as their younger counterparts, Ronald Squire and Jack Buchanan.

"I was able to observe the changing style in drawing-room acting in the London theater," Grant recalled. "The modern gentleman role used to be interpreted in the dancing-master manner, as though it were a part in a romantic costume play. The old-fashioned actor would bow and scrape and always seemed to be taking off an invisible plumed hat with an elegant flourish.

"A. E. Matthews and Ronald Squire changed all that by more natural underplaying. The duke became a human being, a fellow who often talked with his hands in his pockets, and Noël Coward and Freddy Lonsdale wrote comedies in which there was no call for the old stuffiness."

The person influencing Archie Leach the most was Noël Coward, the multitalented actor, playwright, director, composer and lyricist. "As a young actor, I had a thin veneer of pseudosophistication, carefully copied from Noël Coward," Cary Grant said. "I'd carefully put my hand in my pocket, and it would get stuck there with perspiration. My biggest gesture was raising an eyebrow, which ill became me."

By 1927, Archie Leach considered himself ready to make another attempt at conquering America. Gambling all his savings on another steerage ticket, he was on his way.

4

Broadway to Hollywood

Seven years from the time that he first arrived in the United States with the Pender troupe, Archie Leach finally landed in a Broadway show. It was called *Golden Dawn,* but the title was hardly prophetic for Archie's career or for anyone else connected with the musical drama.

Archie got the job in a rather roundabout way, which started with his obsession with Helen Morgan, the torch singer who was famous for performing while perched atop a baby grand piano. Morgan ran a late-night club that Archie frequented, apparently unconcerned that it was often raided by Prohibition agents for drinking violations or by the vice squad because of Morgan's large homosexual following.

One night in the autumn of 1927, Archie dropped in to congratulate Helen Morgan on being signed for one of the leads in Florenz Ziegfeld's upcoming musical, *Show Boat.* While he was there, Archie ran into an actor-friend who introduced him to Reginald Hammerstein, a stage director who was the younger brother of lyricist and libretto writer Oscar Hammerstein II.

What happened next is anybody's guess, but gossip had it that Reggie Hammerstein developed a passion for Archie Leach. At any rate, Archie ended up being signed to a personal contract by Reggie's uncle Arthur Hammerstein, one of Broadway's top producers.

Having earned a multimillion-dollar fortune from his production of the Rudolf Friml operetta *Rose Marie,* Arthur Hammerstein was in the process of spending most of it on a new theatre to memorialize his father, Oscar Hammerstein, who had been New York's foremost impresario until his death in 1919. Situated at Broadway and Fifty-fourth Street, the theatre's cathedral-like auditorium was being lavishly decorated with stained-glass panels depicting scenes from Oscar Hammerstein's triumphs at his illustrious Manhattan Opera House.

To start Archie's contract, Arthur Hammerstein gave him a small role in *Golden Dawn,* the Hammerstein Theatre's inaugural attraction. Just a shadow of the gargantuan shows that Archie worked in at the Hippodrome, it was still a huge undertaking for Broadway, the cast alone numbering 150 people. The book and lyrics were by Otto Harbach and Oscar Hammerstein II, with music by Viennese operetta masters Emmerich Kálmán, Herbert Stothart and Robert Stolz.

The title *Golden Dawn* referred to a beautiful blonde named Dawn (played by opera singer Louise Hunter), who, believe it or not, is the princess of a native tribe in German-controlled East Africa during World War I. While nursing enemy captives in a prison camp, Dawn falls in love with an Englishman, but romance is taboo because she's "colored," or so everybody thinks. Later it turns out that Dawn is really snow white and all ends happily in a spectacular grand finale featuring Broadway's first topless chorus girls (all white, but covered with black makeup to pass for natives)!

Archie Leach, however, was fully clothed as a POW, a role so insignificant that the program listed the character only as Anzac, the term for a soldier of the Australian and New Zealand Army Corps. Still that was better than being called Dago, which was how an Italian prisoner was identified. The play's rampant racism was totally acceptable on Broadway in 1927, although it would start riots today.

Archie's role consisted of just one line of dialogue. Years later, Cary Grant claimed to have also been understudy to Paul Gregory, the highly talented leading man of *Golden Dawn,* but there is no evidence of that in the production records. It hardly seems likely that Arthur Hammerstein would have entrusted such a responsible assignment to a comparative novice.

Golden Dawn opened on November 30, 1927. Except in the cast list, Archie Leach was not mentioned in any of the next day's newspaper reviews. Walter Winchell of *The Graphic* called the play *The Golden Yawn,* and about two thirds of his fellow critics shared a similarly negative opinion. Reactions were tempered by how one felt about the Hammerstein family, which had as many enemies as it did friends.

About all that Archie Leach gained from *Golden Dawn* was some valuable experience and insight into the economics of the legitimate theatre, where the stakes were much higher than in vaudeville. The fate of most shows (264 were produced on Broadway in the 1927–28 season) was in the hands of theatre-ticket agencies, which purchased large blocks of seats in advance and then resold them to the public with a commission added on.

Because Arthur Hammerstein had refused to do business with the majority of brokers during the long sold-out run of *Rose Marie,* they saw a chance to get even when *Golden Dawn* received disappointing reviews. Producers with a less than hit show usually gave the agencies a discount on their buys, but Hammerstein refused with *Golden Dawn* and the brokers dropped the show from their offering lists. Consequently, *Golden Dawn* ran for barely six months, closing in May 1928, after 184 performances.

For Archie Leach, it was just another case of bad luck. But for Arthur Hammerstein, who'd been expecting a run of at least eighteen months, it was the beginning of the end to his producing career. He lost $250,000, a huge sum for those times. *Golden Dawn* also may have jinxed his exquisite Hammerstein Theatre, which never housed a hit, later was converted into a flop nightclub and presently functions as a TV studio.

In 1931, Arthur Hammerstein would declare bankruptcy, but after the closing of *Golden Dawn* in 1928, he still had enough resources to continue in production. His young contractee Archie Leach didn't have to worry about finding another job. Rather than hire a "name" who would cost him more money, Hammerstein decided to gamble by assigning Archie to one of the leading roles in *Polly,* a musical based on *Polly with a Past,* a hit comedy of 1917 that starred the inimitable and ultra-chic Ina Claire.

It was the era of hit musicals with girls' names like *Sally, Irene* and *Rosalie.* Arthur Hammerstein hoped to have another winner by building a similar production around an English singing and dancing star who'd never appeared in America but was supposed to be the equal of Marilyn Miller, the undisputed Queen of Broadway musicals. Her full name was June Howard-Tripp, but she was known professionally simply as June. She dropped the surname because "Tripp" was hardly appropriate for a dancer.

Archie Leach had to portray a rich society playboy, with June as a poor chorus girl masquerading as a French adventuress. The plot didn't make much sense, but neither did most of the musical comedies of the twenties.

Legendary wisecracking comedian Fred Allen, another major player in *Polly*, vividly described preparations for the show. "June arrived from England to great acclaim, which was confined mostly to Mr. Hammerstein's office. As rehearsals progressed, I knew that even if the world were extra dry, this show was not going to set it on fire. The song titles sounded like those you'd expect in a college show. The melodies would never be whistled except by people who were trying to clean their front teeth after a vegetarian dinner."

While *Polly* was trying out in Philadelphia, Archie received the first important press notices of his career, most of which were favorable and hinted that a new star was about to be born. "Archie Leach, as Roy Van Zile, the boyish hero, meets all the requirements for a romantic girl's Prince Charming. He is more than six feet tall, lean, brown and athletically hard, and his fine cut features, gleaming teeth and curly black hair are well calculated to draw forth feminine admiration. His voice is above average for the male lead in a musical comedy," said the critic for the *Evening Bulletin*.

Yet Archie never made it to Broadway. At the end of the Philadelphia engagement, Arthur Hammerstein fired the entire cast with the exceptions of June, Fred Allen and comedienne Inez Courtney. Why Archie was dismissed after getting such good reviews is a mystery. Perhaps the critics were drunk at the time or had had their arms twisted by press agents.

Years later, June gave her version of what happened: "My leading man was tall, dark and handsome, but as far as I could see, he was completely lacking in talent or skill as an actor, singer or dancer. Furthermore, he had a Cockney accent, and his name, Archie Leach, was hardly prepossessing. I liked him personally and he worked hard, but I felt sure he would have to be replaced before our New York opening."

In the end, it turned out a lucky break for Archie because the Broadway critics savaged *Polly* and it ran only two weeks. Robert

Garland of the *Telegram* punned "Oh, to be in England now that June is here!"

Archie's association with Arthur Hammerstein was nearly over. When the producer's archenemy, Florenz Ziegfeld, wanted to hire Archie for the touring company of Marilyn Miller's *Rosalie*, Hammerstein refused. Instead, he sold Archie's contract to Ziegfeld's hated rivals, Lee and J. J. Shubert, who owned a national chain of theatres and also produced most of the attractions that ran there.

The Shuberts gave Archie Leach his first major part on Broadway in *Boom Boom*, a musical comedy that opened at the Casino Theatre on January 28, 1929. Archie's leading lady was a blond soubrette named Jeanette MacDonald, who made a strong impression in previous Shubert shows and seemed on the verge of becoming a major star.

Running for a scant seventy-two performances, *Boom Boom* failed to boost the careers of either Archie Leach or Jeanette Mac-Donald, but it did earn both of them screen tests. The new medium of talking pictures created a huge demand for vocally adept, stage-trained actors. If they could sing and dance, so much the better.

Oscar Serlin, Eastern talent scout for Paramount Pictures, sent Archie and MacDonald to the company's studio in Long Island City for their film auditions, but the results weren't encouraging. MacDonald's test was routinely dispatched to Hollywood, but Archie's received instant rejection. "You're bow-legged and your neck's too thick," he was told.

After *Boom Boom* closed, the Shuberts tried recouping their investment by touring it to some of their out-of-town theatres. While traveling together, Archie and MacDonald became good friends, but no romance developed between them.

Later dubbed Hollywood's "Iron Butterfly," MacDonald still had some consideration for others. She took a sisterly interest in Archie and tried to help him overcome his timidity with the opposite sex. "He was literally tongue-tied around women," MacDonald said later. "I didn't have much luck in changing him."

While *Boom Boom* was running in Chicago, MacDonald received a telegram from the illustrious film director Ernst Lubitsch, who liked her screen test and was coming there by train to see one of her performances. Archie hoped it might be his big break as well, but if the cigar-chomping German saw him as a potential movie star, he never mentioned it. Lubitsch did, however, advise Paramount to sign MacDonald to a contract. As soon as *Boom Boom* closed, she left for California to appear with Maurice Chevalier in *The Love Parade,* Lubitsch's first talkie.

Archie Leach, meanwhile, was doing about as well in the theatre as he would have with comparable work in movies. The Shuberts were paying him four hundred fifty dollars a week. He could afford to buy his first car, a gleaming Packard touring car, then considered one of the finest of American-made automobiles.

That sleek machine seemed to go with the façade of urbane sophistication that Archie Leach was acquiring. Most of his Broadway roles were in the clotheshorse category. He wore white tie and tails impeccably. He studied etiquette books and practiced gestures and poses in front of the mirror.

Archie was one of the regulars at Rudley's Restaurant, a favorite show business hangout at Broadway and Forty-first Street. Contemporaries like Clark Gable, Humphrey Bogart, Spencer Tracy and James Cagney also haunted the place to get job leads, but Archie preferred the company at the so-called "rebels' table," where young writers like Moss Hart, Dore Schary, Preston Sturges, Elmer Rice and Clifford Odets talked and dreamed of revolutionizing the theatre.

Archie was one of the few actors allowed to sit with that group, probably because he was in awe of them and kept silent. "He never was a very open fellow, but he was earnest and we liked him," said playwright Edward Chodorov.

Moss Hart once described Archie as "disconsolate" in those days. Because he never talked much about his background, Archie's English Cockney accent was taken for Australian, like that of his frequent companion Orry-Kelly. The Rudley's crowd had nicknames for Archie like "Kangaroo" and "Boomerang."

At twenty-five, Archie Leach possessed a low opinion of himself as an actor. Cary Grant later said he was ashamed of everything he did on the stage in those early years. Archie was still the confused, troubled boy from Bristol, who through his work sought but did not find the affection he had never received from his parents.

After *Boom Boom,* the Shuberts put Archie into one of their most expensive undertakings, *Wonderful Night,* adapted from *Die Fledermaus.* Copied from Max Reinhardt's famous production of the Strauss operetta in Berlin, it used a revolving stage that turned at five different speeds according to the tempo of the music.

Archie's role of Max (called Eisenstein in the Strauss original) required an operatic voice. How Archie managed is a mystery, but it was suspected that he had an offstage double who did at least part of the singing for him.

Hours before the opening-night performance, Archie's nerves cracked. Between the demands of the role and his fear of being ground to hamburger in the revolving stage mechanism, it was going to be the most cataclysmic event in the history of the world.

En route to the theatre, Archie bumped into his comedian friend Fred Allen, who claimed to know the perfect cure for his jitters and took him to the observation tower of the Woolworth Building. Through the rain and fog, they could scarcely see the street below, let alone the bright lights of the Broadway theatrical district farther uptown. Archie calmed down immediately, realizing how small and unimportant his own problems were.

Wonderful Night was possibly the most beautifully opulent production ever put on by the Shuberts. Despite Walter Winchell's complaint that "it chased itself in circles from 8:30 to midnight," it received generally good reviews, but not for Archie.

"Archie Leach, who feels that acting in something by Johann Strauss calls for distinction, is somewhat at a loss as to how to achieve it. The result is a mixture of John Barrymore and Cockney. He makes a handsome hero, though," critic Arthur Pollack wrote. Percy Hammond noted that "Mr. Archie Leach, as the soprano's straying baritone, brings a breath of elfin Broadway to his role, reminding us that it is 1929."

Unhappily, it wasn't only 1929 but also October 31, just days after the worst financial crisis in American history. Stock market prices had "crashed," wiping out thousands of investors and causing the loss of billions of dollars in capital. *Variety*'s famous headline WALL ST. LAYS AN EGG, ushered in a decade of economic depression that left no one untouched. By the end of 1929, six million people were jobless.

Needless to say, it was not the best time to open an expensive new musical. In New York City, scores of the unemployed were roaming the streets trying to sell apples. Up and down teeming Broadway, competition was so fierce that some vendors were offering five apples for a nickel. The Hearst newspaper chain opened a free breadline in Times Square but had to move it under protest from the theatre owners. The sight was proving too upsetting to those who could still afford to buy tickets.

Under the circumstances, it was remarkable that *Wonderful Night* didn't close immediately. But the Shuberts had so much invested that it was cheaper to keep it running than to mount a new production for the Imperial, their most important theatre. With tickets selling at bargain prices, *Wonderful Night* ran 125 performances, closing in February 1930.

Broadway had opened its first soup kitchen, the Actors Free Dinner Club, but Archie was spared joining the long lines of unemployed that formed there every night. The Shuberts sent him on a tour with *Wonderful Night* that lasted until summer. Traditionally the slow period for theatres, that summer was made worse by the economic conditions. Archie obtained a few weeks' work in vaudeville by renewing his occasional partnership with comedian Don Barclay.

In the autumn of 1930, Archie received a new assignment from the Shuberts, but at a reduced salary. On the verge of bankruptcy, the brothers were packaging streamlined versions of some of their earlier hits to offer to the public at "prewar prices" from three dollars down to fifty cents. As part of a company of sixty-five, Archie went on tour with *The Street Singer*, which had to gross two thousand dollars a night just to break even. The experiment failed and was one of the reasons why the Shubert Corporation filed for receivership in 1931.

Nineteen thirty-one would be the most dismal year for the legitimate theatre in two decades. Nearly half of all Broadway houses were closed. The only job that Archie could get was at the Municipal Opera in St. Louis, Missouri, where J. J. Shubert produced a summer-long series of musical revivals at the 10,000-seat amphitheatre in Forest Park.

Although it was grueling work, with a new role to be learned every two weeks, Archie knew he was lucky to be employed at all. The trade papers were filled with little else but the grim details of the latest Broadway bankruptcies. There was a time when Archie had considered trying his luck in Hollywood, but the Depression had struck there as well. Many stage actors who had moved West at the height of the talkie boom were now coming back, making the competition for Broadway assignments even more cutthroat.

Returning to New York in the fall, Archie found a job right away, thanks to the help of another of his homosexual friends, Phil Charig, composer for the ill-fated *Polly.* Now writing the score for a musical drama called *Nikki,* Charig arranged for Archie to audition for producer William Friedlander, who was looking for a tall, handsome British-aviator type. Friedlander didn't need much convincing when Archie strolled into his office.

Nikki was intended as a showcase for Fay Wray, who had become a silent film star at nineteen in Erich von Stroheim's *The Wedding March.* Now twenty-four, Wray had never gotten a chance to prove herself in talkies and hoped that a success on Broadway would reawaken Hollywood's interest. Helping her toward that goal was her author-husband John Monk Saunders, a former World War I flying ace who wrote *Wings* and many other movies, novels and short stories about war and aviation.

Based on Saunders's magazine serial *The Last Flight,* which had already been made into a film starring Richard Barthelmess, *Nikki* shifted the emphasis to a beautiful French girl pursued by three ex-flying buddies in postwar Paris. Kent Douglass (later a film star under the name Douglass Montgomery) had the male lead, but Archie's role was almost as important and also involved him in two musical numbers.

Most critics panned *Nikki* following the New York opening at the Longacre Theatre on September 29, 1931. The general consensus was that the serious, Ernest Hemingwayish theme of postwar disillusionment was ruined by the addition of songs and specialty numbers ranging from Apache dancing to clattery tap.

Nikki also did nothing for Fay Wray, who had to wait another two years for a giant gorilla named King Kong to rejuvenate her career. Archie Leach, however, got at least one good clipping for his scrapbook. *Daily News* critic Ed Sullivan wrote that he was "a cinch for a movie role."

Perhaps he was, but the best that Archie could get at the time was a single day's work in a musical short subject, *Singapore Sue,* filmed at Paramount's Long Island City studio. Dressed in a white sailor's suit, Archie belonged to a quartet of Americans on shore leave who fall for the title character, the owner of a honky-tonk café. Remembered now solely because it marked the film debut of the eventual Cary Grant, the ten-minute film was really an introductory vehicle for Anna Chang, a singing and dancing Chinese bandleader whom Paramount rather incredibly hoped to develop into another Anna May Wong!

Meanwhile, the producers of *Nikki* tried to save the show by moving it to the smaller George M. Cohan Theatre, where it soon expired on Halloween night after a grand total of thirty-nine performances.

Working together on stage for the last time, Archie and Fay Wray were sitting at a table in the background, supposedly making small talk appropriate to the scene while the main action swirled around them. But what Archie really said to Wray was "Well, what now? Know of any jobs—a good bootblack, bricklayer or hoofer wanted?"

"Why don't you go to Hollywood?" Wray answered. "I should think you'd go over big in pictures."

"Who, me?" Archie said. "I'm no pretty boy."

A few weeks after *Nikki* closed, Wray was surprised to receive a souvenir postcard from Archie, scribbled in haste in El Paso, Texas. For better or worse, he'd decided to take her advice after all.

5

Introducing Cary Grant

In November 1931, Archie Leach was a few months away from his twenty-eighth birthday. Roughly half his lifetime had been spent working, yet what did he have to show for it besides a scrapbook of press clippings and a three-year-old Packard that guzzled more gasoline and oil than he could afford? He lived in furnished rooms and could fit all his clothes and belongings into one wardrobe trunk.

Clearly, he had nothing to lose and everything to gain by heeding Horace Greeley's proverbial "Go West, young man!" after *Nikki* closed. Encouraging him was his friend Phil Charig, whose fellow composers were heading for Hollywood in droves to cash in on the craze for musicals. Neither man wanted to risk making the trip on his own, so they decided to share expenses by driving out in Archie's Packard.

It was an experience they never forgot, although not for the usual tourist reasons. With the whole continent in the grip of the Great Depression, they witnessed scenes of squalor and human misery that equaled anything from the pen of John Steinbeck or the camera of Walker Evans.

For Archie, Hollywood turned out to be the Land of Oz. There are several versions as to how he landed a studio contract, but one can be dismissed immediately. Contrary to a legend perpetuated by the lady herself, Mae West never "discovered" him, although

she did have a major influence on his career. But he had made
seven movies before that happened.

A more likely story was told by Phil Charig. Soon after they
arrived in Los Angeles, Charig went for an interview at Paramount's music department and took Archie with him so that he
could see the interior of a movie studio. Charig didn't get the job,
but the interviewer took a gander at Archie and said, "Who's your
good-looking friend?" Archie was sent to the casting department,
screen-tested and eventually signed.

It's possible that the Paramount casting department was already interested in Archie. Casey Robinson, who directed *Singapore
Sue* back in New York, claimed that Archie had so impressed him
that he wrote to the studio brass urging them to screen the short if
they were looking for a "surefire star."

According to Cary Grant himself, a New York agent gave Archie a letter of introduction to a Hollywood agent whose client,
director Marion Gering, just happened to need an actor to play
opposite his actress-wife in a screen test. When the test was made
at Paramount, Mrs. Gering failed to impress, but Archie was offered a long-term contract.

Paramount envisioned a future for Archibald Alexander
Leach, but not under that name or any variation of it. His contract
specified that a new professional name had to be selected.

Fay Wray and John Monk Saunders, who by this time had
returned to California, suggested that Archie call himself Cary
Lockwood, the name of his character in *Nikki,* the last play he did
on Broadway. It would be a sentimental gesture, a link to his
theatrical past.

But Cary Lockwood had a short life. Paramount accepted
"Cary" but "Lockwood" was discarded to avoid confusion with
another film actor named Harold Lockwood. Running through a
list of surnames drawn at random from the Hollywood telephone
directory, an executive stuck a pin in "Grant" and there it stayed.
When someone noticed that Cary Grant's initials were the same as
Clark Gable's and the reverse of Gary Cooper's, it seemed a good
omen. Gable and Cooper were the top matinee idols of the day.

Cary Grant was born on December 7, 1931, the day that he
signed his Paramount contract and effectively laid Archie Leach to
rest at the age of twenty-seven years, eleven months. The contract
ran for five years, starting at four hundred fifty dollars a week,

certainly a good salary for those depressed times but no more than Archie had been earning on the stage. But a movie deal did offer greater security. No more worrying where his next job would come from when his present show closed. No more road tours or living out of a wardrobe trunk.

When Cary Grant first reported to work at Paramount, he felt as Archie Leach had upon entering Fairfield Secondary School. He doubted whether he'd ever make the grade, let alone graduate to the level of a so-called "star." The studio had a superabundance of those already, including Marlene Dietrich, Gary Cooper, Maurice Chevalier, Ruth Chatterton, Fredric March, Nancy Carroll, Tallulah Bankhead, Kay Francis, Sylvia Sidney, Jack Oakie, the Marx Brothers, W. C. Fields, Miriam Hopkins, Claudette Colbert, Carole Lombard and Harold Lloyd. The only one that he knew personally was Jeanette MacDonald, but her option had not been renewed and she was leaving Paramount. That left him with no friends that he could consult for help or advice.

Paramount, however, had no intention of starting Cary Grant in leading roles. The company owned the largest circuit of theatres in the world, which it kept supplied by producing about sixty features a year, more than any other studio. Operating like a factory, it finished and shipped at least one new picture every week, so there was always a place for a new contractee somewhere along the assembly line. If he proved capable and the public liked him, he would be promoted to the premium merchandise and to pampered "star" treatment.

But as a beginner, Cary Grant would have to work extremely hard for four hundred fifty dollars a week. It was a six-day schedule, Monday through Saturday, with no extra pay for overtime, which came almost as regularly as the sunset.

Cary Grant's first feature-length movie was *This Is the Night*, produced in January 1932. Comic actors Roland Young and Charles Ruggles worked so well together in Ernst Lubitsch's *One Hour with You* that Paramount decided to reteam them in a similar bedroom farce, with Lili Damita and Thelma Todd as the female leads.

Playing the supporting role of an Olympic javelin-thrower whose wife is having an affair with a millionaire playboy, Cary Grant was described in the ads for *This Is the Night* as "the new he-man sensation of Cinemerica!" There was slight evidence of that in the film itself. Director Frank Tuttle left Grant to his own devices, which were still those of a stage-trained actor, and he hammed it up terribly. He had yet to learn the importance of underplaying. In the theatre, everything had to be exaggerated in order to reach the last rows of the balcony. In movies, where the camera enlarged everything a thousand times, the opposite was true.

When Cary Grant saw himself on-screen for the first time at a preview of *This Is the Night,* he was so appalled that he sneaked out of the theatre before it was over. He went straight back to his apartment, packed all his belongings and was getting ready to drive back to New York when some friends who'd also attended the screening arrived to congratulate him. It took them a solid hour to persuade Grant to stay. It wasn't that they convinced him that he was good. In his own mind, he was still lousy, but if others considered his work acceptable, he might as well go along with it.

Paramount next tossed Grant into a secondary part in *Sinners in the Sun,* a melodrama with Carole Lombard and Chester Morris. Lombard had yet to establish herself as a "screwball" comedienne, so this was just another in a series of films in which she modeled stunning clothes designed by Travis Banton and suffered romantic torments that invariably ended happily. As a playboy gambler, Cary Grant had little to do, but proved that he could wear black tie and tails as elegantly as Lombard did her sequined evening gowns.

He literally walked through his third film, *Merrily We Go to Hell,* never even encountering the stars of the drama, Fredric March and Sylvia Sidney. Dressed and bewigged as an eighteenth-century nobleman, Grant acted in a scene from a play that was supposedly written by Fredric March, a reporter turned dramatist.

Brief though his participation was, *Merrily We Go to Hell* marked the only time in Cary Grant's career that he worked under a female director, always a rare bird in Hollywood and especially in the 1930s. The mannish, allegedly lesbian Dorothy Arzner was assigned to the film in the hope that she could control temperamental Sylvia Sidney (the mistress of studio head B. P. Schulberg) better than some of her male counterparts. But the two women fought bitterly and Sidney subsequently returned to working with her usual director, the more easily dominated Marion Gering.

An easygoing Polish immigrant who got along with everyone, Gering was usually handed the troublesome projects that other Paramount directors shunned, which was how he inherited *The*

Devil and the Deep, Cary Grant's fourth film in as many months. The sexually charged melodrama had more than its share of problems, namely Gary Cooper, Tallulah Bankhead and Charles Laughton, which gave Grant his first real taste of the intrigues and eccentric behavior that often made working conditions on a movie set unbearable.

Gary Cooper, the biggest box-office draw of all the Paramount stars, was threatening to walk out if he didn't get a raise in pay. Tallulah Bankhead, already unhappy about her failure to achieve a major success in films, was also nursing an unreciprocated case of the hots for Gary Cooper. Working in Hollywood for the first time, Charles Laughton was so neurotic about his blubbery appearance that he practically had to be dragged from his dressing room to face the cameras.

Cary Grant sat on the sidelines, trying to be as pleasant and diplomatic as he could with the three stars. His role was minimal— a navy lieutenant stationed at a submarine base in West Africa— and he just wanted to get through it without being dragged into the constant squabbling.

While he'd now made four films, Cary Grant had yet to appear with one of Paramount's top women stars, although in retrospect it seems that he did. But Carole Lombard was considered just another leading lady then, and Tallulah Bankhead had been in one flop movie after another since quitting the stage to pursue a Hollywood career.

The first real test of Cary Grant as a romantic consort came in his fifth film, *Blonde Venus,* starring Marlene Dietrich. The nearest thing to a true "goddess" that Paramount Pictures had at the time, she was treated as such, with a sumptuous four-room dressing suite built for $300,000 (sixty times the cost of an ordinary family dwelling in 1932!).

Blonde Venus was the fifth collaboration between Dietrich and Josef von Sternberg, the Austrian-American director whose German-made *The Blue Angel* had turned her into a world sex symbol. Herbert Marshall (who lost a leg fighting in World War I and always wore a prosthesis) was the leading man, playing a research chemist dying of radium poisoning.

But Cary Grant's role was almost as important. He portrayed a wealthy playboy who starts housewife-mother Dietrich on the path of sin and degradation as she tries to raise money to pay for medical treatments that could save her husband's life. It was one of the most bizarre scripts ever filmed, with Dietrich eventually becoming a Paris nightclub star who pops out of a white gorilla costume to sing "Hot Voodoo" to an astonished audience.

Cary Grant said later that *Blonde Venus* gave him his first good role, but he must have been referring to the impact it had on his career rather than to its quality. Director Von Sternberg was a master of lighting and camera angles, and Cary Grant was never more exquisitely photographed than in *Blonde Venus,* made when he was twenty-eight years old.

No detail was too minor for Von Sternberg to notice. On the first day of production, he stopped everything, whipped a comb from his pocket and proceeded to change the part in Grant's hair from the left to the right side. Cary Grant wore it that way for the rest of his life.

But Von Sternberg failed in his attempts to turn Grant into a better actor. "Joe bemoaned, berated and beseeched me to relax, but it was years before I could move with ease before a camera. Years before I could stop my right eyebrow from lifting, a sure sign of inner defenses and tensions," he said.

Grant was grateful to Marlene Dietrich, who "smilingly accepted my immaturity and inexperience with comforting patience."

Impressed by the glowing sensuality that Grant projected in *Blonde Venus,* Paramount announced plans to star him in a remake of Rudolph Valentino's *Blood and Sand.* Hollywood had been looking for a successor to its greatest romantic idol ever since his premature death from peritonitis in 1926, but if Cary Grant was to be the new Valentino, he never got the chance to prove it. Paramount went bankrupt, and the expensive bullfighting spectacle was one of the first projects canceled in the studio reorganization that followed.

The sudden reversal in Paramount's fortunes (going from a profit of $6 million in 1931 to a loss of $21 million in 1932!) actually helped Cary Grant's position at the studio instead of hurting it. Still the new boy in school, he couldn't be blamed, as certain other actors and actresses could, for contributing to Parmount's losses. As the new studio management started weeding out such weak box-office draws as Tallulah Bankhead, George Bancroft, Buddy Rogers, the Marx Brothers, Richard Arlen, Jeanette Mac-

Donald and Maurice Chevalier, it needed replacements. Cary Grant was one of the first to be promoted to star status from within the ranks. From outside, Paramount acquired the talents of Bing Crosby, George Raft and Mae West.

Cary Grant's stardom fell upon him when Gary Cooper refused to appear in *Hot Saturday*. Cooper's buddy and fellow contractee Fredric March, who kept up on all the Paramount scripts, advised him not to do it because there was a supporting male role that was better written and that would grab all the attention.

Though it seemed a rather incongruous substitution, Cary Grant took over Gary Cooper's role. That displeased leading lady Carole Lombard, who asked for another assignment. Replacing her was flame-haired Nancy Carroll, the first star created by talking pictures, who was in danger of being dropped by Paramount as a result of her waning popularity.

Fredric March proved correct in his estimation of *Hot Saturday*. The supporting part of the heroine's childhood sweetheart did win the audience's sympathy, giving Cary Grant plenty of reason to hate the actor who "stole" his first starring vehicle from him. But the opposite turned out to be true. It sparked a close personal relationship between Grant and Randolph Scott, a recent Paramount contractee who possessed some of the all-American appeal of Gary Cooper and was being groomed for a career along similar lines.

Cary Grant and Randolph Scott discovered that they had a lot in common, but what it was beyond their mutual employment at Paramount soon became a matter for conjecture and gossip. In any case, they decided to pool their resources and live together.

Gary Cooper and Fredric March, meanwhile, continued to exert a major if unintentional influence on Cary Grant's career. Again taking March's advice, Cooper rejected the part of Lieutenant Pinkerton in *Madame Butterfly* because the man's caddish behavior caused the heroine to commit suicide, hardly a role to please an actor's female fans.

Since he was not yet important enough to be able to get away with turning down assignments the way Gary Cooper did, Cary Grant found himself drafted into the U.S. Navy in his place, with Russian-Jewish-American Sylvia Sidney portraying the Japanese geisha girl Cho-Cho-San. The film was done as a straight drama and used Puccini's operatic score mainly as background music. But before the action turned grim, Grant crooned "My Flower of Japan, I Love You" to his little cherry blossom.

With Cockney-sounding Cary Grant as an American and Sylvia Sidney singsonging pidgin English dialogue like "You're the most best nice man in all world," the lavish and expensive *Madame Butterfly* seemed doomed from the start. Why Paramount even bothered to make it at a time when the company was in dire financial straits can only be explained by a type of wheeling and dealing that still thrives in Hollywood today.

In order to get B. P. Schulberg to vacate his post of production chief at the time of the bankruptcy and reorganization, Paramount had to agree to give him his own independent production unit. It seemed only logical (at least to Schulberg) that he should choose *Madame Butterfly* as his first production. His paramour, Sylvia Sidney, who excelled at portraying tragic, long-suffering types, had been hounding him to let her play the part because she thought it suited her slightly oriental appearance.

The first major break in a successful career often comes as a result of being in the right place at the right time. For Cary Grant, it happened one day in the autumn of 1932 while he was making *Madame Butterfly* and strolling toward the Paramount commissary to have lunch. Dressed in the dazzling white linen uniform of Lieutenant Pinkerton, the deeply tanned six-footer turned many heads, including that of peroxide-blond Mae West, who was just leaving a production meeting in the administration building. Plump, bosomy and only five feet four inches tall, she still towered over the cigar-chewing runt with her, Emmanuel Cohen, Paramount's new production chief.

As might be expected of the self-proclaimed "world's foremost authority on men," she trailed Grant with her eyes until he passed from view. "*Who* was *that?*" she finally asked Cohen when she caught her breath.

"Oh, that's Cary Grant. He's making *Madame Butterfly* right now."

"I don't care if he's making Little Nell," Mae West said. "If he can talk, I'll take him."

"For what?" Cohen asked. With Mae West, her interest in a man could be personal, professional or both.

"For the lead, of course." She was getting ready to make her first starring film for Paramount and had total control over cast, director and script, which she adapted from her self-written stage hit *Diamond Lil.*

Naturally, Cary Grant got the part, a Bowery missionary who tries to reform Lady Lou, "one of the finest women who ever walked the streets," but ends up her conquest instead. In the original play, Captain Cummings belonged to the Salvation Army, but Paramount feared reprisals from that organization and made him nondenominational.

Under orders from movie censorship czar Will Hays, the title and character name *Diamond Lil* also had to be discarded. The play created a scandal when it was first produced on Broadway in 1928 and was considered "too hot" to be filmed in its original form. West toned down a subsidiary plot dealing with white slavery and changed the title to the much more suggestive *She Done Him Wrong,* which surprisingly raised no objections from the Hays office.

Cary Grant proved to be the perfect foil for Mae West. He had an aloof charm and naïveté about him that contrasted well with her brash sexuality, making her seem less the insatiable maneater than she did in subsequent films where her leading men tended to be as tough and coarse as she was.

When Grant first comes to plead with West in the saloon where she entertains, he says, "I'm sorry to be taking your time." To which West replies, leering, "What do you think my time is for?" Later, when Grant turns out to be a police undercover agent and starts putting West in handcuffs, she asks, "Are those absolutely necessary? You know, I wasn't born with them."

"No, but a lot of men would have been safer if you had," Grant says.

"I don't know. Hands ain't everything," West replies.

Cary Grant also became permanently identified with the line that became Mae West's trademark: "Come up and see me sometime." Only she never said it quite that way. After appraising Grant's physical assets from head to toe, West drawled, "You can be had." Then she added, "Why don't you come up sometime, see me? . . . Come up. I'll tell your fortune."

About his working experience with Mae West, Grant later said: "I learned everything from her. Well, no, not quite *everything,* but almost everything. She knows so much. Her instinct is so true, her timing so perfect, her grasp of the situation so right. It's the tempo of the acting that counts rather than the sincerity of the characterization. Her personality is so dominant that everyone with her becomes just a feeder."

Not released until February 1933, *She Done Him Wrong* was by far the most successful of the eight films that Cary Grant made in 1932, his first year at Paramount. Within six weeks, it earned rentals of two million dollars (ten times its negative cost) and became the biggest factor in Paramount's return to profitable operations.

At the rather ripe age of forty-one, Mae West suddenly became Hollywood's top box-office attraction and an international sex symbol. The association helped Cary Grant enormously. More people saw *She Done Him Wrong* than all his previous films combined, so there was a public awareness of him that hadn't existed before. Even more important, Grant became eligible for idolization in his own right. If Mae West desired him, then he must be a pretty hot number worthy of every woman's interest.

Yet after Grant's success with West, Paramount still didn't know what to do with him. If he'd been employed by MGM, Grant would have been given a big publicity buildup and teamed with all the studio's major female stars, as the fledgling Clark Gable was with Joan Crawford, Norma Shearer, Jean Harlow, Greta Garbo, et al. Unfortunately, Paramount lacked women in that category and also had too many men to go around. Gary Cooper, Fredric March, Bing Crosby, George Raft and even W. C. Fields were considered more important than Cary Grant, who got the leftovers.

Paramount also couldn't figure out a public image for Cary Grant. Was he to be a he-man like Gable, an aesthete like Fredric March, an average guy like Gary Cooper? Then there was his personal life to be considered. After going through his childhood, education and stage career, what was there to excite the interest of fan magazine readers? Gary Cooper, for example, owed much of his fame and popularity to his scandalous romances with sexpots Clara Bow and Lupe Velez and the notorious adventuress the Countess di Frasso.

When Cary Grant was interviewed about women and romance, he declined comment or gave evasive answers. Consequently, the fan magazines titillated readers with hokey stories about his early "loves," which read as though Grant had concocted them with the help of the studio publicity department.

An article in *Movie Classic* cited a shipboard romance with "Ruth," a brief summer fling with "Ann" and irreconcilable differences with "Ethel" and "Adele" over career and social status. None of the ladies were fully identified, perhaps to protect their privacy, more likely to prevent anyone from finding out whether the alleged romances ever happened. "Ann," by the way, came nearest to fulfilling Cary Grant's ideal of what a sweetheart should be: "A good sport, willing to ride in a Ford or Rolls-Royce, as happy as a hotdog stand as in the best restaurant in town."

Julie Lang Hunt, who supervised Paramount's magazine publicity at the time, said that getting coverage for Cary Grant was the most difficult and frustrating experience in her career as a press agent. Grant not only never had anything important to say to reporters, but he also usually got upset when the innocuous interviews appeared, claiming that he'd been misquoted or misrepresented.

Hunt believed that Grant had a real phobia about seeing his name in print that had started in his lonely childhood. Growing up without any close personal ties, he developed the habit of keeping his thoughts and beliefs locked up inside, which made him reluctant to reveal anything about himself to the public.

Interestingly, Grant told everyone then that his mother had died suddenly when he was ten years old. He either believed that, or, if he did know Elsie Leach's whereabouts by that time, thought it was better than admitting the truth. Having a mother in a lunatic asylum wasn't exactly the ideal kind of family history for a romantic idol.

Nor did Grant's association with Randolph Scott help to establish a positive image. A year older than Grant, the tall, blue-eyed, blond Scott came from an affluent Southern family. He studied engineering in college and eventually dropped out to study acting with the Pasadena Community Players, where he was "discovered" by a Paramount talent scout. Grant and Scott were so different from each other that their oppositeness may have been the initial attraction.

Grant and Scott briefly shared a small rented house in Westwood but soon moved to an eight-room Spanish hacienda high in the winding Hollywood Hills. With a splendid view from downtown Los Angeles to the Pacific Ocean, it was quite private and secluded. The fan magazines, which loved to put labels on everything, dubbed the domicile "Bachelors' Hall," while Grant and Scott became known as "Hollywood's Damon and Pythias." No one explained who was who, but it probably didn't matter. If Grant and Scott were as devoted to each other as their ancient Roman counterparts, then either one would sacrifice his life for the other if it ever came to that.

Since neither Grant nor Scott had any serious female attachments at the time, Paramount started using their living arrangement as an angle for publicity stories and picture layouts. Instead of the hackneyed theme of girl starlets, here were two handsome male equivalents, helping each other along and sharing expenses while they climbed the ladder to success. Paramount didn't seem to care that the relationship could be interpreted as homosexual. In 1933, the average person didn't know what the word meant.

Ben Maddox was one of the first journalists invited to visit Grant and Scott in their new home. "A late supper was served by an old-fashioned Negro mammy cook who came with the house and referred to her new employers as 'the young gentlemen,' " Maddox said, sounding as though Hollywood never heard of the Emancipation Proclamation.

After spending a couple of hours with the two "success boys," Maddox concluded that "Cary and Randy are really opposite types, and that's why they get along so well. Cary is the gay, impetuous one. Randy is serious, cautious. Cary is temperamental in the sense of being very intense. Randy is calm and quiet. Need I add that all the eligible (and a number of the *in*eligible) ladies-about-Hollywood are dying to be dated by these handsome lads? Cary tears around in a new Packard roadster and Randy flashes by in a new Cadillac. Oh-oh-oh, how the girls want to take a ride!"

Within a few months, such press coverage started to backfire. Photographs of Cary Grant and Randolph Scott wearing aprons while they washed the dishes together and made up their twin beds suggested a couple of newlyweds. Columnist Jimmie Fidler sniped that Grant and Scott were "carrying the buddy business a bit too far."

Paramount called off its publicists and waited for the air to clear. Cary Grant went one step farther and found himself a real live girlfriend.

6

Cary Takes a Wife

Like everybody who was anybody in public life during the 1930s, Cary Grant invariably got invited to the extravagant parties and receptions given by Marion Davies, whose dual status as movie star and mistress of publishing tycoon William Randolph Hearst made her Hollywood's hostess of hostesses. It was at Ocean House, Davies's palatial seven-million-dollar beach retreat at Santa Monica, that Grant met the woman who became his first wife. She was a blond actress named Virginia Cherrill, quite celebrated at the time for her portrayal of the blind flower seller in Charlie Chaplin's *City Lights*.

That night at Ocean House, Grant became entranced by the way Cherrill's flaxen hair curled into ringlets in the sea air. He fell in love with her almost instantly. That Cherrill was fair and blue-eyed, the opposite of Elsie Leach, could have been the reason. Many years later, Grant said that he avoided dark women like his mother for most of his life, subconsciously punishing her for abandoning him as a child.

Grant and Cherrill made a stunning couple. Besides the contrast in coloring, he was a foot taller and outweighed her by a hundred pounds.

Four years younger than Grant, Cherrill typified thousands of poor but attractive young women who flocked to Hollywood in the 1920s to dig for gold via career, marriage or both. Born on an Illinois farm, she had an ambitious mother who paid for her tuition

at a swank Chicago finishing school by working in the kitchen as a
cook.

At eighteen, Cherrill was voted Queen of the Chicago Beaux
Arts Ball, which led to marriage with attorney Irving Adler. Divorced a year later, she headed for Hollywood at the urging of
former classmate Sue Carol, who had already made it big as a fast-
stepping movie flapper and inspiration for the hit song "Sweet
Sue."

Charlie Chaplin "discovered" Cherrill when he spotted her in
the crowd at a boxing match and offered her a screen test. Cherrill
later claimed there was no sexual motive involved and she was
probably right. Twentyish and a divorcée, she was too mature for
Chaplin, who preferred teenage virgins.

Although Cherrill had never acted in her life, Chaplin made
her his leading lady in *City Lights.* Her work in the initial scenes was
so inept that his financial backers wanted to fire her, but Chaplain
couldn't find a replacement that pleased him. Instead, he started
over again, this time wrenching a poignant performance from
Cherrill that became one of the highlights of a movie often considered to be Chaplin's masterwork.

Had it been made earlier, *City Lights* might have turned Virginia Cherrill into a star, but it only caused her hardship. While the
King of Pantomime could still get away with releasing a silent film
in 1931, Cherrill had no future unless she could handle speaking
parts in talkies. Unluckily, despite her angelic looks, she sounded
like a gangster's moll, with a high-pitched voice and a nasal Chicago accent. Her career really was over before it had begun.

But you could coast along in Hollywood for quite a while on
one big success, and *City Lights* was still fresh in memory when Cary
Grant and Virginia Cherrill met. Soon they were an item in all the
gossip columns, but whether it was a real romance or an arrangement of convenience, no one really knew except the two people
involved.

Grant needed a woman in his life to bolster his image. The
exquisite protégée of Charlie Chaplin was a definite catch. Cherrill, conversely, had appeared in two badly received talkies by that
time and knew that her moviemaking days were numbered. Just
before meeting Grant, she'd been engaged to marry millionaire
William Rhinelander Stewart, but the wedding was mysteriously
canceled on the day it was to take place. While Grant lacked

Stewart's wealth, he had prospects. Cherrill could only benefit from such an association.

The relationship developed gradually. Cary Grant appeared in eight films in 1932 and would make six in 1933, with little time to spare for socializing. Cherrill hardly worked at all. It took her a long time to accept the fact that Grant was much more successful than she was and probably always would be. The only offers coming her way were from minor Poverty Row companies like Monogram and Pinnacle.

Cherrill also had to contend with Grant's friendship with Randolph Scott. The two men had deserted the Hollywood Hills for the Santa Monica beachfront strip known as Millionaires' Row, where they were renting a sumptuous "bungalow" that belonged to silent-pictures star Norma Talmadge. Every morning, they worked out together in their private gymnasium and swimming pool before driving to Paramount.

Virginia Cherrill thought that Grant spent too much time with his housemate. When Grant and Cherrill went out together, he usually insisted on dragging Scott along, so they were more often a trio than a couple. Cherrill wouldn't have minded so much if it had been a foursome, but Scott lacked female friends. If he had to attend a movie premiere or nightclub opening, Paramount was always ready to arrange a date with a starlet who needed publicity.

Throughout 1933, Grant and Cherrill kept fairly constant company. Marriage rumors circulated every other week, but were just as quickly denied. Grant claimed that he was too busy with his career to make such a serious commitment.

The success of *She Done Him Wrong* helped Grant's status at Paramount considerably. He inherited the dressing room formerly occupied by silent-pictures star George Bancroft, who had been demoted to the ranks of supporting players. Paramount's top dozen stars were quartered side by side, with an implied order of importance. Mae West occupied dressing room number 1, followed by the other women: Claudette Colbert, Marlene Dietrich, Sylvia Sidney, Miriam Hopkins and Carole Lombard. Then came the men: Gary Cooper, Fredric March, Bing Crosby, George Raft, Grant (in 11) and Charles Laughton.

But Paramount's choice of roles for Cary Grant showed no improvement. For his first film in 1933, the studio reteamed him with Nancy Carroll in *The Woman Accused*. As a promotional gim-

mick, ten popular writers of the day, including Rupert Hughes,
Vicki Baum, Zane Grey and Irvin S. Cobb contributed to the script,
but the result was a trite mystery thriller that proved to be one flop
too many for Nancy Carroll, whose contract was soon terminated.
Just three years earlier she'd been the most popular star in movies.

Paramount then decided to pair Grant with Fredric March in
The Eagle and the Hawk, another World War II aviation story by John
Monk Saunders, author of *Nikki* and *Wings.* Carole Lombard appeared in the film as well, but her role was written in at the last
minute to add some romantic interest and she had only one short
scene.

In *Gambling Ship,* his third film of 1933, Grant played Ace
Corbin, "big shot gambler," a part that seemed like a Clark Gable
reject. Britisher Benita Hume, who later quit acting to marry Ronald Colman, co-starred with Grant in a melodrama that invited
moviegoers to "Come where the scarlet lights blink an invitation to
wink at the law!" Most stayed home to listen to the radio.

If Grant's career seemed in a decline, it suddenly leveled off
when Mae West requested him again for *I'm No Angel,* the story of
"a girl who lost her reputation and never missed it." West portrayed a carnival hoochy-coochy dancer who becomes the toast of
Broadway as a lion tamer!

Grant, playing an attorney who has to defend himself against
West's breach-of-promise suit, inspired one of her most frequently
quoted wisecracks: "When I'm good, I'm very good. But when I'm
bad, I'm better."

Some of their exchanges, all written by Mae West, were considered obscene at the time.

Grant: "Do you mind if I get personal?"

West: "I don't mind if you get familiar."

Also, Grant: "If I could only trust you."

West: "Hundreds have."

One of the main reasons the movie industry had to adopt a
self-censorship code to protect itself from pressure groups like the
Catholic National Legion of Decency, *I'm No Angel* was the raciest
of all Mae West films, earning over a million dollars more than *She
Done Him Wrong.* And thanks to Mae West's choosing him, Cary
Grant had the good luck to appear in the two biggest grossers of
1933.

Except for the public exposure, however, the films did nothing to help Grant's bargaining power with Paramount. Mae West received all the credit for their success and undoubtedly deserved it. She not only saved Paramount from disaster, but also gave the entire industry its first reason for box-office optimism since the onset of the Depression.

After *I'm No Angel,* Paramount loaned Grant to the recently formed Twentieth Century Pictures, headed by former Warner Brothers production chief Darryl F. Zanuck and Joseph Schenck. Most of the major studios were helping the new one get started by loaning it talent, not for humanitarian reasons but because they were coerced into it by Nicholas Schenck and Louis B. Mayer of Loew's/MGM, who had a financial stake in the new enterprise.

Grant was assigned to *Born to Be Bad* with Loretta Young, whom Zanuck brought with him from Warners to become one of the first contractees of the company (which later became 20th Century–Fox when it merged with Fox Films). The melodrama of fraud and blackmail was probably the worst of Cary Grant's early films. *Variety* found the story so unpleasant that it wondered why Zanuck even bothered to make it. As a wealthy trucking executive, Grant had "the weakest and most uninteresting part he has ever played," according to *Film Daily.*

Returning to Paramount, Grant was pressed into service as a last-minute replacement for Bing Crosby in *Alice in Wonderland.* Ridiculous as it might seem for Grant and Crosby to be interchangeable, it didn't really matter *who* played the part of the Mock Turtle. Looking like a fugitive from a Halloween party, Grant was completely hidden in a man-sized turtle shell and rubber mask. What amounted to about three minutes of screen time could have been enacted by anyone, with Grant dubbing in the voice later, but that would have been too easy.

Why Paramount decided to make *Alice in Wonderland* as a live-action film rather than with puppets or as an animated cartoon is anybody's guess. With nineteen-year-old Charlotte Henry playing a rather wordly-wise Alice and a huge supporting cast that also included Gary Cooper as the White Knight and W. C. Fields as Humpty Dumpty, it was one of the most expensive flops in Hollywood history up to that time. Hardly the best way for Cary Grant to close out his second full year in films.

During those twenty-four months in Hollywood, Grant made fourteen pictures back to back. In November 1933, he asked for some time off to take a trip to England, and Paramount approved, since it was an opportunity for Grant to do some publicity for his latest pictures in New York and London. Randolph Scott worked out a similar arrangement so that he could accompany his friend.

Although Archie Leach had been born there, Cary Grant had never been to England. But the movie star of only two years' standing longed to return to the country of his birth to play the conquering hero. Also, Virginia Cherrill just happened to be heading there in hopes of finding work in British films. Grant thought it would be a good time for them to try to come to some understanding about their relationship. Randolph Scott presumably could act as referee if tempers flared too fiercely.

Grant and Cherrill had already been through one skirmish that hurt him deeply. A few months earlier, while in Hawaii making a low-budget quickie called *White Heat,* Cherrill had become involved with another man. As if that weren't enough to make Grant furious, gossip had it that his competition was a notorious Waikiki Beach hustler. When Cherrill returned to Los Angeles, she had a lot of explaining to do before Grant would take her back. Apparently she had wounded his ego as much as his feelings.

When Virginia Cherrill sailed from New York to England on the *Champlain* in November 1933, Cary Grant went on board to wish her bon voyage. Reporters covering the liner's departure wanted to know if the two movie stars planned to be wed.

"If we were to be married, I'd say so. I see no reason for lying about such things," Cherrill declared. "Nor I," Grant chimed in.

Although it was common knowledge that Grant also planned to visit England, no one bothered to ask why he wasn't traveling on the same ship as Cherrill. Together with Randolph Scott, he sailed on the *Paris* a few days later.

What Cary Grant planned as a few weeks' vacation turned into a three-month misadventure with elements of mystery, melodrama and screwball comedy. Shortly after arriving in England, he took Cherrill and Scott to Bristol to show them around Fairfield School and the theatres where Archie Leach broke into show business. Archie's reappearance as a Hollywood movie star, traveling in the company of two other well-known personalities, created a sensation in the provincial city.

In mid-December, Cary Grant landed in a London nursing home. Depending on what newspaper account you read, he was suffering either from pneumonia or from the aftereffect of a minor concussion that he sustained when a bomb accidentally went off while he was filming *The Eagle and the Hawk.*

But the truth was that the tensions of the previous recent weeks had proved too much for Grant. He had a nervous collapse, started drinking heavily and was put away for drying out.

Virginia Cherrill caused some of his distress. She kept pressing Grant to marry her, but he couldn't make up his mind. While it appealed to him in theory, he doubted whether he could fulfill the sexual and emotional demands of marriage. He knew, too, that if it didn't work out, Cherrill would have a legal claim on him. He earned good money now and didn't want to part with it needlessly. He wanted to put the relationship to a test by living with Cherrill first, but she refused.

Grant also opened up some old psychological wounds during his visit to Bristol. He discovered that his father had become a hopeless alcoholic. Even more upsetting was the revelation that his mother was not only alive but locked away in a mental institution.

Most actors have a tendency to overdramatize everything in their own lives. Grant became obsessed with the idea that he had probably inherited some or all of his parents' problems. He was hospitalized in London for a month. No one knows what went on in his mind during that time, but shortly after being released he announced that he intended to marry Virginia Cherrill.

The wedding took place on February 4, 1934, at Caxton Hall registry office in London. Randolph Scott had returned to Hollywood by that time, so there was no best man. For a while, it had looked as though there wouldn't be a bride, either.

Grant arrived first, followed by a mob of reporters and photographers. As the crowd grew larger, Grant became visibly upset and went to a telephone box to make a call. Twenty minutes later, Cherrill arrived in a taxi. All too aware of the reasons for Grant's recent breakdown, she had deliberately delayed her arrival to avoid the embarrassment of being left in the lurch in case he suddenly changed his mind about marrying her.

People in that fashionable district of London, who were accustomed to seeing wedding parties in formal array, were disappointed by the raffish dress of the visitors from Hollywood. Grant wore a beige herringbone suit, with a woolen scarf knotted foppishly around his neck. Cherrill's sable coat partly concealed a black-and-yellow checked suit that matched her cloche hat.

By the end of the civil ceremony, the throng outside Caxton Hall had become so thick that the newlyweds were sucked into it and divided as they headed for a taxi. Each separately hailed a cab and then couldn't find the other to make a getaway. Eventually they were reunited in a mad race across London to catch the boat train to Southampton, where they took the *Berengaria* back to the United States that same day.

Mr. and Mrs. Cary Grant rented a house in Santa Monica, not far from the one he used to share with Randolph Scott, who still lived there alone. Absent from filmmaking for five months, Grant had to report to work immediately. Cherrill was "at liberty." Producers weren't deluging her with job offers, which soon became a major source of contention between the couple.

Grant's extended leave hadn't changed Paramount's attitude toward him. The studio still thought of him mainly as window dressing for its female stars. In the first of five pictures that Grant made in 1934, he was reunited with Sylvia Sidney and her usual director, Marion Gering, for *Thirty-Day Princess.*

An attempt to change Sidney's serio-dramatic image, the comedy of mistaken identity gave her a chance to play a double role. Critics found little to laugh at, one complaining that the script "must have been written in ancient Sanskrit." Cary Grant fans would remember his role as a newspaper publisher as the beginning of a black-tie-and-tails period. He wore formal clothes in five consecutive pictures.

Grant's next film, *Kiss and Make Up,* marked the first time that Paramount made him the star attraction. The two leading women, Helen Mack and Genevieve Tobin, were hardly big names, and the story centered around Grant, a Paris beauty expert "whose treatments were the talk of the town!"

With Grant singing "Love Divided by Two" and the 1934 Wampas Baby Stars putting on a lingerie fashion show, the semimusical was an unsuccessful attempt to duplicate some of the frothy French and German farces of that period. But American audiences didn't know what to make of the film or of Cary Grant, whose limp-wristed portrayal of the cosmetician was far too campy for a star trying to establish a strong masculine identity.

Grant received another chance to prove his box-office drawing power in *Ladies Should Listen,* with the leading female part played by Frances Drake, whose expressive eyes made her eligible for parts rejected by Sylvia Sidney. Paramount reused most of the sets from *Kiss and Make Up* and this time turned Grant into a Parisian playboy who falls in love with a busybody telephone operator.

Although it was yet another flop, *Ladies Should Listen* at least won Grant some recognition in the right quarters. The influential industry magazine *Script* said that "Like Clark Gable in *It Happened One Night,* Cary Grant surprises everyone with his delightful flair for light comedy."

Grant's next film, *Enter Madame,* was Paramount's attempt to imitate Columbia's highly successful *One Night of Love,* which starred grand opera's Grace Moore. Since dropping Jeanette Mac-Donald, Paramount no longer had a resident diva, so it tried to create one by combining Elissa Landi, Italy's answer to Garbo and Dietrich, with the dubbed singing voice of Nina Koshetz. Playing Landi's husband in the romantic farce, Grant had nothing much to do but look elegant in between long stretches of scenes from *Tosca* and *Cavalleria Rusticana.*

In *Wings in the Dark,* the last of the five films he made in 1934, Grant got his first chance at a big dramatic role playing opposite Myrna Loy, who was loaned to Paramount so that MGM could get Fredric March for Garbo's *Anna Karenina.*

Grant portrayed a pilot who is literally blinded while experimenting with a device for flying blind! Myrna Loy, who is also a pilot and secretly in love with Grant, hires herself out for all sorts of dangerous missions to raise money so that he can buy a Seeing Eye dog and continue with his experiments. To no one's surprise, Grant's research not only saves Loy's life when she gets lost in fog on a history-making flight between Moscow and New York, but he also miraculously regains his sight.

Although it now sounds like a travesty on aviation films, *Wings in the Dark* was hailed at the time for its "persuasive living conviction." *Variety* said that "Cary Grant tops all his past work. The part gives him dimensions to play with and he takes it headlong."

Wings in the Dark was Cary Grant's last picture for six months. One of the reasons was that Paramount had a backlog of Grant films; two of the five that he made in 1934 weren't released until the following year.

The second reason for prolonged inactivity was that Cary Grant's marriage was beginning to crumble.

7

Free Lance

"I doubt if either of us was capable of relaxing sufficiently to trust the happiness we might have had," Cary Grant said of his marriage to Virginia Cherrill. "My possessiveness and fear of losing her brought about the very condition I feared: the loss of her."

Although he had just turned thirty when he married Cherrill, Grant lacked emotional maturity and was too self-centered to make a success of the relationship. His idealistic concept of marriage must have been derived from some of his own movies.

For Grant, getting married really meant settling down. After a day's work, which meant rising at the crack of dawn and usually not getting home until late evening, he wanted nothing more than to relax, memorize his lines for the next day and retire early. If Cherrill worked as regularly as her husband did, she could have accepted that routine. But she was bored by idleness and wanted to go out for a good time when her husband returned from the studio.

The Grants had been married for only seven months when their troubles became public knowledge. In September 1934, after accepting an invitation to join a Hollywood delegation to a cultural festival in Mexico City, they were forced to cancel when Paramount decided it couldn't give Grant time off. Cherrill blew up, a screaming match followed and she moved out of the house to stay with her mother.

The press quickly learned of the separation and demanded an

explanation. "I'm still in love with Cary and I hope and feel certain that we'll be able to patch things up and continue with our marriage," Cherrill said.

The next day, Grant retorted: "It's silly to say that Virginia and I have separated. We've just had a quarrel, such as any married couple might have. I hope when I get home tonight Virginia will be waiting for me."

But Cherrill didn't return, and three days later millions of Americans picked up their morning newspapers to read that Cary Grant had attempted suicide.

At two in the morning on October 3, 1934, the Filipino houseboy telephoned police to send an ambulance for Grant. Wearing only shorts, he was discovered lying unconscious across his bed, with a bottle of tablets marked POISON beside him on a table. The doctor who pumped out Grant's stomach told reporters that he admitted to swallowing one tablet. Later, police said the mysterious bottle was sealed and had never been opened.

As soon as Grant was brought home from the hospital, Cherrill rushed to see him but left within a few minutes. Terribly embarrassed, Grant provided his own version of the alleged suicide attempt.

"I was drunk," he told reporters. "I didn't take any poison at all. The fact is, I was dead drunk. I'd been drinking most of the day before and all that day. You know what whiskey does when you drink it all by yourself. It makes you very, very sad. I began calling people up. I know I called Virginia. I don't know what I said to her, but things got hazier and hazier. The next thing I knew, they were carting me off to the hospital."

Reminded of the incident years later, Grant laughed it off. "The whole suicide story was a big joke. Believe me, when I lost a love, I always thought, 'Well, I'll go on living.' "

In December 1934, Cherrill filed suit for separate maintenance, charging that Grant used liquor excessively and threatened her life by choking and beating her. After moving out, she claimed that she had had to pawn her jewelry to cover living expenses. The court ordered Grant to pay her $167.50 a week and $2,500 on account, pending division of their community property, estimated to be worth $50,000.

Three months later, Cherrill applied for a divorce, toning down her complaints by dropping all references to physical abuse.

She charged that in the first months of their marriage, Grant was "sulky and morose, and then took to drinking . . . He would argue with me on every point. He said I was lazy and ought to go to work. He refused to pay my bills because he said I could earn my own money. But when I tried to get work, he discouraged me and refused to let me work."

According to Cherrill's testimony, Grant finally avowed that he was tired of her and didn't want to live with her anymore. "Cary was really married to his career," she said later. "And he was terribly jealous—even of my mother!"

A gentleman to the end, Grant kept a public silence and never tried to deny Cherrill's allegations. He did not appear in court when the divorce was granted on March 26, 1935, thirteen months from the day of their wedding. Cherrill soon left Hollywood to work in England. In 1937, she married into nobility and as the Countess of Jersey became renowned for her charity work during World War II.

Returning to bachelor life, Grant moved back in with Randolph Scott, who had not taken another housemate while his friend tested the matrimonial waters. Telling everyone that he would never marry again, Grant kept his word for eight years.

The divorce left Cary Grant even more ill-humored than Cherrill claimed he had been while married. The most obvious cure for his unhappiness was to plunge back into work, but Paramount had nothing at the moment. The studio tried "loaning" him to Warner Brothers as a last-minute replacement for the ailing Robert Donat in *Captain Blood*, but Grant was rejected as "too effete." Errol Flynn got the part, which made him a major star virtually overnight.

Grant moped around feeling sorry for himself for two months before Paramount finally assigned him to *The Last Outpost*, which Gary Cooper had already rejected as an intended follow-up to his highly successful *Lives of a Bengal Lancer*.

Just about the only new element in *The Last Outpost* was the mustache that Cary Grant grew for it. Most of the sets, costumes and action footage were left over from Cooper's British Colonial epic. Looking like a bronzed version of Clark Gable, Grant played a tank corps officer, with co-star Claude Rains as a sort of Lawrence of Arabia adventurer who dies in his arms during a climactic battle with enemy tribesmen in the Sahara Desert.

Continually handed such inappropriate parts in second-rate productions, Grant was becoming increasingly despondent over the way Paramount ran his career. He reached the boiling point when informed that he was being loaned to Paramount's next-door neighbor, RKO Radio, for a *supporting* role in the Katharine Hepburn vehicle *Sylvia Scarlett*. The demotion in status wounded Grant's pride, but it proved to be a turning point in his career.

Sylvia Scarlett was reportedly a private joke between Katharine Hepburn and director George Cukor to see what they could put over on the RKO bosses and movie censors. With Hepburn masquerading as a boy through most of the film, it was audaciously ahead of its time in its sexual implications.

Men and women alike fell in love with the she/he character. The artist-hero, played rather swishily by Brian Aherne, falls strongly for Hepburn in her male drag, muttering, "There's something very queer going on here." In another scene, a maid kisses Hepburn and tells her, "You're very attractive."

Cary Grant portrayed a Cockney con man who teams up with Hepburn and her father, Edmund Gwenn, in various embezzlement schemes. Director Cukor, who worked in the Broadway theatre before going to Hollywood, was well aware of Grant's background and wanted him for the part from the beginning.

"Cary knew the kind of life we showed in the picture, when the Scarletts join a traveling fair. He had started his career walking on stilts," Cukor said. "He'd had enough experience by this time to know what he was up to, and suddenly the part hit him, and he felt the ground under his feet."

But Cukor also encountered problems with Grant. Made in an era when foreign location filming was rare, a scene taking place at the foot of the White Cliffs of Dover was actually photographed north of Malibu Beach. The script required Grant to dash into what was supposed to be the Strait of Dover to rescue a drowning girl.

Grant refused. He took one look at the pounding Pacific surf and told Cukor, "No, I won't go in there! I won't!"

Meanwhile, actress Natalie Paley, in real life an exiled Russian princess who aspired to be a movie star, kept bobbing up and down in the freezing water, looking as though she really were in danger of losing her life.

"Oh, go in, Cary, she's drowning," Cukor said.

Grant stamped his foot. "I won't. It's too cold!"

Katharine Hepburn, also appearing in the scene, started laughing so hard that she nearly collapsed. Cukor finally said, "Oh, Christ!" turned his back on Grant and—to get the shot—sent Hepburn in to rescue Paley instead.

Romancing Hepburn at the time was millionaire industrialist Howard Hughes, who often flew to the oceanside location in his biplane to have lunch with her. Hughes usually invited Grant to join them and it was the beginning of a lifelong friendship between the two men.

Grant also had a new lady friend, a nineteen-year-old blonde named Betty Furness, whom he had met at Paramount while she was working with George Burns and Gracie Allen in *Here Comes Cookie.* Gossip columnists spotted a physical resemblance to Virginia Cherrill and predicted that Furness would be the next Mrs. Grant.

Although Grant and Furness kept close company for about a year, she denied that they were romantically involved. "We were never in love. We did have a lot of fun together. I was fond of him and he of me. That's all there was to it," Furness remembered.

When Grant completed *Sylvia Scarlett,* he had no idea that the film would prove such a boost to his career. In fact, the first preview was such a disaster, with people rushing out of the theatre before it was even half over, that he thought his acting days might be over.

Adding to Grant's pessimism was Paramount's rejection of an offer from MGM to borrow him for *Mutiny on the Bounty.* Although it was another supporting role, Grant believed that working with Clark Gable and Charles Laughton more than offset the possible diminution of his status as a leading man.

It would be easy to say that Paramount turned down the request for that reason, but the studio never really cared whether a film was right for Cary Grant or not. The real reason was simply that *Sylvia Scarlett* encountered production delays and Paramount didn't think that Grant would be finished in time to meet MGM's schedule. Not only did Franchot Tone get the part instead, but he later won an Oscar for his performance, which made Grant livid.

Grant proved partly correct in his feelings about *Sylvia Scarlett.* While the film was a critical and box-office failure, it became a personal triumph for Cary Grant, whose relaxed, ingratiating performance overshadowed everything else in the comedy-drama. *Variety* said he stole the picture. *Time* claimed that "the film is made remarkable by Cary Grant's superb depiction of the Cockney."

Hollywood, but not necessarily Paramount Pictures, suddenly woke up to Grant's abilities, discovering a brash, engaging dimension of him that hadn't been evident before.

Grant was slow to realize any benefits from *Sylvia Scarlett.* By the time the reviews started to appear at the close of 1935, he was in England making *The Amazing Quest of Ernest Bliss.*

Since Paramount had nothing waiting for him when he finished *Sylvia Scarlett,* the studio had loaned him to an independent British company, Garrett Klement Pictures, which was trying to break into the world market by hiring Hollywood names. Grant was happy for the opportunity, sensing that he might have a bigger future in his native country than in his adopted one. Also, it gave him the chance to deal with family problems that were left unresolved when marriage took priority on his last visit to England.

While boarding the *Aquitania* for England in November 1935, Grant told reporters that he was looking forward to spending time with his father and teenaged brother, Eric. So little was known about Grant's family history that the question of how an only child could have a brother never came up.

But Grant really meant his illegitimate half-brother, born to the woman with whom Elias Leach lived after his wife was institutionalized. Grant later changed his story and always described Eric Leach as "my favorite cousin" to spare them both unpleasant publicity. (When Eric Leach died in 1982, Grant attended the funeral, personally making sure that there was no press coverage that would reveal the long kept family secret.)

Grant's reunion with his father never took place. On December 2, 1935, Elias Leach died in a Bristol hospital, aged fifty-nine. The cause was given as "extreme toxicity," a polite way of saying that Leach died of acute alcoholism.

"It was more probably the inevitable result of a slow-breaking heart, brought about by an inability to alter the circumstances of his life," Grant said years later.

But at the time of his father's death, the son's only public comment was "I worshipped him, and I learned a lot from him." It sounded like a press agent's handout, but no one could have expected Grant to mention the pain and loneliness that Elias Leach caused him as a child.

Elias Leach's death had one very happy result. It brought about Elsie Leach's return to a world from which she'd been locked away for twenty years. As her newly designated next of kin, Grant had to assume responsibility for her care. It didn't take him long to realize that his mother didn't belong in an institution.

Grant arranged for Elsie to stay with relatives awhile and then set her up in a house of her own in Bristol. Although he wanted to take her back to California with him, doctors advised against it because the double shock of cultural readjustment might prove too great for her. Just getting back to a "normal" life in Bristol would be difficult enough.

Elsie Leach was fifty-eight years old, her son thirty-two. She could barely remember young Archie. The sun-tanned giant who called himself Cary Grant was a complete stranger. It took her years to understand and accept that they were the same person.

Grant didn't know what to expect when his mother was released from the asylum, but he was pleasantly surprised by her liveliness and well-groomed appearance. She acted timid and nervous, but who wouldn't after being institutionalized for two decades?

Relatives informed Grant that Elsie had developed a morbid fear of men. "I'm a virgin," she protested to them again and again. The quickest way to get her off the subject was to ask her, "In that case, Elsie, how did you come to have Cary?"

Her phobia posed a real danger, however, because Elsie locked every door behind her and barricaded herself in her bedroom at night. If a fire broke out, she might have been trapped. Still, it was no worse a fate than spending the rest of her life in the asylum, so Grant tolerated her eccentricity. Her freedom, no matter how long it lasted, merited the risk.

With so many personal matters to occupy him, it was a wonder that Grant found time to make a movie while in England. On that score, he might just as well have stayed in Hollywood. *The Amazing Quest of Ernest Bliss* boosted neither his career nor the British film industry. With Grant as a millionaire trying to prove that he can support himself without using any of his inherited fortune, the lackluster comedy fared poorly in England and was withheld from American release until 1937, retitled *Romance and Riches*.

While making the film, Grant became romantically linked with his leading lady, Mary Brian. Stereotyped as "the sweetest girl in pictures" after playing Wendy in the silent *Peter Pan*, the Texas-born brunette never overcame that image in adult roles. Like Grant, she went to England to try to change her luck, but was similarly disappointed.

When Grant and Brian returned to Hollywood, they dated frequently, but the relationship remained platonic. For the sake of his image, Cary Grant needed to be seen in the company of women, and he couldn't have selected a prettier or more charming partner.

Despite the rave reviews he'd received for *Sylvia Scarlett*, Paramount welcomed Grant back as if nothing had changed in his absence. His first assignment was to add name value to *Border Flight*, a "B" programmer designed to showcase two new contract players, Frances Farmer and John Howard. Grant balked and declared war.

By that time, Grant's five-year contract with Paramount was coming up for review. In four years, he had made twenty-two films, including three loan-outs. His salary rose from $450 to $2,500 a week, certainly an adequate wage when $43 a week was the national average but still a long way from the $6,000 a week that Paramount paid Gary Cooper. If Grant stayed on at Paramount, he wanted more money plus script approval. Without the latter, he was convinced that he'd continue to be relegated to Cooper's rejects and other unsuitable material.

While willing to raise Grant's salary to $3,500 a week, Paramount wouldn't knuckle under to his demand for script approval. The studio already had its hands full with Gary Cooper, Mae West, Marlene Dietrich and Claudette Colbert on that score and didn't want any more problems, especially from an actor who had yet to prove that he could be a box-office draw. Paramount urged Grant to reconsider, promising to find him better roles in the future.

Instead of *Border Flight*, Grant received what Paramount considered an acting plum in the latest effort by Walter Wanger, who headed his own production unit within the company. But "lemon" might have been a better word for *Big Brown Eyes*, a trite detective story whose biggest mystery was why the title role went to blond and blue-eyed Joan Bennett (clue: she later married the producer).

Bad as the film was—critic Paul Jacobs called it "an imbecilic dose of moronic piffle"—Cary Grant was genuinely thrilled by getting a chance to work with director Raoul Walsh. As nineteen-year-old Archie Leach, he had stood on a Hollywood set watching Walsh guide his idol, Douglas Fairbanks, through *The Thief of Bagdad*, never dreaming that one day he'd be taking direction from the same man.

Paramount next tried to prove that it had Cary Grant's best interests at heart by loaning him to MGM for a Jean Harlow film. He couldn't have been more delighted. Besides the chance to work with one of the top box-office stars, he hoped it might lead to MGM offering to sign once his Paramount contract ended.

But Grant's elation faded quickly when the role in *Suzy* turned out to be secondary to one played by Franchot Tone. In the World War I drama, "Suzy" Harlow was an American entertainer in Paris who marries French aviator Grant after inventor-husband Tone has apparently been murdered by a German spy. When Tone later turns up alive, husband number two has to be eliminated to satisfy the movie censorship code. It's Grant's misfortune to be killed by the same spy who didn't quite succeed in rubbing out husband number one.

Grant and Harlow shared one memorable scene in a Paris cabaret, where she performs "Did I Remember?" and he sings part of the haunting ballad back to her from the audience. The Harold Adamson-Walter Donaldson composition became permanently identified with both stars, and was played at Harlow's funeral when she died only a year later from uremic poisoning at the age of twenty-six.

While working at MGM, Grant gave up hope of being employed by the studio on a permanent basis. With Clark Gable, Robert Taylor, William Powell, Robert Montgomery, Spencer Tracy, Robert Young, James Stewart and Franchot Tone already signed to MGM contracts, there seemed little chance of Cary Grant's getting anything but the dregs. That happened with *Suzy*, produced at a time of peak activity when all the other MGM regulars were spoken for.

Grant's experience at MGM was one of the reasons why he finally left Paramount, where he competed against Gary Cooper, Bing Crosby, George Raft, Henry Fonda and Randolph Scott, plus newer contractees like Fred MacMurray, Ray Milland and Robert

Cummings. As Grant recalled: "They had a lot of leading men over there with dark hair and a set of teeth like mine, and they couldn't be buying stories for each of us."

It was Grant's opinion that Paramount had also failed to keep its promise about assigning him to better roles. To induce him to sign a new contract, the studio offered him one of the leads in *Spawn of the North*, a big-budget seafaring epic intended as one of its major releases of the year. But Grant couldn't picture himself playing the owner of a salmon cannery fighting against Russian poachers. The proposal only confirmed his belief that Paramount hadn't the foggiest notion of how to cast him effectively.

In retrospect, all of Cary Grant's Paramount films create a sort of blur. "He didn't have a strong enough personality to impose himself on viewers, and most people don't remember Cary Grant for those roles, or even much for his tall-dark-and-handsome stints with Mae West," said critic Pauline Kael.

Grant ended his Paramount contract with *Wedding Present*, again teamed with Joan Bennett but this time with billing second to hers. Now that he was leaving, the studio seemed to care even less about his treatment. He played a scatterbrained newspaper reporter who stops his sweetheart from marrying another man by disrupting the wedding and then eloping with her himself in an ambulance stolen from the city psychopathic ward.

After that sad mess of a comedy, it was small wonder that Cary Grant decided to become a free agent instead of tying himself down to a single studio. While there was no guarantee of steady work *or* a steady salary, he would be his own boss, able to choose his scripts and to set his own price.

8

Topper Turns the Trick

Although he'd gained his freedom, Cary Grant took some spills before he made any progress. More ready and willing than discriminating, he latched on to a couple of projects that suggested that he was no more adept at picking winners for himself than Paramount had been.

In October 1936, Grant signed with Columbia Pictures for *When You're in Love*, starring opposite former Metropolitan Opera singer Grace Moore. Moore had already made several hit films for Columbia, but the novelty was starting to wear off because the public could only take so much of her insufferably regal demeanor.

When You're in Love attempted to humanize Grace Moore by making her seem more like a regular gal than an overbearing diva. For one of her big musical numbers, she jazzed her way through Cab Calloway's "Minnie the Moocher," with Cary Grant, suitably dubbed, accompanying her at the piano.

Robert Riskin, who proved he knew something about ordinary people with his screenplays for Frank Capra's *It Happened One Night* and *Mr. Deeds Goes to Town*, made his directorial debut with *When You're in Love*. Since he also wrote the script, he created a character for Cary Grant that effectively used the actor's easy, casual style to offset Moore's stiltedness.

But the pairing might have worked better if Grant and Moore were more physically suited to each other. Since the platinum-blond Moore was six years older than Grant and also rather plump,

Grant's role made him appear more like a gigolo than a man who was supposed to be moved by love alone.

Grant started another movie before he even finished *When You're in Love,* made possible by RKO filming much of *The Toast of New York* at night to accommodate him and borrowed leading lady Frances Farmer, who was shooting *Ebb Tide* at Paramount during the day. Farmer later cited such rapid changing back and forth between characters as a cause of her lifelong psychiatric problems, but it didn't seem to do Cary Grant any harm. He didn't "live" his roles the way Farmer did, which enabled him to leave them behind at the studio when he went home.

After working with Grant in *The Toast of New York,* Frances Farmer said that he was "aloof and remote, solely intent on remaining 'Cary Grant,' the personality." To her way of thinking, that had nothing to do with acting, and she often told him that to his face. Grant appeared undisturbed and unaffected by her outbursts, but the love scenes between them lacked any emotional or sexual charge.

The Toast of New York was a highly romanticized biography of Jim Fisk, the notorious robber baron of post-Civil War America, who was portrayed by Edward Arnold, with Grant as his business partner and rival for Frances Farmer's affections. Grant got the girl, but Arnold won the audience's sympathy with a bravura performance that made mincemeat of everybody else in the cast.

A master at stealing scenes, Arnold deliberately blew his lines in take after take, until the other actors started faltering from exhaustion and he suddenly became letter perfect. The exasperated director, Rowland V. Leigh, then had to accept any take that Arnold completed, no matter how unsatisfactory the other actors might have been.

When Grant finished *When You're in Love* and *The Toast of New York,* Columbia and RKO both offered to sign him to contracts. Still pained by his experience at Paramount, Grant was reluctant to tie himself down again, although circumstances weren't quite the same. Neither Columbia nor RKO had a strong roster of leading men, so Grant could see opportunities for himself that he wasn't likely to get at the bigger "star factories" (MGM, Paramount, Warner Brothers and 20th Century–Fox).

Through his agent, Frank Vincent, Grant worked out a deal whereby he would work for both Columbia *and* RKO, making two pictures for each of them every eighteen months. In other words, each studio would get Grant for at least one picture a year and sometimes two, depending on whose turn came next in the rotating time schedule.

Grant's financial demands almost killed the deal. He made *When You're in Love* and *The Toast of New York* for his former Paramount salary of $2,500 a week. But now he wanted a flat fee of $75,000 per picture, which Columbia and RKO considered exorbitant. The custom in Hollywood, as in many businesses, was to determine compensation by what someone received in his last job. In Grant's case, there was no precedent, since he'd never worked on a picture-by-picture basis before.

The only way to break the stalemate was for Grant to prove to Columbia and RKO that he could get $75,000 per picture elsewhere. That proved impossible, but Grant did find a $50,000 buyer. Columbia and RKO were then willing to accept that as a starting fee, with provision for gradual increases if the arrangement worked out to everyone's satisfaction.

If Grant thought he sold himself cheap in order to close the deal with Columbia and RKO, the one-picture contract that he signed with independent producer Hal Roach turned out to be well worth the sacrifice. Roach took a Thorne Smith short story, "The Jovial Ghosts," and transformed it into a classic comedy called *Topper*, which became Cary Grant's first undisputed hit and the beginning of his reputation as Hollywood's most gifted light actor.

Hal Roach wanted Jean Harlow and W. C. Fields for the other leading roles in *Topper*. But Harlow was ill (she died soon afterward) and Fields couldn't be persuaded, so Roach settled for Constance Bennett and Roland Young, who seemed much better suited to the parts anyway. Grant and Bennett played a couple of reckless socialites killed in a car crash, who come back as ghosts to complicate the life of their timid banker friend, Cosmo Topper.

Making *Topper* was one of the easiest assignments that Cary Grant ever had. Since he and Bennett were supposed to be invisible much of the story, they were spared going to the studio every day and could record their voice tracks whenever it suited their convenience. The really hard work fell to the special-effects men. Fountain pens wrote, furniture floated in air, shower spray bounced off Bennett's invisible body, all through camera tricks that were as old as Hal Roach's silent slapstick comedies. But in the context of a sophisticated bedroom farce, audiences responded to them as if they were brand new.

Finishing *Topper*, Grant reported to Columbia for the first film under his new contract. Not too surprisingly for those times of assembly-line production, the script was still in the process of being written, but Grant and his co-star, Irene Dunne, read enough of it to beg studio head Harry Cohn to reassign them to another picture. Cohn refused. Too much money had been invested in the project. The sets were all ready and waiting to be used.

Believing that he'd made the worst mistake of his life by signing with Columbia, Grant started *The Awful Truth* in a hostile mood. "Cary was afraid because he'd never done a comedy like that," said director Leo McCarey. "I remember he argued, 'Any man married to a lovely lady like Irene Dunne could not be unfaithful to her— it's totally unbelievable.' "

After a week of filming, Grant sat down at a typewriter and composed an eight-page memorandum entitled "What's Wrong With This Picture." He sent it to Harry Cohn together with an offer of five thousand dollars to be released from his contract. Cohn threw it in the wastebasket.

Although the plot didn't make much sense, the "awful truth" was that Grant and Dunne should have stayed married instead of getting divorced at the beginning of the film. Before they finally realize how much they still love and need each other, a great many zany things happen, most of which hinge on a custody battle over Mr. Smith, their Scottish terrier.

It all worked because of the lightning pace and the chemistry between Grant and Irene Dunne. Leo McCarey, who started in the movie business as a gag writer for silent two-reelers, piled laugh upon laugh so that the audience rarely had time to catch its breath.

Cary Grant's rapid-fire delivery and his ability to throw away lines, which sometimes made it sound as though he were talking to himself, made him the perfect foil for Irene Dunne's calm, relaxed style. Dunne was best known then for romantic and emotional "weepers." The director capitalized on the incongruity of involving such an obviously genteel lady in screwball happenings.

By the end of 1937, Cary Grant had more than established himself as a free-lance star. *Topper* and *The Awful Truth* were among the biggest box-office hits of the year, bringing him more job offers than he could possibly handle. Their success also renewed the public's curiosity about Grant's private life, which had been more or less a closed book in the two years since his divorce from Virginia Cherrill.

Gossip columns said that Grant was dividing his time between Ginger Rogers and blond starlet Phyllis Brooks. Since Grant and Rogers both worked for RKO, cynics considered their association more publicity-oriented than romantic.

Whatever was going on between Grant and Brooks, a former model under contract to 20th Century–Fox, continued for several years. Grant said at the time: "I'm an awfully poor Romeo. When I go courting, it's a pretty sad performance. I guess I'm too deadly intense, and I can't express, in words, the deep feelings I'm trying to convey. So I'm just a muddle-tongued boob."

But apart from his mother, the most important woman in Grant's life then was the Countess di Frasso, whose noble title belied one of Hollywood's most profligate characters. Short, plump and sixteen years older than Grant, the American-born Dorothy Taylor was an heiress to a leather-goods fortune. She'd been married twice, first to the famous British aviator Claude Graham-White (who left her for vaudeville star Ethel Levey) and then to Italy's Count Carlo Dentici di Frasso.

The countess's second marriage was strictly a matter of convenience. She wanted a title and the count needed money to restore his family's decaying sixteenth-century Roman palace to its former splendor. Villa Madama became a main watering hole for the international social set. At one of her own extravagant parties in 1931, the countess fell in love at first sight with visiting movie star Gary Cooper and followed him back to California, where she established a second residence in Beverly Hills.

For three years, Di Frasso played Cooper's "sponsor" and traveled everywhere with him. The affair ended when too much sordid publicity caused image-conscious Paramount to intervene by advising Cooper to find himself a more suitable companion. When Cooper married socialite Veronica Balfe, the countess decided to stay in Hollywood, quickly becoming one of moviedom's most popular hostesses and the first outsider to be accepted into that smart social set.

Cary Grant partially replaced Gary Cooper in the life of Countess di Frasso. Grant never served stud as Cooper had, but in other ways he filled the countess's need for a handsome companion and protégé.

Grant owed much of his initial success as a free-lancer to Di Frasso. Always singing his praises in the right places, she was the one who sold George Cukor on the idea of casting Grant in *Sylvia Scarlett.* She also introduced him into privileged high society, eventually becoming his marriage broker as well.

Grant later described Dorothy di Frasso as "a friend whose rare ability to laugh at herself so often dispelled my own gloom." Not afraid to admit that she was getting too old for the younger men she preferred, she loved to recount her latest escapades in finding companionship. Her favorite sport was driving up and down Hollywood Boulevard late at night in her chauffeured limousine, picking up hustlers or an occasional serviceman in uniform. She also frequented the wild parties given by director Edmund Goulding, which were notorious for sado-masochistic activities.

While Di Frasso was Grant's closest woman friend, he still spent most of his spare time with Randolph Scott, with whom he'd resumed living after his divorce from Virginia Cherrill. A year later, in March 1936, it was Scott's turn to get married, the bride being Marion duPont Summerville, a wealthy divorcee and sportswoman. Fan magazines quickly pointed out that she was older than Scott, homely and rather mannish-looking, hardly the kind of wife that a Hollywood dream prince would be expected to choose for himself.

Cary Grant moved out of the Santa Monica house he'd been sharing with Scott and rented one right next door to the newlyweds. How long that arrangement lasted is unknown, but within a year Grant and Scott became housemates again. The reunited duo caused a lot of gossip and snickering when they made a grand entrance—identically dressed as circus acrobats in white satin pantaloons—at the costume ball thrown by Marion Davies in honor of William Randolph Hearst's seventy-fourth birthday.

According to the newspapers, Scott and his wife had filed for a legal separation, due to an incompatibility of interests. His work kept him anchored in Hollywood, while she had to spend most of the time on her farm in Virginia, where she raised racehorses.

When Grant and Scott first started living together in 1932, the reason supposedly was to economize. "We're living as we want to, as bachelors with a nice home at a comparatively small cost," Grant said at the time. "If we got married, we would have to put up a front. Women, particularly Hollywood women, expect it."

Actress friend Carole Lombard found the arrangement rather amusing. After visiting the Grant-Scott ménage and watching them handle the household accounts, she said that "Cary opened the bills, Randy wrote the checks and if Cary could talk someone out of a stamp, he mailed them."

Broadway playwright Moss Hart, who was sometimes a houseguest of theirs, said that if he stayed more than a few days, Grant and Scott presented him with an itemized bill at the end of the week for his laundry, phone calls and incidentals.

After Grant and Scott had been living together off and on for five years, the arrangement started to bother the gossip columnists and other guardians of Hollywood morality. Although it was understandable when they started out in the business, the two men were successful enough now to afford separate residences. To counteract rumors that they were possibly lovers, stories started appearing in the fan magazines that stressed their masculine, he-man qualities.

The campaign focused more on Grant than Scott, probably because Grant was the more successful of the two and stood to lose more if fans started to avoid his films because they disapproved of his private life. Also, Grant tended to be a bit too dandified and came from England (homosexuality was often called "the English disease" because of its prevalence in British public schools).

"Randy says the guy's regular," stated an article in *Movie Mirror,* but it was left to the reader to decide whether that meant Cary Grant was heterosexual or simply had "normal" masculine interests. Scott cited a fishing trip they took together along the McCloud River in Shasta National Forest. Grant foolishly wore tennis shoes, and kept slipping and sliding on the boulders and finally removed them to go barefoot.

"By the time we got back, his dogs were plenty sore and bruised. But not once was there one yap or complaint out of him," Scott said.

Scott also claimed that Grant "is easy to live with, considerate of others, doesn't interfere or try to give advice however well meant, has the courage to fight for his convictions, is a graceful winner and a good loser, never outfumbles in doing his share, and has a punchy sense of humor."

Archibald Alexander Leach, age four, in Bristol, England. (UPI/Bettmann Newsphotos)

A poster advertising Bob Pender's troupe of knockabout comedians, which Archie Leach joined when he was thirteen. The figure on the far right was said to represent him. (The Museum of Modern Art/Film Stills Archives)

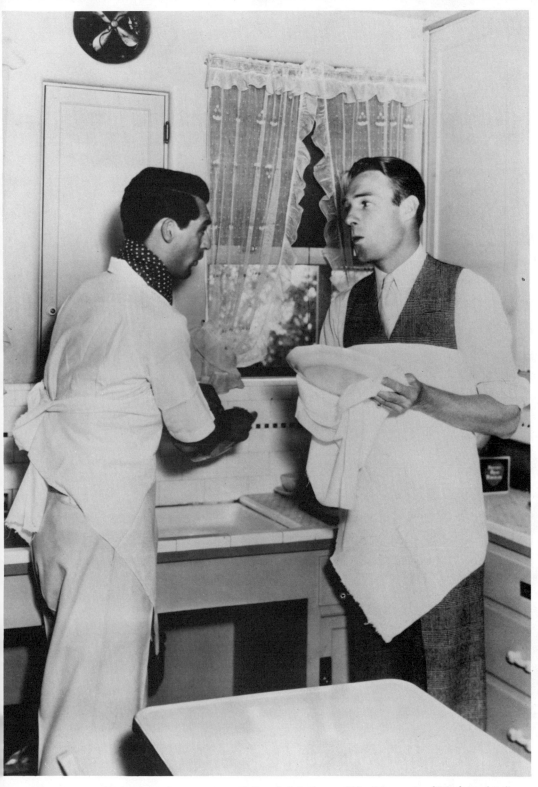

Cary Grant with his longtime roommate, Randolph Scott. (The Museum of Modern Art/ Film Stills Archives)

Above, the first Mrs. Cary Grant,
Virginia Cherrill,
with her husband.
(The Museum of Modern Art/
Film Stills Archives)

Left, Cary Grant and his second wife,
Barbara Hutton,
on their wedding day.
(Culver Pictures, Inc.)

Actress Betsy Drake became the third Mrs. Grant.
(The Museum of Modern Art/Film Stills Archives)

Dyan Cannon was the only one of Grant's wives to bear him a
child. In their first family portrait, Grant, sixty-two, and Cannon,
twenty-eight, pose with their 3½-month-old daughter, Jennifer.
(AP/Wide World Photos)

Cary Grant with his fifth wife, Barbara Harris, in September 1986. (AP/Wide World Photos)

Marlene Dietrich and Cary Grant in *Blonde Venus,* 1932. (The Museum of Modern Art/ Film Stills Archives)

The young star with Mae West in *She Done Him Wrong,* 1933. (The Museum of Modern Art/Film Stills Archives)

Cary Grant with co-stars Roland Young and Constance Bennett in *Topper*, 1937. (The Museum of Modern Art/Film Stills Archives)

A reporter visiting the set of *The Awful Truth* described Grant as "rather standoffish, with an invisible but definite barrier you can't get by. Cary hides off in a corner when he's not needed, with a handkerchief over his face. Sometimes he suddenly warms up, sputtering wisecracks, banging out a mad medley of tunes on the piano and interspersing them with snappily executed tap dances."

Louella Parsons said that Grant "falls in love like a tumble bug. He idealizes all women yet treats *the* woman of the moment with a casual offhandedness that sometimes amuses them, more often burns them up." The woman of the moment was again starlet Phyllis Brooks, who had returned to Hollywood after an unsuccessful attempt at a Broadway stage career.

Randolph Scott, meanwhile, stirred up romantic news with Paramount contract player Dorothy Lamour, with whom he appeared in *High, Wide and Handsome*. Lamour said later that the studio publicity department arranged their dates, that she and Scott were "really just good friends."

Grant and Scott often invited Lamour to the Sunday dinner parties they gave at their Santa Monica beach house. During one of those meals, she praised the chicken dish served as the main course. Grant looked at her and said, "Dottie, that wasn't chicken, it was rabbit." Imagining all the adorable bunnies that went into the meal, Lamour had to run for the bathroom.

Noël Coward usually stayed with Grant and Scott during his visits to California. Coward's homosexuality was so widely known that whenever he stopped over in Santa Monica, the Hollywood smart set had a saying that "Cary and Randy have the queen in residence again."

A man who knew everybody, Noël Coward arranged Cary Grant's famous and ill-fated meeting with Greta Garbo. One day while Coward was a houseguest, he called Grant at the studio: "Try to get home in time to meet her, dear boy. She'd like to be introduced."

As Grant put down the phone, he broke into a cold sweat. He so idolized Garbo that Archie Leach had once followed her for several blocks when he saw her leaving the Astor Hotel in New York. Garbo was such a living legend that he couldn't work up the courage to go home to meet her. All day he invented things to do, just to keep him at the studio.

It was dark when Grant finally arrived home. As he walked into the living room, the "Divine Swede" was standing there, getting ready to leave. "Greta, I'd like you to meet Cary Grant," Noël Coward gushed.

Grant opened his mouth but nothing came out. He shook hands with the visitor and bowed. Garbo grinned, tried to engage Grant in conversation, but finally gave up when he didn't utter a single word.

Bewildered, Noël Coward escorted Garbo out to her car, with Grant trailing after them. Just as she was about to drive away, Grant found his tongue. "Very pleased to meet you," he said, ten minutes after the occasion called for it. "How dod you do?"

His friends kidded him about the incident for years. For one of the few times in his life, Cary Grant was tongue-tied, struck dumb by admiration and awe.

9

Lucky Streak

Starting with *Topper* and *The Awful Truth* in 1937, Cary Grant's career hit a lucky streak that continued through the decade. In the field of screwball comedy, he reigned as king. With his newborn freedom to pick and choose roles, he proved equally adroit at romantic melodrama and high adventure. Top directors like Howard Hawks, George Cukor, George Stevens and Leo McCarey lined up waiting for his next availability.

Syndicated columnist Ed Sullivan called Grant "the biggest name in Hollywood right now." Howard Hawks said, "I've seen it happen time and again. A performer goes along for years and is never better than satisfactory. Then, suddenly, he becomes brilliant. It's all a matter of confidence. Cary Grant became a star when he became confident of himself. He's doing things now, little gestures, facial expressions, that he wouldn't have dared to do when he first came to Hollywood because then he lacked confidence. Now he's got it. Confidence brings poise and polish and what I call 'style' to a player. Once a performer has it, his reading of lines and his reactions take on sparkle. Right now, Cary is hot."

In September 1937, Hawks became the first director to work with Grant since the actor had signed his semi-exclusive contract with RKO. Because Grant had worked so effectively with Katharine Hepburn in *Sylvia Scarlett*, production executive Pandro S. Berman talked him into teaming with her in a screwball comedy designed to make Hepburn more appealing to that large majority of moviegoers who weren't buying her in dramatic parts.

Cary Grant's role in *Bringing Up Baby* had already been turned down by Ronald Colman, Robert Montgomery and Ray Milland. Grant almost rejected it himself, claiming that he wasn't the intellectual type and didn't know how to play the earnest, bespectacled paleontologist.

"You've seen Harold Lloyd, haven't you?" Howard Hawks asked him. Grant nodded. That was all the guidance he needed. Whenever he had any problems with interpretation, he just summoned up a mental picture of the deadpan antics of one of his early film idols.

In the first weeks of shooting, Hawks had problems with Katharine Hepburn, who thought that she had to *act* funny to *be* funny. Time and again, Hawks stopped the action to explain to her that the great clowns like Lloyd, Chaplin and Keaton never ran around making funny faces. They were serious, sad and even solemn, with the humor springing from what happened to them and how they reacted. Grant understood that immediately, but Hepburn didn't.

In desperation, Hawks asked Walter Catlett, the veteran character comedian who had a featured role in the film, to give Hepburn some lessons. Catlett played a whole scene of Hepburn's with Grant, first mimicking her mistakes and then showing her how she should really do it. Hepburn was entranced. From then on she played perfectly, not trying to be funny but acting her natural self.

Bringing Up Baby was probably the screwiest of all screwball comedies, the two basic jokes being that the seemingly wacky heroine isn't much crazier than any of the other characters and that human and animal behavior are virtually identical. Hepburn, the owner of a pet leopard named Baby, leads Grant a merry chase while he's trying to persuade her rich aunt to contribute a million dollars to his museum. Hawks directed the farce at such a fast clip that his earlier screwball classic, *Twentieth Century*, seemed like a relic of the Victorian age.

When released in February 1938, *Bringing Up Baby* received excellent reviews but proved too sophisticated for the mass audience, barely earning back its production cost. The film's disappointing grosses contributed to theatre exhibitors' branding Katharine Hepburn "box-office poison." Although she joined elite company—Greta Garbo, Marlene Dietrich and Joan Crawford were also on the list—Hepburn thought her film career was over and left Hollywood for New York to resume working in the theatre.

But before that happened, Cary Grant and Katharine Hepburn got another chance to work together. Prior to the film's release, reaction to *Bringing Up Baby* within the industry was so favorable that it seemed good business sense to team them again as soon as possible.

The main stumbling block was that Grant owed his next picture to Columbia. Since Hepburn wasn't any too happy with RKO's plans to next star her in *Mother Carey's Chickens*, she bought her way out of her contract and then persuaded Columbia to make *Holiday*, with Cary Grant as her leading man.

Hepburn had a sentimental attachment to the Philip Barry play. After serving as understudy to leading lady Hope Williams in the original 1928 Broadway production, she had tested for the 1930 film version but lost out to Ann Harding. Now Hepburn finally had the chance to prove herself in a role that seemed tailor-made, an idealistic rich girl opposed to her family's materialistic views.

Portraying a happy wanderer with no steady job, Cary Grant received an opportunity to show that he was as skilled an acrobat as he was a light comedian. Required to perform handsprings in one of the scenes, he ended up giving lessons to Hepburn as well. She proved such a good pupil that he took to tossing her in the air as a prelude to teaching her more difficult stunts. Whenever Grant was due on the set, Hepburn had to run and hide, out of fear that she'd break her neck.

Hepburn got back at Grant with a prank of her own. He occupied a small portable dressing room in which he could barely turn around. Hearing much laughter outside one day, he emerged to find that Hepburn had plastered a sign on the door that said "Grant's Tomb."

Directed by Hepburn's staunch friend George Cukor, *Holiday* blended a polite comedy of manners with a slight touch of screwball to liven the pace. Although future generations of movie buffs would treasure it for Grant and Hepburn's delightful performances, the film was even less successful in its day than *Bringing Up Baby*. Quite talky and far removed from the experience of ordinary moviegoers, it ended up playing as a second feature to Columbia's "B" Western *Law of the Plains*, in rural areas.

Released in June 1938, not long after the Independent Theatre Owners Association had named Hepburn one of the box-office-poison stars, *Holiday* seemed to confirm their selection. Amazingly, Columbia tried to use the condemnation as a selling point for *Holiday* by adopting the advertising slogan, "Is it true what they say about Hepburn?" Apparently the public thought so. It would be three years before any new Hepburn films reached the screen, and then only because Cary Grant made it possible.

With his co-star of two consecutive films branded a pariah, it was amazing that Cary Grant escaped a similar fate. But in the eyes of the industry, Grant hadn't quite crossed the dividing line between leading man and major star. *Bringing Up Baby* and *Holiday* were considered Hepburn vehicles; Grant just happened to be along for the ride. His commendable performances augured well for the future.

When RKO's turn at using Grant came around again, he was offered one of the leads in *Gunga Din*, a two-million-dollar epic that would be the most expensive film in the studio's history. Grant needed no coaxing. He loved the script, which gave him a chance to break out of the usual comedy mold, and he also realized what the association with such a prestige production could do for his career. Furthermore, he saw a good luck omen in the fact that Rudyard Kipling's poem (with the immortal line, "You're a better man than I am, Gunga Din"), was schoolboy Archie Leach's favorite recitation piece.

With Kipling's heroic water-bearer doing little more than lending his name to *Gunga Din*, Ben Hecht and Charles MacArthur wrote an original story that combined elements of their own *The Front Page* with *The Three Musketeers* and *Lives of a Bengal Lancer*. Grant, Victor McLaglen and Douglas Fairbanks, Jr., were three British soldiers in nineteenth-century India, the first two trying their damnedest to stop the third from quitting the service to get married and run a tea plantation.

As boisterous Archibald Cutter (he picked the first name himself), Grant finally got a chance to emulate his idol, Douglas Fairbanks, Sr., leaping through the air, performing somersaults and brandishing a sword against hostile hordes.

According to writer Sheilah Graham, who visited the set, Grant deliberately cheated Douglas Fairbanks, Jr., out of one of the most memorable moments in the picture. In a rooftop scene, Fairbanks had to wrestle with a native foe, pick him up and hurl him into the street below. Grant coveted the bit himself, so he told his co-star, "Doug, you really shouldn't do this. It looks like you've killed the guy. It wouldn't help your image. And you know your father would never have done such a thing on the screen."

Convinced that Grant was right, the worried Fairbanks begged director George Stevens to assign the chore to someone else. When Stevens agreed, Grant jumped forward and said, "George, I'll do it!"

Gunga Din took 104 days to shoot, twice the average for those times, and had a company of twelve hundred actors and workers. Most exteriors were filmed not in India but two hundred miles northeast of Los Angeles in Lone Pine, California, between Mount Whitney and Death Valley.

For weeks, everybody lived outdoors in a city of canvas tents, awakened every morning at five-thirty. On his way to breakfast, Grant saw one of the strangest sights of his filmmaking career. Since there was a shortage of dark-skinned extras who could pass for natives, hundreds needed to have their bodies covered with brown liquid makeup. Starting at daybreak, they lined up to take their turns on revolving platforms that were operated by makeup artists armed with spray guns.

The monotony of location living finally got to Grant and he couldn't wait to return to Hollywood. Near the end of filming, he blew up when George Stevens ordered him to stay over another day or two. Victor McLaglen had gotten into a drunken brawl the night before and had received a whopping black eye that prevented him from working in scenes with Grant that day. Grant thought for a moment and then asked, "Which eye? Right or left?"

When Stevens said the left, Grant replied, "So what's the problem? We do over the shot with the horses, put Vic on foot to the camera's left, eliminate him from the crowd scene and he doesn't have to show the bruised side of his face until tomorrow, when the swelling should have gone down." Stevens followed Grant's suggestion exactly, saving RKO the ten thousand dollars it would have cost to cancel production for the day.

Grant was more pleased about the time he saved for himself. In another six weeks he had to start a new picture at Columbia. In the interim, he intended to visit his mother in England, a trip that he would have been forced to cancel if *Gunga Din* had gone over schedule.

Nearly three years had passed since Grant's reunion with his mother. Although he'd promised to return to Bristol every year, his work prevented it. He had made ten pictures since his last visit, with not enough time in between for the long coast-to-coast, trans-oceanic trip that a took a minimum of ten days each way then before the era of high-speed air travel.

But Grant wrote to his mother regularly, supported her and sent large hampers of canned goods on her birthday and special occasions. Many of them remained unopened for years. When friends urged Mrs. Leach to use them before they went bad, her stock reply was "I want to save them until they're really needed. You never know, Cary might be hard up one day."

That she now called him Cary instead of Archie showed that Elsie Leach had finally come to terms with her son's new identity. Although she was shy and didn't encourage the attention herself, Bristol townsfolk treated her like a celebrity because she was Cary Grant's mother. Theatre managers invited her to the openings of his films. Everybody fussed over her when she went shopping or for her afternoon strolls.

In November 1938, Grant spent two weeks with his mother in Bristol, taking her sightseeing and making frequent visits to fish-and-chips shops. Both were addicted to the greasy fried fare that was traditionally served up in wrappings of old newspapers. Causing lots of amusement in Bristol for years was the sight of Cary Grant and his mother sitting in the back seat of his rented limousine, sharing one of their cheap meals and washing it down with hot tea brought from home in a Thermos bottle.

The menu was more upscale on the French superliner *Normandie*, on which Grant returned to America at the end of his visit. During one of the lavish *cordon bleu* dinners, the captain introduced him to an attractive blonde who nibbled Ry-Krisp and sipped black coffee while everyone else gorged on lobster Thermidor and champagne.

She was the Countess Haugwitz-Reventlow, better known as Barbara Hutton. Grant didn't need to be told that she was one of the world's richest women. He'd been hearing and reading about the Woolworth heiress since his earliest days in America. In fact, they had a close mutual friend in Countess Dorothy di Frasso.

Hutton complimented Grant on his performance in *Holiday,* which the Countess di Frasso had taken her to see at the Venice Film Festival. The new acquaintances chatted briefly and went their separate ways. As far as Grant was concerned, Barbara Hutton was just another name to add to the list of famous people he ran into all the time. Little did he know that Hutton had a crush on him.

"Barbara's amorous daydreams weren't much different from those of the girls who clerked in Woolworth's," said close friend Elsa Maxwell. "She imagined that being involved with Cary Grant could be as much fun as what took place on the screen in one of his romantic comedies."

After the *Normandie* docked in New York, Grant found himself trapped in a major scandal when the U.S. Justice Department subpoenaed him to testify in the investigation of William P. Buckner, Jr., a securities broker accused of using the mails to defraud. Buckner, who claimed to be the ex-fiancé of actress Loretta Young, allegedly had sold one million dollars' worth of phony bonds in the Philippine Railway Company through mail solicitations that carried the endorsement of Cary Grant and other movie stars.

Questioned for fifteen minutes, Grant testified that he'd never met Buckner and knew nothing about the charges brought against the man. Crooked schemes involving the unauthorized use of celebrities' names were all too common in the hard times of the 1930s, so no further action was taken against Grant.

But he still had to suffer the embarrassment of being used by the press to sell newspapers. All across the nation, huge front-page headlines linked Cary Grant to a million-dollar fraud, but the fact of his apparent innocence was buried inside at the bottom of the stories.

Back in Hollywood, Grant received a job offer that seemed like a dream come true. Ernst Lubitsch, the undisputed master of sophisticated comedy, wanted him to play opposite Greta Garbo in MGM's *Ninotchka.* Lubitsch was so eager to get Grant that his writers, Billy Wilder and Charles Brackett, were standing ready to tailor the role to the actor's exact specifications.

But Grant owed his next picture to Columbia and Harry Cohn refused to postpone the commitment so that he could accept Lubitsch's offer. Since Columbia didn't own theatres as the bigger companies did, the studio depended on revenues from advance block bookings to cover production costs. Since exhibitors had already been promised "a Cary Grant picture," Columbia was bound by contract to deliver.

Melvyn Douglas got the part in *Ninotchka*, depriving Cary Grant of his only chance to work with Greta Garbo, who retired from acting after making only one more film after that. Instead, Grant reported to Columbia for *Plane Number Four*, which sounded suspiciously like another of those aviation programmers from his Paramount days.

The script, in fact, was being written day by day. Most of it still remained in the head of director Howard Hawks, who based the story on one of his own experiences as a flyer. Hawks had known a pilot who parachuted from a burning plane, leaving his co-pilot behind to die in the crash. Spending the rest of his life shunned by other pilots, the man was finally killed in an attempt to redeem himself.

With Cary Grant and vivacious Jean Arthur as the leads and Columbia starlet Rita Hayworth thrown in for an extra touch of glamour, Hawks and scriptwriter Jules Furthman couldn't allow the film to be too serious or tragic. With the title changed to *Only Angels Have Wings*, it became a hybrid drama, romantic comedy and sky thriller, enshrouded in the steamy, foglike atmosphere that was the hallmark of many Howard Hawks movies.

Portraying the owner of an airline flying mail and cargo over the Andes Mountains in South America, Cary Grant further established himself as a male sex object. "He drew women to him by making them feel he needs them, yet the last thing he'd do would be to come right out and say it," Pauline Kael remarked.

Dressed like a sexy Lindbergh in a leather jacket and baggy trousers, Grant drives stranded showgirl Jean Arthur into an advanced state of heat while she waits for him to make the first move. Many Cary Grant fans believe that he reached the zenith of his physical perfection in the film, made around the time of his thirty-fifth birthday.

In 1939, Grant made three films. After *Only Angels Have Wings*, he returned to RKO for *In Name Only*, based on a romantic novel that the studio purchased for Katharine Hepburn before she fell from favor. RKO still hadn't selected a female lead when Carole Lombard heard it was available and put in a bid. Recently married to Clark Gable, she was anxious to get back to work while he filmed

Gone With the Wind. The couple made a pact that each would work only when the other was working so that they could have more free time together.

RKO needed women stars so desperately at the time that Lombard was able to negotiate a four-picture contract at $150,000 each, plus a percentage of the profits. While admiring her business acumen, Cary Grant blew his stack, not least of all because Carole Lombard got top billing. His deal with RKO paid him only half of what Lombard received: $75,000 a picture and no profit participation.

He demanded more and thought he was worth it since the recent success of *Gunga Din,* the biggest grosser in the studio's history. RKO conceded, raising Grant's fee to $100,000, with promises of additional benefits to come later.

A slick "woman's picture," *In Name Only* neither advanced Cary Grant's career nor harmed it. The soap-opera melodramatics seemed a waste of the talents of Grant and Lombard, the best screwball comedians in the business. Compared with Lombard and Kay Francis, who competed for his love and million-dollar fortune, Grant had very little to do except appear to be worth their efforts to land him.

While making *In Name Only,* Grant joined members of Hollywood's British colony in a special radio program honoring King George VI and Queen Elizabeth, broadcast at the exact time the visiting royalty were having a Sunday afternoon picnic with President and Mrs. Roosevelt at their estate in Hyde Park, New York.

Grant, David Niven, Laurence Olivier, Vivien Leigh, Errol Flynn, Ronald Colman and others rehearsed for days and put on a dazzling show. Years later, Grant discovered that the picnickers never heard it. The batteries in FDR's portable radio ran down just before the broadcast began, and no one had thought to bring replacements.

In that summer of 1939, Cary Grant's mother was very much in his thoughts. Although British Prime Minister Neville Chamberlain returned from conferences with Adolf Hitler predicting "Peace in our time," the prevalent feeling was that a second world war could break out at any moment.

Fearing for his mother's safety, Grant made his second trip to England within a year. He wanted Elsie Leach to come to live with him in California, if not permanently, at least until the dangerous situation in Europe resolved itself.

Mrs. Leach refused, but Grant had to admire her for the reason she gave. Confined to an institution during the last war, she was determined to see the next war through by doing her patriotic best for king and country.

When Grant returned to New York on the *Île de France*, he received a surprise welcome from Phyllis Brooks, whom fan magazines had been calling "the next Mrs. Grant" for over three years. Dockside reporters speculated that the couple planned to elope.

Grant and Brooks lingered in New York for two weeks while he publicized *In Name Only* and they visited the newly opened World's Fair at Flushing Meadows. Legend has it that Grant first started taking a romantic interest in Barbara Hutton when he saw an exquisite photograph of her in a display of contemporary personalities in the General Motors Pavilion.

Still in the company of Phyllis Brooks, Grant next turned up at the annual racing season at Saratoga Springs, reviving rumors of an impending wedding. Instead, the couple announced their engagement.

The betrothal sputtered on for months, with breakups and reconciliations every few weeks. It eventually died on the vine when Grant became involved with Barbara Hutton. Brooks reportedly vented her anger over that development by smashing a framed picture of herself over Grant's head during a party at his house.

But in the summer of 1939, romance had to take a second place to more urgent matters. On September 1, Germany's invasion of Poland signaled the start of World War II (the United States, of course, didn't enter the war until December 8, 1941). A few days later, Hollywood's large community of British actors, writers, producers and directors assembled to determine a course of action now that their native country was involved in the conflict.

Cary Grant, who'd once applied for American citizenship but never followed through for his final papers, not only attended but was also delegated, together with Laurence Olivier and producer Herbert Wilcox, to fly to Washington to get a directive from the British ambassador.

Herbert Wilcox, husband of actress Anna Neagle, remembered the trip to Washington as "a nightmare flight through continuous thunder and lightning storms. Larry Olivier slept through it all, not bothered in the least by Cary Grant trying to calm my terror by singing old music hall ditties."

During the meeting at the British embassy, the ambassador, Lord Lothian, asked each of the visitors how old they were. Laughing, Grant said, "For years, I've been stepping it down. Now I'd better step it up." Noticing that Lord Lothian wasn't at all amused by the jest, he confessed to being thirty-five. Olivier was thirty-two, Wilcox forty-eight.

"Go back and get on with your jobs," Lord Lothian told them. "It's important to keep the English idiom and way of life before American audiences. Don't violate the Neutrality Act, but do everything you can to promote the British cause. And tell those of military age to get back to England and take their part."

Grant and Wilcox took the ambassador's advice, but Olivier chose not to. Telephoning inamorata Vivien Leigh back in Hollywood, he told her to start packing for a return to England. Leslie Howard, David Niven and Richard Greene were among the first to follow Olivier's example.

With his gift for making people laugh, Cary Grant decided that he could do more as a morale booster than as a soldier and went back to work in *His Girl Friday,* which turned out to be one of the funniest films he ever made. Howard Hawks cleverly reworked Ben Hecht and Charles MacArthur's *The Front Page* so that one of the two contentious newspapermen could be played by a woman. The addition of a sexual subtext was such a daring change from the original much-revered play that no one wanted to take the title role. Irene Dunne, Claudette Colbert, Carole Lombard and Jean Arthur had turned it down before Columbia gambled on Rosalind Russell, who hadn't quite made it into the top ranks despite many fine performances.

Since Grant and Russell both excelled at improvisation and extemporaneous delivery, Howard Hawks let them run riot. One of Grant's cleverest interpolations came when he remarked to one of the minor characters, "The last person to say that to me was Archie Leach just before he cut his throat." In another scene, Russell saw room for extra comic business, hurled her handbag at Grant and missed. Improvising, Grant quipped, "You used to be better than that." Hawks was smart enough to keep it in the final cut.

During the filming of *His Girl Friday*, Grant had a houseguest named Frederick Brisson, who was the son of famous Danish entertainer Carl Brisson and the London representative for Grant's agent, Frank Vincent. On his latest transatlantic crossing, Freddy Brisson saw *The Women* and fell in love with one of the actresses in the movie. When he got to Hollywood and discovered the very same Rosalind Russell working with his host, Cary Grant, it seemed like fate.

Grant tried to play Cupid by arranging an introduction for Brisson, but Russell said she was busy and kept putting him off. She turned down an invitation for Christmas dinner and also to a cozy New Year's Eve celebration. Grant and Brisson had twenty-four bottles of champagne sitting on ice in the bathtub, but Russell never showed up, choosing to go out on the town with Jimmy Stewart instead. But Brisson never lost heart and his perseverance eventually paid dividends.

At least for the time being, Grant had ended his living arrangement with Randolph Scott and now owned the beach house which the two of them had rented for years from Norma Talmadge. The two-story, twelve-room stucco house seemed rather large for one person, but Grant employed a live-in staff of three.

Frank Horn, an ex-actor of similar age whom Grant had met during his stage days, served as secretary and also managed the household. A married couple had combined duties of cook-maid and butler-chauffeur.

A dismal failure at doing anything for himself, Grant even had trouble preparing meals for his two Sealyham terriers, Archibald and Cholmondeley. But he was a penny-pinching overseer who always made sure that he received the full value for his money.

When Frank Horn presented the monthly bills to his employer, he had to attach the ones for the previous month so that Grant could make sure that expenses weren't getting out of hand. Horn was also required to use his own car for shopping and errands, with Grant reimbursing him at the rate of four cents a mile upon presentation of a weekly itemized travel log.

Visitors to Grant's home detected a distinctly feminine tone, probably because he made few changes in Norma Talmadge's original decor. It was antique French, predominantly in gold, blue and burgundy, not surprising for an actress made famous by her portrayal of Madame DuBarry.

Grant rarely used the overly formal living room, preferring to relax and entertain in what he called "the bar," which stretched the whole width of the house and looked out on the ocean. The furnishings included a grand piano, a radio-Victrola console and a coffee table that opened up into a backgammon board. Several floor-to-ceiling cabinets contained Grant's collection of records and sheet music of show tunes and English music-hall songs.

Grant completely renovated the master bedroom on the top floor, decorating it himself with walls, ceiling and carpet in a rich chocolate brown, accented by beige trimmings and furnishings. Because of his height, Grant had never owned a bed in which he felt comfortable, so he ordered one specially built that was large enough for four people.

Over the wood-burning fireplace hung an abstract oil painting that Grant boasted of purchasing for ninety-three cents in a flea market. There were no photographs of Cary Grant anywhere except for one in the bathroom on the wall behind the toilet, which he felt was the only correct place for it.

At one end of the master bedroom, Grant kept a separate haberdashery room. Except for historical movies, Grant had established the practice of wearing his own clothes, guided, of course, by instructions from the designer working on the film. He charged the studio a hefty wardrobe fee each time, which meant, of course, that most of his clothes cost him nothing in the end.

Grant's closets contained dozens of suits, hats and accessories, and an even larger number of shirts. The latter were made to order for him in New York, with a special collar that he designed himself to minimize his short "bull" neck.

To image-conscious Hollywood, Grant's seaside hermitage seemed to lack one important component—a wife. In one of her frequent articles, Hearst feature writer Adela Rogers St. Johns offered Grant some advice from the nineteenth-century American humorist Artemus Ward: "The happy married man dies in good style at home, surrounded by his weeping wife and children. The old bachelor don't die at all—he sort of rots away, like a polliwog's tail."

But the nearest Cary Grant came to matrimony at the time was in films, where he'd just started making *My Favorite Wife*. Since the success of *The Awful Truth*, Leo McCarey had been trying to reteam Grant and Irene Dunne in another screwball comedy. With scripters Sam and Bella Spewack, the director concocted a new version of Alfred Tennyson's "Enoch Arden." Written in 1864, the tale of a shipwrecked sailor who's given up for dead and later returns to find his wife remarried had provided the plot for countless movies since early silent days.

Unfortunately, just before production began, Leo McCarey got drunk one night and was seriously injured when he smashed up his car on Sunset Boulevard. RKO wanted to cancel the film, but McCarey insisted on supervising production via telephone from his hospital bed while another director did the actual floor work. Garson Kanin got the director's job, with McCarey billed as executive producer.

As a result of the secondhand manner in which it was made, *My Favorite Wife* lacked the sparkle and spontaneity of *The Awful Truth*. Grant played a newly remarried man whose first wife returns from the dead, not alone but with a man with whom she was marooned on a desert island for seven years. Irene Dunne had the pivotal role, while Grant's required him to do little more than look bewildered and perform skittish double takes.

My Favorite Wife marked the second time that Cary Grant competed with close friend Randolph Scott for the same woman. Of course, it was all make-believe, but this time the actors were less evenly matched. Since their early contract days at Paramount, Grant's career had skyrocketed, while Scott still played supporting roles or leads in "B" Westerns.

The professional rivalry between the two men reportedly caused the breakup of their house-sharing arrangement for a time, but they made peace while working on *My Favorite Wife* and resumed living together. Although they managed to keep it secret from the press at the time, Noël Coward later spilled the beans when he described a late 1939 visit to Los Angeles.

"Cary Grant met me at the airport and drove me to his house by the sea in Santa Monica," Coward said. "He was friendly and cheerful as usual: the house was comfortable, he gave me a car and chauffeur and a valet of my own so that I should be in no way dependent on his own comings and goings and could drive about, elegantly pressed and groomed, to visit the studios and call upon my friends. Cary and Randolph Scott shared the house, which was on the beach, and we lay in the sun, swam in the redundant pool, relaxed and gossiped."

Coward finally started feeling pangs of guilt over vacationing in the California sunshine while his beloved London was threatened by attack from Nazi bombers. When Coward announced he was returning immediately, Grant and Scott hastily arranged a farewell cocktail party.

Ironically, while Noël Coward headed back to England, another acquaintance of Cary Grant's, who would cause a revolution in his life, started an ocean journey in the opposite direction.

10

War Clouds

At the advice of Joseph P. Kennedy, the American ambassador to Great Britain, Barbara Hutton shut down her sixty-room mansion in London and returned to the United States to sit out the war that threatened to engulf the rest of the world.

By the spring of 1940, "the poor little rich girl" had wandered from New York to Palm Beach to San Francisco, where she took a cruise to Hawaii with her four-year-old son, Lance Reventlow. Cary Grant flew up from Los Angeles to attend a bon-voyage party given by the Countess di Frasso. Afterward, Grant took Hutton dancing at the Mark Hopkins Hotel. They had a delightful evening and promised to see each other again when she returned from Hawaii.

In the months that followed, the promise went unkept because Hutton settled in San Francisco for a time. But she started writing to Grant and soon developed the habit of calling him on the telephone every night. Mellowed by cocktails and Seconals, she would ramble on for hours about her life and her unhappy experiences with men, all of whom she claimed were only after her money. Flattered that "Princess Barbara" trusted him enough to confide in him, Grant listened sympathetically but wondered where it was all leading.

Unbeknown to Grant, Hutton was in the midst of trying to change her image as "America's most hated woman." Born on November 4, 1912, she hit the news headlines at the age of five, when her thirty-three-year-old mother committed suicide and Barbara became heir to one third of the seventy-eight-million-dollar fortune left by her maternal grandfather, five-and-ten-cent-store pioneer Frank Winfield Woolworth.

Barbara's father, Franklyn Laws Hutton, stockbroker brother of financial wizard E. F. Hutton, took his daughter's twenty-six-million-dollar inheritance and ran it up to $39 million, being astute enough to liquidate just before the 1929 stock-market crash. In 1930, Barbara Hutton made her formal debut into society with a sixty-thousand-dollar bash for a thousand guests at New York's Ritz-Carlton Hotel. French omelets, caviar and champagne were served until eight the next morning, while hundreds of the destitute lined up for free bread and gruel at a Salvation Army kitchen just around the corner.

Few people in history have experienced revilement such as the American public heaped on Barbara Hutton throughout the Depression years as she unashamedly flaunted her extravagant lifestyle. In 1933, the symbol of capitalist injustice married notorious fortune hunter Prince Alexis Mdivani, paying *him* $2 million for the privilege. When the outraged public started to boycott Woolworth stores, Hutton had to sell out her interest in the company to save it from financial ruin.

To escape a constant barrage of poison-pen letters and death threats, Hutton moved to Europe in 1935, when she bought a $1.5 million divorce from Mdivani and married Count Court Haugwitz-Reventlow, settling on him another $1.5 million. Ironically, most of the millions that Hutton had paid Mdivani reverted to her when he was decapitated in a car crash a few months after their divorce. She was the principal beneficiary of his will.

In London, Hutton purchased a decaying twelve-room mansion near Regent's Park, added on forty-eight rooms at a cost of $4 million, and dubbed it Winfield House after her grandfather's middle name. Following the birth of her son, Lance Reventlow, by a cesarean delivery in February 1936, Hutton developed health problems that plagued her for the rest of her life.

But if that won her any sympathy from the American public, it quickly evaporated when she renounced her U.S. citizenship to become a Danish subject like her husband. Hutton regretted the decision when she obtained a legal separation from Reventlow in 1938, supposedly due to irreconcilable differences over their son's upbringing and education. But Hutton also had developed a romantic interest in Baron Gottfried Von Cramm, the German tennis star.

Needless to say, the welcome mat wasn't out for Barbara Hutton when the million-dollar war refugee returned to the land she'd once rejected. But her good friends and surrogate mothers Elsa Maxwell and Countess di Frasso soon placed her in the hands of Steve Hannagan, a high-powered press agent who specialized in laundering the soiled reputations of the rich and famous. Hannagan thought he could create a more "lovable" Barbara Hutton and help her to regain American citizenship if she toned down her lifestyle and tried to avoid the romantic entanglements that had gotten her into so much trouble in the past.

Admiring Hannagan for his audacity in telling her how to run her life, Hutton promptly hired him, demonstrating her intention to follow instructions by giving the gate to Bob Sweeny, a handsome American sportsman and well-known gigolo who'd been living with her.

Soon newspapers abounded with accounts of Barbara Hutton's charitable works. She gave one hundred thousand dollars to the American Red Cross, donated a fleet of ambulances to the British war effort, and knitted socks and sweaters for refugees.

Press photographs portrayed Hutton as a loving mother as she took her little son, Lance, sightseeing at the New York World's Fair. Under-the-table payments (usually ten thousand dollars at a time) to society-columnist pals Elsa Maxwell, Cobina Wright and Maury "Cholly Knickerbocker" Paul ensured an endless stream of babble about the "new" Barbara as a paragon of American motherhood.

Whether it was intentional or not, Cary Grant became the master stroke in the Barbara Hutton public relations campaign. Since Hutton was never without a man for very long, Steve Hannagan believed that her enemies were just waiting for her to start another unsavory relationship so that they could renew their attacks. No one knows whether Hannagan actually advised Hutton to pursue Cary Grant, but he did tell her what he saw as the advantages to such a liaison.

Cary Grant was most of the things that Hutton's previous husbands and lovers weren't. As a romantic idol of women and men alike, he had the admiration and respect of the public. More important, while not rich by Hutton's standards, he earned a huge salary and seemingly had no motive for being a fortune hunter.

Grant, however, didn't appear to be in any hurry to extend his friendship with Hutton beyond conversing on the telephone. Work took up most of his time—he made four films in 1940—and world events weighed heavily on his conscience. He was torn between becoming an American citizen or remaining British. Although he preferred the first course of action, he feared condemnation in England for deserting the country of his birth in time of crisis.

Like so many others in those turbulent times, Grant took a neutral course. He thought that if the United States joined forces with England, which seemed inevitable, no one could accuse him of being a shirker if he switched citizenship from one allied country to the other. In the meantime, he tried to do whatever patriotic service he could for both countries.

In his eagerness to help, Grant made an unwise choice of vehicles in *The Howards of Virginia,* produced by Columbia in the spring of 1940. Anticipating that the war climate would create a demand for patriotic subjects, the studio purchased Elizabeth Page's Revolutionary War novel, *The Tree of Liberty,* as the basis for the film. Budget-conscious Columbia could only afford to make the epic because it received ten million dollars' worth of sets for nothing. Eager to promote tourist interest in his recently completed restoration of Williamsburg, Virginia, John D. Rockefeller, Jr., gave director Frank Lloyd full access to the site for the exterior scenes.

Decked out in buckskin and Revolutionary uniforms, and with his long hair tied with a ribbon in a pigtail, Grant played a hot-blooded freedom fighter with more gusto than conviction. When he saw the results, he vowed to never make another costume picture again (he changed his mind sixteen years later, with equally unhappy results).

Grant never quite forgave Harry Cohn for talking him into making *The Howards of Virginia.* Whether he deserved it or not, Grant took most of the blame for the film's flop at the box office. He was the only major star in the cast, which featured Martha Scott as leading lady and Sir Cedric Hardwicke and Richard Carlson in the top supporting roles.

Grant's next attempt to help the war effort turned out marvelously, thanks to friends Katharine Hepburn and Howard Hughes.

After triumphing on Broadway in *The Philadelphia Story*, Hepburn returned to Hollywood to negotiate a movie deal. Longtime suitor Hughes, who put up 25 percent of the financing for the stage production, saw to it that she also received control of the film rights. Warner Brothers offered her $225,000, but only if the film were a starring vehicle for Bette Davis, not Katharine Hepburn.

MGM finally came up with the best offer: $175,000 for the rights and $75,000 for Hepburn as the star. But because Hepburn still had that stigma of "box-office poison" attached to her, MGM insisted that she must pick two major male names as co-stars before the deal could be finalized.

MGM wanted its own contractee James Stewart to play one of the roles. Hepburn accepted that, but she didn't warm to the studio's suggestion that Clark Gable, Robert Taylor or Spencer Tracy should play the other part. The problem seemed insurmountable until Howard Hughes interceded and suggested Cary Grant.

Grant accepted the assignment on three conditions: that his salary should be donated to a British war charity, that his part be built up to equal James Stewart's (in the original play it was decidedly secondary), and that he get top billing over both Hepburn and Stewart. Joseph L. Mankiewicz, who produced *The Philadelphia Story*, said later that MGM would never have made the movie if Grant hadn't signed.

News accounts at the time said that Cary Grant donated his $137,500 salary to the British War Relief Fund. Hollywood insiders doubted that, however, because Grant's asking price then was $100,000 a picture. Later, Internal Revenue files revealed that the gift amounted to $62,500, which was what remained of Grant's salary after he deducted the income tax that had to be paid on it.

Working for the third time with Hepburn and director George Cukor, Grant gave one of his best performances as C. K. Dexter Haven, the playboy ex-husband. Since there was so much chemistry between Grant and Hepburn, movie fans often wondered why they never made another film together after *The Philadelphia Story*. The simple answer is that nobody ever asked them. Hepburn soon became almost a permanent team with Spencer Tracy. By the time that screen partnership ended, producers considered Hepburn too old for Cary Grant, whose leading ladies by then tended to be at least half his age.

While Grant was filming *The Philadelphia Story* in the summer of 1940, Barbara Hutton decided to move to Los Angeles and asked him to help her find a place to live. At his suggestion, she rented a mansion in Beverly Hills that had formerly belonged to the now bankrupt silent-film star Buster Keaton. The walled-in "Kingdom of Hutton" soon became a mecca for all the rich and titled British and European war exiles who were pouring into Hollywood at the bidding of the Countess di Frasso and another American with a purchased title, Lady Mendl (Elsie de Wolfe, ex-actress and interior decorator to the *haute monde*).

Cary Grant found himself drawn more and more into that circle as Hutton, Di Frasso and Mendl tried to outdo each other with lavish dinners and parties that seemed to share the same basic guest list. As one of Hollywood's most eligible bachelors, Grant's attendance at those functions was considered a coup for the hostess. When in a good mood and under the influence of a few cocktails, he could be counted on to end the evening by performing at the piano, delighting everyone with improvised naughty lyrics to current hit songs. Like most women, Barbara Hutton was enchanted. It reinforced her belief that Cary Grant could be just as "delicious" offscreen as he was on.

Hutton longed to spend more time with Grant so they could get to know each other better, but his work kept interfering. In November 1940, he started work on *Penny Serenade* and virtually dropped out of the party circuit during production.

Penny Serenade, Harry Cohn's peace offering to Grant after the fiasco of *The Howards of Virginia*, again teamed him with Irene Dunne. The story of a young married couple who suffer the death of two children, the first one their own and the second adopted, hardly fitted into the category of Grant and Dunne's screwball comedies, but director George Stevens injected enough funny moments to keep it from becoming a maudlin tearjerker.

Irene Dunne later told what it was like working with Cary Grant: "He was very apprehensive about nearly everything. So apprehensive, in fact, that he would get almost physically sick. If the script, the director, an actor or a particular scene displeased him, he would be greatly upset. I remember one scene in *Penny Serenade* where he had to plead with a judge to keep an adopted baby. He was so disturbed. I had to talk to him and talk to him. By the time I had finished my diatribe, Cary did a perfect scene, but I was a total wreck."

In the midst of filming *Penny Serenade*, Grant received some horrifying news from England. During an air raid on Bristol, a Nazi bomb made a direct hit on a house containing three generations of his relatives. Killed instantly in the basement shelter were an aunt and uncle, Mr. and Mrs. John Leach, their daughter, son-in-law and young grandson.

Devastated by the incident, Grant became even more concerned for his mother's safety. Each time he learned about a new raid on Bristol—bombs destroyed more than half the city by war's end—Grant wondered how long it would be before he received a telegram that Elsie Leach had been killed or maimed.

In Hollywood, however, life continued the same as ever, and Barbara Hutton threw a huge party to celebrate Cary Grant's birthday (his thirty-seventh, a fact left unmentioned on the engraved invitations). Louella Parsons interpreted the event as Hutton's way of staking a public claim on Grant as her exclusive property.

The three hundred guests came from so many different national, social and business spheres that not everyone knew the hostess or the guest of honor. Composer-performer Hoagy Carmichael, who had become friendly with Grant when they worked together on *Topper*, was tinkling at the piano when a blonde asked him to play something faster to enliven the party. "I told her to get lost and she very quickly did," Carmichael remembered. "Later I discovered it was Barbara Hutton."

Herb Stein, gossip columnist for *The Hollywood Reporter*, described the scene: "Hundreds of yards of white satin decorated with tiny white feathers draped the walls and ceilings of the house, and covered the cafe tables out by the pool that were centered with red roses in crystal vases. The waiters wore red-and-white color-coordinated uniforms. Two silver-stringed orchestras played until dawn. The hostess wore a shimmering gold Oriental gown and glimmering emeralds. Cary Grant wore his rosewood suntan and familiar smile. They make a smashing couple, even by Hollywood standards. And they seem to know it."

Grant was about to make his first film with Alfred Hitchcock, a collaboration suggested by their mutual friend David O. Selznick. But Grant felt uncertain about the public accepting him in the role of a callous wife murderer in the script based on Francis Iles's novel *Before the Fact.* Hitchcock shared Grant's concern, so he turned it into a psychological thriller in which the audience would never be quite sure whether Grant really intended to kill his wife or if it was all in her imagination. From that came a new title, *Suspicion.*

Halfway through production, Grant decided that the wife, played by Joan Fontaine, really dominated the movie. Envy, coupled with Fontaine's swollen ego over rave reviews she received in Hitchcock's *Rebecca,* caused a definite chill between Grant and his leading lady on the set. More than once, he was heard muttering to other co-workers that her bitchy behavior made it perfectly understandable that her husband could murder her.

Later, when Fontaine won an Academy Award for her performance and Grant didn't even get nominated for his, he thought he'd been sold down the river. He avoided Fontaine for the rest of his life and swore never to work with Hitchcock again, although, fortunately, he changed his mind five years later.

In March 1941, Barbara Hutton's long pending divorce from Count Reventlow became official after King Christian of Denmark signed the final decree. While Reventlow received no financial settlement, he was placed in charge of a 1.5-million-dollar trust fund in their son's name. The count also got jurisdiction over Lance's upbringing, with the right to approve governesses, tutors, schools, etc.

Later that month, during a New York shopping spree, Barbara Hutton bought twenty-five thousand dollars' worth of handmade silk sheets and pillowcases, raising speculation that she was refurbishing her hope chest for a new marriage. As Walter Winchell put it, "Looks like another case of a man who's coming to dinner and will decide not to leave."

Winchell obviously aimed the jibe at Cary Grant, who'd just signed with Warner Brothers for the title role in the film version of the hit play *The Man Who Came to Dinner.* As he had done with *The Philadelphia Story,* Grant intended to contribute his salary to British War Relief, but the casting was roundly criticized by the press and many of his fans. The notion of Cary Grant playing pompous, caustic-tongued drama critic Sheridan Whiteside didn't make sense to anyone but Jack Warner, who finally capitulated by hiring the original Broadway star, Monty Woolley.

That left Cary Grant in a very embarrassing position because of his promise to donate his salary to the war effort. Jack Warner had no choice but to offer him another assignment, which was the lead in another hit play that Warner Brothers owned called *Arsenic and Old Lace,* to be directed by Frank Capra. But one problem created another. Grant's role was a comparatively minor one in the stage version, so he demanded a rewrite before production could begin.

Grant took advantage of the delay by traveling to Mexico with Barbara Hutton in August 1941 to visit the Countess di Frasso, who had been spending lots of time in Acapulco since the international social set adopted it as a sort of wartime replacement for the French Riviera. Also staying as Di Frasso's houseguests at the same time as Grant and Hutton were ex-King Carol of Rumania and his mistress, Magda Lupescu, reputed Nazi collaborators who were *persona non grata* in the United States.

While Grant and Hutton wandered around Mexico for several weeks, it was one of the few times in their relationship that the press didn't follow them every minute. But unbeknown to the couple, agents of the American FBI trailed them wherever they went as part of an investigation into the activities of Countess di Frasso, who was suspected of being an Axis spy.

More likely, Di Frasso was just an incredibly gullible and politically naïve woman who got her kicks by mingling with notorious characters. For years, she had an intimate relationship with Mafia big gun "Bugsy" Siegel. Before the war, she often entertained Benito Mussolini and other Fascist leaders at her Villa Madama in Rome. But the FBI never found sufficient evidence to prosecute Di Frasso for espionage or any other illegal activities and terminated the investigation in 1945.

During Grant and Hutton's visit with the countess, the FBI became alarmed when someone started placing phone calls to Nazi Germany via neutral Switzerland. It turned out to be Barbara Hutton, trying to reestablish contact with her friend Baron Gottfried von Cramm, who'd just been released from prison after serving a year's sentence for an alleged homosexual offense. Hutton and many others believed that Von Cramm had been framed for publicly criticizing the Hitler regime.

Cary Grant said later that he knew Hutton made the calls to Von Cramm: "I didn't question it. The Baron was a very dear and old friend of Barbara's. And he was not a Nazi."

Grant failed to mention, however, that Hutton was in love with

Von Cramm. Her friend Elsa Maxwell believed that she might never have become involved with Grant if there had been a way of getting Von Cramm out of Germany. But even the Hutton millions couldn't arrange that (Von Cramm did, however, become Hutton's sixth husband in 1955).

In the autumn of 1941, Grant began working on *Arsenic and Old Lace,* which had suddenly become a project of great urgency. Frank Capra was in a rush to get finished so that he could accept an invitation from the U.S. Signal Corps to make military training films. Furthermore, Capra wanted to use three of the main actors from the Broadway production—Josephine Hull, Jean Adair and John Alexander—and could only get them during their three weeks' vacation from the play, which was still running on Broadway.

Ironically, though Capra made *Arsenic and Old Lace* in record time, the negative went into cold storage in the studio vaults for three years. The contract with Warner Brothers prohibited the release of the movie until the Broadway production closed, which didn't happen until the summer of 1944!

In the macabre comedy about a drama critic whose two seemingly harmless spinster aunts have poisoned at least a dozen men and buried them in the cellar, the scriptwriters expanded Grant's role out of all proportion to the original play. Allowed to make full use of his gifts for pantomime, slapstick and rapid-fire delivery of lines, Grant had a field day making the film, which contained reminders of his past. Jean Adair, who played one of the murderous aunts, was the actress who twenty years earlier had helped to nurse Archie Leach back to health when he came down with rheumatic fever while touring with the Pender troupe. As a joke, Grant arranged for Archie Leach to be officially laid to rest by putting his name on one of the gravestones in a cemetery scene.

In October 1941, Grant served as best man at the wedding of his friend Frederick Brisson to the long pursued Rosalind Russell. With Barbara Hutton keeping him company, Grant took part in one of the longest weddings on record. Festivities went on for three days in the picturesque Danish community of Solvang in the Santa Ynez Valley, where Brisson and Russell took over three hotels to accommodate all their relatives and friends.

With Solvang swarming with reporters and sightseers, the presence of Cary Grant and Barbara Hutton had everyone wondering if they would be the next to wed. Cary Grant's standard response to that question was: "Our personal affairs are none of your goddamned business."

But privately, he was having second thoughts about the relationship. He told a friend that if he did marry Hutton it would be because "Neither of us can afford to have it said that the other walked out."

The Japanese attack on Pearl Harbor on December 7, 1941, and the official entry of the United States into the Second World War soon made considerations of marriage seem unimportant. Bred on drama anyway, people of the movie industry pitched into the war effort with a spirit that became legend.

Cary Grant didn't know what a non-U.S. citizen of thirty-eight might be required to do, but he realized that he'd better find out fast. In the meantime, he joined the actors' division of the Hollywood Victory Committee and plunged into the job of helping to coordinate bond rallies, camp shows and hospital tours.

No one on the committee, not even chairman Clark Gable, could have foreseen that Carole Lombard Gable, one of the first stars to be dispatched, would never return from her bond-selling mission. In Hollywood on January 19, 1942, all activities at the movie studios halted at noon as taps were sounded in Lombard's memory. Grant had just started work that day at Columbia in a new film called *The Talk of the Town*, but director George Stevens sent everyone home early when the atmosphere on the set turned funereal.

Grant took on *The Talk of the Town* with great reluctance because he was unaccustomed to working alongside another top male star, especially one as revered as Ronald Colman, who, though thirteen years older, was at least his equal in playing light romantic comedy. Since Colman also had misgivings about working opposite Cary Grant, George Stevens cleverly capitalized on the rivalry between the two actors by making it a real guessing game as to who would win leading lady Jean Arthur in the final reel.

Stevens shot two different endings and left it up to several preview audiences to decide which one would be used in the final version. Cary Grant came out the winner.

In February 1942, Grant received his first nomination for an Academy Award, for his performance in *Penny Serenade*. He was none too pleased when the victor turned out to be former Paramount rival Gary Cooper, who won the Best Actor Oscar for *Sergeant York*. Grant's competition also included Orson Welles for *Citizen Kane*, Robert Montgomery for *Here Comes Mr. Jordan* and Walter Huston for *All That Money Can Buy*.

That spring, Grant caught some of the patriotic spirit of the times and participated in the Hollywood Victory Caravan, a three-week whistle-stop tour by train to promote the sale of war bonds. As part of the largest contingent of entertainers to ever tour the country in a single group, Grant joined Bing Crosby, Laurel and Hardy, Groucho Marx, Bob Hope, James Cagney, Pat O'Brien, Charles Boyer, Merle Oberon, Claudette Colbert, Joan Blondell, Joan Bennett, Olivia de Havilland, Bert Lahr, Desi Arnaz, Jerry Colonna and many others.

Grant never worked harder in his life, marching in a street parade every afternoon, playing straight man to Bert Lahr in the nightly three-hour stage show and collecting cash donations from the audience in a bucket. He also began to understand the mythical power of the movie star on the public's imagination. In Topeka, a man leaped out of a street crowd and shouted angrily at Grant: "You've ruined my marriage! My wife's so crazy about you that she wants a divorce!"

Despite the aggravations, Grant and the other stars had so much fun on the trip that they hated to see it end. The group had an entire train to themselves, and though each personality occupied a compartment of his own, a card game, party or something wilder was always going on. The tour's resident doctor quickly ran out of sleeping pills and stimulants and kept sending out for more at each stop.

When Claudette Colbert's navy-officer husband paid a surprise visit, the couple didn't emerge from her compartment for two days. When they finally came out, they discovered that Groucho Marx had posted a sign on the door: "Isn't this carrying Naval Relief too far?" The day after the tour ended, Grant and the other men received telegrams jointly signed by Joan Blondell and Joan Bennett that asked the simple question, "Are you getting much?"

If Cary Grant was, he kept quiet about it, but his relationship with Barbara Hutton seemed headed toward a resolution. Late in June 1942, he became a United States citizen and also legally changed his name from Archibald Alexander Leach.

The press immediately assumed that the new citizen intended

to do his patriotic duty by joining the Army Air Force. The previous week, Grant had taken a physical examination at March Field, but it turned out to be merely publicity for an army recruitment drive. For whatever reason, Cary Grant decided to remain a civilian. At thirty-eight he was too old to be drafted.

Gossip had it that Grant's motive for becoming an American citizen was to clear the way for marrying Barbara Hutton. Since she still had millions of dollars in property and capital in England, her holdings would be heavily taxed and frozen for the duration of the war if she wed a British subject.

In July 1942, Grant started working at RKO with Ginger Rogers in the Leo McCarey comedy *Once Upon a Honeymoon.* Early one Monday morning, Grant held a private meeting with studio publicity director Perry Lieber and told him, "Barbara and I are going to be married Wednesday. I have the day off."

All too aware of how the wedding could turn into a circus if the press and public found out, Grant demanded total secrecy. He also knew that he would enrage the news media if he cut them off entirely, so a studio publicist and photographer were delegated to cover the event and to "service" the material afterward. Security was so tight that the publicist and photographer believed they were going to cover Grant's enlistment in the armed services.

With only a few close friends in attendance, Grant and Hutton were married near Lake Arrowhead on July 8 at the secluded mountain hideaway of his agent, Frank Vincent. Held outdoors in the shade of an enormous oak tree, the ceremony was performed by a Lutheran minister whose church later received a new pipe organ as a token of Barbara Hutton's appreciation.

Cary Grant was attired in a dark blue double-breasted pinstripe suit and dark blue tie; he sported a large pearl stickpin from Cartier, his wedding present from the bride. Hutton wore a blue silk suit with a cyclamen blouse and matching hat, all designed by Stella Hanania of I. Magnin in Beverly Hills.

Photographs taken by RKO still man John Miehle showed the newlyweds to be an oddly matched pair. Although she was not yet thirty years old, Hutton's wistful, rather matronly appearance made her look like Cary Grant's older sister, if not his mother.

The couple drove back to Beverly Hills to spend their wedding night at Hutton's rented mansion. Not one to miss a chance for publicity, RKO sent out a press release noting that the star of *Once*

Upon a Honeymoon didn't have any. Grant reported back to work the next morning, though director Leo McCarey gave him permission to come in an hour later than usual.

While visiting the set that day, columnist Sheilah Graham overheard Grant telling McCarey, "This marriage is really going to work. I've never had such a wonderful night in my life!"

11

Cash and Cary

"My marriage with Barbara Hutton had little foundation for a promising future," Cary Grant recalled. "Our backgrounds—family, educational and cultural—were completely unalike. Perhaps that in itself was the initial attraction. But during war years, and my absence from home on entertainment and hospital tours, we had little opportunity to discuss, or to learn from and adjust to, each other's divergent points of view. Had we been able to close the wide gap between our individual beliefs and upbringings, it could have benefited us both.

"I doubt if anyone ever understood Barbara," Grant continued. "But then I doubt if Barbara ever understood herself. But I remain deeply obliged to her for a welcome education in the beauties of the arts and other evidences of man's capability for gracious expression and graceful living."

A widely published wedding photograph showing Grant carrying Hutton over the threshold into their host's living room caused the press to dub them "Cash and Cary." Infuriated, Grant let it be known that his IRS return for 1941 showed an income of $256,250, that he didn't need Barbara Hutton's money and that he had signed a premarital agreement relinquishing any claims to it in the unlikely event that they ever divorced.

"If Barbara wants to buy diamond overshoes, that's her privilege. But all routine household items such as rent and groceries will be strictly on me," Grant said.

Years later, Grant recalled that he always tried to protect Hutton from publicity. "I think I did the best that could be done," he said. "God knows, I've had some idiotic notoriety and I realized she could hide behind that. It took the onus off her and it was helpful. During that time, she was moderately happy. She was only recognized when she was out with me. People asked 'Who was that?' and they were told 'That's his wife.' "

Elsa Maxwell compared the married life of the Grants to a temperamental fireplace: "Sometimes it blazes cheerily, sometimes there's smoke." Right from the beginning, Hutton found it difficult to adjust to Grant's being a working man. Her previous husbands and lovers were always at her beck and call twenty-four hours a day.

While Grant made *Once Upon a Honeymoon,* he left the house at dawn and didn't return until evening. Although Hutton didn't usually get out of bed until midafternoon, that still left her with too many lonely hours to spin jealous fantasies, such as of Grant having an affair with his leading lady, Ginger Rogers. He had a lot of convincing to do before Hutton would believe otherwise.

Hutton never learned to adapt to the alien ways of the movie world. Shortly after the wedding, the Grants had to attend the world premiere of his new film, *The Talk of the Town,* which raised funds for the Hollywood Canteen. Hutton spent days turning herself into her idea of what a movie star's wife should look like, with a gold lamé evening suit and upswept hairdo.

But screaming mobs of common people, photographers' flashbulbs and pesky autograph hunters proved too much for her. And being thrown into the company of Lana Turner, Betty Grable, Rita Hayworth, Ann Sheridan and so many other women she considered more beautiful than herself only intensified the feelings of inferiority that Hutton had suffered all her life. After that night, the Grants seldom turned up on the Hollywood social scene.

Grant persuaded Hutton to give up her rented Beverly Hills house. Too small for them and their combined retinue of twenty-nine servants and secretaries, it was also too open to invasion. Although Hitler, Hirohito and Mussolini now outranked her as hated public figures, Hutton still had to contend with threats of personal violence or the kidnapping of her son, who lived with her part of the time.

In the autumn of 1942, the Grants leased Westridge, the secluded twelve-acre estate belonging to his friend Douglas Fairbanks, Jr., who had gone into active service with the Naval Reserves. With views of both the ocean and the blue-purple Pacific Palisades, the gracious English-style house had exquisite gardens with rare and exotic plants, tennis courts, a swimming pool and a sauna. Except for problems keeping domestic help, who were constantly being drafted or quitting for higher-paying defense jobs, the Grants never experienced the pinches or shortages of war.

Hutton's society friends, most of them refugees from England and Europe, visited in such numbers that Grant later remarked, "If one more phony Earl had come in, I'd have suffocated."

As a counterbalance, he started bringing around some of his married film-business cronies like Freddy Brisson and Rosalind Russell, Alexander Korda and Merle Oberon, Constance Moore and agent Johnny Maschio, Ida Lupino and Louis Hayward. While they played charades, danced or sang around the piano, Hutton usually stayed in the background, shyly protesting that she had no special talent in such a crowd of professionals.

One night, however, Grant coaxed Hutton into showing his friends some of the oriental dances that he knew she practiced in private. "Barbara put some Chinese music on the record player, kicked off her shoes and started dancing in time to the music," Grant remembered. "None of us knew what we were looking at, but she explained the significance of each step and hand movement. It was delightful, but I could never persuade her to repeat the performance."

For the sake of making conversation, Grant tried to interest Hutton in what was going on in the movie industry. When she started talking about becoming an actress, Grant indulged her by saying, "Oh, sure," figuring that she'd soon forget about it. The next thing he knew, however, Louella Parsons ran an item predicting that Barbara Hutton would be signed to play opposite Cary Grant in his next RKO film, *Mr. Lucky*.

It turned out that Hutton stole a peek at her husband's script, decided that the leading female role of a glamorous heiress suited her perfectly, and telephoned RKO head Charles Koerner to apply for it. Koerner was delighted, not only by the enormous publicity potential of such a teaming, but also by Hutton's offer to work for nothing. But Grant considered the idea absurd and refused to even discuss it. Laraine Day got the role instead.

Grant later admitted that he made a mistake in denying Hutton a chance to express herself, to contribute something more to life than just signing checks. While he was preoccupied with making *Mr. Lucky,* she spent a lot of her time writing poetry, an avocation that she started in childhood; her output amounted to about two thousand compositions by that time.

Hutton sometimes showed Grant her work but he didn't know what to make of it. "Unfortunately, and to my shame, I had little knowledge of poetry," he remembered. "Barbara had a need for expression, but I had little patience for it. I'm sorry I gave her no encouragement, and few people did. That was as much responsible for her unhappiness as anything. She had nothing to fall back on, nothing to do."

Right from the start of the marriage, Hutton insisted on having her own bedroom. Grant occupied a separate one, not adjacent to hers but at the other end of the hall. The reason for the arrangement was Hutton's incurable insomnia, no doubt caused by the thirty cups of black coffee and six packs of Chesterfield cigarettes that she went through in an average day. She spent most of the night pacing the floor or walking alone in the garden.

Grant also soon became aware of her dieting problems, a classic case of *anorexia nervosa* before the psychosomatic disorder became widely known. Whenever they sat down for a meal together, Grant's five-foot-four-inch, 101-pound wife ate nothing but Ry-Krisp. Grant always had a hearty appetite himself and felt ashamed of it. Feeling her ravenous eyes watching him as he ate only made matters worse.

Grant and Hutton did develop a strong common bond through Lance, who adored his stepfather and dubbed him "The General," after another famous Grant of the American Civil War era. Fair and blond like his mother, the six-year-old boy started calling himself Lance Grant, which enraged his father. By that time, Count Reventlow had married another rich American, Margaret Astor Drayton, and resided with her at a posh hotel in Pasadena so that he could see Lance during the six months of the year that Hutton had custody.

Friends believed that the main reason Grant and Hutton stayed together for as long as they did was for Lance's sake. The scandal of a divorce too soon after they married would have given

Reventlow grounds for trying to gain full custody of the boy by having her declared an unfit mother.

From the beginning, the Grants tried to have a baby of their own. When attempts failed, they consulted a Hollywood specialist who put Hutton on estrogen and also recommended that they consider artificial insemination. But it was probably all wasted effort anyway, because Hutton had had one ovary removed during the unnecessary cesarean section that brought Lance into the world.

"Barbara was cut to ribbons before I knew her," Grant said. "She was covered with scars, few of which showed when she was dressed. There's no surgeon or doctor who ever approached her who didn't want to cut immediately. They weren't doing it for Barbara's sake. They were doing it for themselves. Those scars were all because of that bankroll."

Meanwhile, marriage and the war had a neutralizing effect on Cary Grant's career. To placate his wife, he cut down on the number of films he made so that they could have more time together. Not that Grant missed any great opportunities, because the projects offered to him weren't up to prewar standards.

The sort of light, sophisticated froth that became known as "a Cary Grant movie" was replaced by a broader, less refined type of comedy in the vein of Abbott and Costello and the Bing Crosby–Bob Hope "Road" pictures. Also, most of the top writers and directors with whom Grant had worked earlier were involved in the war effort or making serious "message" films that didn't suit him.

Grant's first films of the World War II years were all stamped with wartime fervor. *Once Upon a Honeymoon,* with Grant as an American radio correspondent in Europe trying to rescue ex-burlesque queen Ginger Rogers from a disastrous marriage to a Nazi baron, sounded the death knell for screwball comedy. A sequence in which Grant and Rogers are mistaken for Jews and held in a concentration camp caused everything but laughter in those harrowing times. In *Mr. Lucky,* Grant played a draft-dodging gambler who redeems himself by solving the fund-raising problems of a faltering war relief charity.

Grant kept busy with war work himself, taking to the backwater military camps that missed the big touring shows and offering his own brand of entertainment. Instead of the typical song-and-dance routine, he talked to servicemen about Hollywood and moviemaking and answered any questions they had. He also served as president of The Masquers, an organization of celebrities that gave parties for servicemen. With participating restaurants and caterers providing food and drink at cost, The Masquers could entertain a group of 250 for about $350.

At Grant's instigation, Barbara Hutton pitched in as well, endowing army medical clinics in San Francisco and Santa Barbara and a navy canteen in San Pedro. The Grants frequently opened their home for fund-raising parties for the American Red Cross, British War Relief and France Forever, an organization supporting Charles DeGaulle's Free French movement.

Because of all his war activities, six months passed before Grant started another film, *Destination Tokyo*, in June 1943. It was part of a wacky deal in which Columbia loaned Grant to Warner Brothers in exchange for Humphrey Bogart, who took over a part already rejected by Grant in the tank warfare thriller, *Sahara*. At Warners, Grant stepped into a role turned down by Gary Cooper, that of the captain of an American submarine gathering information vital to a planned bombing of Tokyo Bay.

Delmer Daves, who made his debut as a director with *Destination Tokyo*, became the first of several important filmmakers to get their start with Cary Grant's help. With his contractual right to approve directors, Grant picked Daves on the basis of his earlier successes as a screenwriter, believing that if he could write good films, he could also direct them. Recalling how Mae West gave him his first big opportunity, Grant said it was time he did the same thing for others.

After *Destination Tokyo*, Grant sought lighter material and let Harry Cohn talk him into *Once Upon a Time*, based on a whimsical radio play about a caterpillar who gets up and dances on his hind legs whenever he hears "Yes, Sir, That's My Baby" being played. Grant portrayed a theatrical producer who tries to turn Curly the wonder worm into a star.

Unfortunately, Curly performs inside a shoe box, and while people in the film see him, the audience only gets a glimpse of him at the end, when he emerges as a beautiful butterfly and escapes to freedom through an open window. Leaving too much to the imagination, the movie failed at the box office, despite its attempt to uplift the spirits of a war-weary public.

By the time he finished *Once Upon a Time* in November 1943,

Grant and Barbara Hutton had been married for a year and a half. Since they steadfastly refused to give press interviews about their life together, the gossip mongers had them pegged as a pair of "million dollar recluses" who were miserable together and on the verge of divorce. When Igor Cassini, the new writer of the "Cholly Knickerbocker" column, dubbed Mrs. Grant "The Huttontot" and described Cary as a "former Coney Island hot dog salesman," Grant decided it was time to put a stop to the malicious publicity.

Grant arranged a meeting with Hearst columnist and feature writer Louella Parsons, better known to Hollywood insiders as "Mrs. Velvet Finger" because she was married to a proctologist. Parsons had been pestering the Grants for an "exclusive" for months. The interview that they gave her for *Photoplay* became a classic of manipulated journalism.

After describing a visit to Westridge during which Barbara Hutton knitted argyle socks while Cary Grant romped with his young stepson, Parsons concluded that "the richest couple in Hollywood presented a picture that might have been any young couple on a Sunday afternoon anywhere in America."

According to Parsons's account, Hutton denied rumors that the Grants dressed formally every night and dined off solid gold plates. "Isn't it ridiculous?" Hutton said. "We're in a war and we're living like everyone else on our coupon rations. And there's always the Victory garden. Our tomatoes weren't so good this year—but, oh, the corn on the cob!"

Whether Parsons knew it or not, most of the food in the Grants' larder came from a black marketeer who charged prices like two dollars a pound for butter and twenty dollars for prime beef.

Despite the glowing picture painted by Louella Parsons, Grant found trying to live with Barbara Hutton extremely difficult. His wife was dominated by two older women who rarely left the house, her former childhood governess, Germaine "Ticki" Tocquet, and her personal secretary Margaret "Sister" Latimer.

When Grant started living under the same roof with them, he soon understood what Hutton's previous husband, Count Reventlow, meant when he said "Those two cooked my goose." Hutton did not seem to want to participate in an active life. She was content to stay in bed most of the day, protected by her two guardians and behaving like a fairy-tale princess.

But some of the Grants' domestic problems were caused by him and not by her. "I don't care how many six-figure donations Cary Grant made to the war effort, he was stingy as hell," said Dudley Walker, his valet at the time. "He ran around the house turning off lights to save electricity. When he discarded his shirts, he cut off the buttons first. He claimed it was because his shirts were made with a particular kind of button and he wanted to save them to replace buttons that fell off of other shirts. The truth is that he was too cheap to enjoy his own wealth."

According to Walker, Grant had four crystal-and-silver liquor decanters that he marked with a line after each use to make sure that no one drained them off in his absence. "It was all Barbara's liquor anyway. The pantry bill alone, what with help, came to $3,500 a month, and all that was being paid by her. But Grant was still worrying about it. He begrudged the help every bottle of Coke they took from the pantry. His rule was no soda between meals, only with your meal. If he caught you drinking a soda, he docked it out of your pay," Walker recalled.

"Barbara was extraordinarily generous about everything, but Grant was entirely out of her class," Walker said. "He would sit at dinner and eat and put his fingers in his mouth and suck his fingers. He would eat very heavily, and Barbara would barely touch her food. And he was a bad drinker. He would get real nasty and cold. He would become sadistic. He could be a terrible bastard, that one."

At the beginning of the marriage, Hutton tried to avoid her former cronies from the international social set because Grant felt uncomfortable in their company. "For a long time, I protected myself from my friends," Hutton recalled. "But finally, Hollywood was too tough a place. I didn't feel I belonged there. It's part of the disease of the outcast. You feel you never belong to any place or to anyone. For a time, it gave me infinite solace and strength to belong to Cary. I prayed my feelings for him would endure forever. But 'forever' is hardly in my vocabulary."

While Grant made *Destination Tokyo* and *Once Upon a Time*, his wife felt left out and sought the company of old cronies like the Countess di Frasso, Lady Mendl, Baron Eric Rothschild, Baroness Renée Debecquer and especially Elsa Maxwell, whose spectacular parties were actually paid for by Hutton. Grant, who kept a strict schedule and insisted on retiring by eleven on working days, had a low tolerance for such activities.

"Cary was extremely different from his screen image, the way he was in *The Philadelphia Story*—fun, laughing and naughty all the time. He was really a serious man," Hutton said.

While she was married to Grant, Hutton discovered that drinking consoled her. A few gin and Dubonnet cocktails conquered the feelings of disappointment and frustration that usually arose when hubby was late coming home from the studio.

"I don't know if Barbara can accurately be described as an alcoholic, but in ordinary social terms she drank too much," said Frederick Brisson. "And because she had difficulty sleeping she was on tranquilizers. The two together screwed her up. Cary said that she hadn't slept with him in months. And when they had made love, she didn't want her hair mussed up."

A major source of unhappiness for Hutton was that people never saw her as a woman but as one of the world's wealthiest citizens and therefore a freak. "People could not treat her normally," Cary Grant said. "People who were otherwise intelligent froze up and became absolute idiots. They said stupid and ridiculous things like 'My God, for all that money you're quite normal.' They probably expected her to be a raving idiot."

Grant remembered a dinner party where one of the Hollywood moguls asked Hutton how it felt to be so rich: "Barbara gave him a shy smile and replied, 'It's wonderful.' I felt like raising her hand and shouting 'the winner!' "

If it was Grant who helped Hutton to gain confidence, she gave him an appreciation of art and the finer things in life. "Barbara had a marvelous word for anything that lacks taste," Grant said. " 'My God, isn't that *ig*,' she'd say."

One day the couple visited a house that was done in delightful taste except for a huge apricot-colored bar stretching across one whole end of the living room. "The owner was exceptionally proud of it and finally said to me, 'Don't you just love the bar?' " Grant recalled. "There was a pause and I said, 'Yes, it's so wonderfully *ig*.' Well, Barbara got hysterical with laughter. She staggered around the room shrieking, and she was still doubled up when we got to the car. What that poor woman who owned the house thought of us, I shall never know."

In January 1944, Cary Grant turned forty, a disquieting birthday for anyone and particularly for an actor specializing in romantic leading roles. From the standpoint of his appearance, Grant really had little to fear about his career coming to an end. He could easily pass for thirty with the proper lighting and camera angles.

But psychologically, Grant's marital problems caused him to be morose and pessimistic about the future. That unhappiness was reflected in his next project, *None but the Lonely Heart*, the gloomiest movie that Cary Grant ever made and probably the only one that revealed any of his innermost feelings about himself.

How Grant became involved with the film is a story that could only have happened in Hollywood. While looking for a property for Cary Grant, RKO head Charles Koerner ran into a friend who'd just attended a party where he overheard Grant raving about a new novel called *None but the Lonely Heart*. Without stopping to read the book, Koerner purchased the film rights for sixty thousand dollars as soon as he discovered the author to be Richard Llewellyn, whose *How Green Was My Valley* had been a huge hit for 20th Century–Fox the previous year.

When Koerner telephoned him with the news, Cary Grant expressed astonishment. Everything he'd said about *None but the Lonely Heart* was merely repetition of what a friend told him. He'd never read the book himself. But if RKO would pay him one hundred fifty thousand dollars plus 10 percent of the profits, he'd be willing to take a chance on the property. Koerner agreed immediately, since Grant's last RKO release, *Mr. Lucky*, was the studio's biggest grosser since *Gunga Din*.

Meanwhile, eminent Broadway playwright Clifford Odets needed to earn some quick money before going into the Army and asked his agent to find him some work in Hollywood. When RKO offered him the adaptation of *None but the Lonely Heart*, Odets accepted, but it wasn't until he arrived at the studio for a script conference that he discovered it was to be a vehicle for Cary Grant.

As Clifford Odets recalled the scene: "I was silent for a moment and asked, 'Has anyone read this book?' It seemed that no one had. Well, it was about a 19-year-old boy with pimples whose two desires in life are to have a girl friend and to get a new suit of clothes. 'Are you sure it's right for Cary Grant?' I said. It seemed they were, so I had to change the concept of the book considerably."

When Grant read Odets's screenplay, he was impressed

enough to insist that the writer should also direct the film. Although Odets's experience was primarily on the stage, his reputation as an innovator convinced Grant that he could bring a fresh viewpoint to filmmaking.

"Cary Grant's a remarkable man," Odets said later. "If he believes in you, he'll gamble his entire career with you."

Transformed by Clifford Odets, *None but the Lonely Heart* became the story of a restless Cockney drifter trying to make a better life for himself and his aged mother, who runs a secondhand store in London's East End slums. The tale of deprivation and loneliness had parallels to Cary Grant's own life. The plight of Ernie Mott might very well have been that of Archie Leach if he'd never run away to become an acrobat, while "Ma" Mott was a crusty eccentric reminiscent of Elsie Leach.

Grant made sure that the casting of that role was done with as much care as if it had been his own mother. He wanted to hire the great American stage actress Laurette Taylor. Sadly, when RKO made a screen test, the beer-guzzling star had gained so much weight that she photographed like a huge blob of bloated flesh. After losing the part, Taylor took a drinking cure and scored one more triumph on Broadway in Tennessee Williams's *The Glass Menagerie* before she died in 1946.

The part of "Ma" Mott ended up going to another great lady of the theatre, Ethel Barrymore, who hadn't made a movie in twelve years and was currently touring the country in the hit play *The Corn Is Green*. Before RKO could sign her, the studio had to promise to pay all the road company's salaries during the time it closed down and also reimburse the producer and the theatres for revenues lost. Barrymore herself received seventy-five thousand dollars, pretty good pay for two weeks' work in 1944. Her scenes were shot all in a bunch so that she could rejoin her play as quickly as possible.

For all that Cary Grant, Ethel Barrymore and Clifford Odets brought to *None but the Lonely Heart,* it divided the critics and failed dismally at the box office.

Time magazine said "Cary Grant makes a gallant and winning fight against such natural handicaps as maturity, physique, handsomeness and the conditioned expectations of his audience." James Agee of *The Nation* noted that "Cary Grant plays the far from

Cary Grantish hero so attentively and sympathetically that I all but overlooked the fact that he is not well constituted for the role."

The movie's main benefit for Cary Grant was his second Academy Award nomination, competing for Best Actor against Charles Boyer in *Gaslight,* Alexander Knox in *Wilson* and Bing Crosby and Barry Fitzgerald in *Going My Way.* Although Crosby turned out the winner, Grant at least had the satisfaction of seeing Ethel Barrymore get the Best Supporting Actress Oscar for her performance.

None but the Lonely Heart was one of the few attempts that Grant made at stretching his abilities and playing deeper character parts. But at the age of forty, his development as an actor had essentially ended. He went on playing variations on the standard Cary Grant character for the rest of his career.

Except for *Road to Victory,* a ten-minute short promoting the sale of war bonds, Grant didn't make another movie for over a year, the longest break he'd ever taken. While disappointment over *None but the Lonely Heart* contributed to the layoff, the main cause was matrimonial problems. No longer able to cope with them, he was just waiting for the moment when he could bow out gracefully.

Grant and Hutton tried to be understanding of each other but aggravating incidents kept happening. Stirring up nasty headlines was a case involving a handsome young Latin named Carlos Vejarano Cassina, whom Hutton had met during a trip to New York with the Countess di Frasso and had brought back to Los Angeles with the promise of finding him a job. When the FBI later arrested Cassina as a suspected Nazi agent, he was found to be carrying a letter of recommendation from Mrs. Cary Grant.

Although Grant became furious at having his name dragged into it, he supported Hutton when she told the FBI that she didn't really know Cassina and had only given him the letter as a favor to her friend, Countess Dorothy di Frasso, who introduced them. The trail went cold when Di Frasso also claimed to have been duped.

Whether or not Grant had any extramarital attachments at the time, the mere hint of it in a gossip column could drive Hutton into a frenzy. "I was most unreasonably jealous of all those girls who threw themselves on Cary. I was often in despair," Hutton recalled. "Any time we went out to an affair or dinner, those sirens stuck to Cary like glue, all under the pretext of discussing their roles and directors. Women are very sly and cunning, and love to have what someone else has, especially someone they envy, and they envied me."

Many stories circulated about open disharmony in the Grant household. According to Elsa Maxwell, Hutton gave a party for some society friends and Grant stubbornly refused to attend. When Hutton insisted, Grant reportedly put on a pair of stilts and thumped into the room, exclaiming, "Cold enough to freeze up here!"

Cobina Wright recalled a dinner where each of Hutton's foreign guests was represented on the menu by his or her country's most popular dish. Assuming an exaggerated Cockney accent, Grant supposedly disrupted the meal by pounding on the table and demanding fish and chips.

Hostilities were suspended in June 1944, when eight-year-old Lance Reventlow was due to be returned to Hutton's custody after spending six months with his father. Grant and Hutton planned a big welcome-home party, but on the scheduled day of arrival, Reventlow fled to Canada with the boy. In an attempt to gain permanent custody, Reventlow's attorney served Hutton with papers charging that during Lance's last visit she neglected his health and education, encouraged him to use vulgar language and tried to poison his affection for his father.

Realizing how much Hutton loved Lance, Grant felt obligated to maintain an appearance of marital harmony until the dispute was settled. Grant also considered himself partly to blame for Count Reventlow's complaints, most of which were true and might have been avoided if he'd taken a stronger hand in his stepson's upbringing. But he had learned early on that trying to tell Hutton anything was useless and that scolding her only made her more defiant.

Hutton offered Count Reventlow five million dollars to return Lance and to step out of their life forever. When Reventlow refused to even consider the deal, Hutton's lawyer, expert strategist Jerry Giesler, petitioned the Los Angeles district attorney to issue a kidnapping warrant. But nothing came of it, and as the weeks dragged on without further court action, the main beneficiaries were the highly paid attorneys.

By August 1944, Cary Grant had lost patience with playing Sir Galahad and decided to be on his way, leaving it up to Hutton to make the announcement. "There is no thought of a divorce at the present time," she said in a press release written by Jerry Giesler. "Cary and I are remaining the fondest of friends. He decided to stand by me in my present legal dispute, but I think it's best we part now. Besides, it's dishonest and unfair to take advantage of his name and protection because I am fighting for my child."

The United Press report of Grant's attempted departure from Westridge left Hollywood and the rest of the nation tittering. According to the wire service dispatch, Grant became victim of the wartime housing shortage. He couldn't move out of Hutton's rented mansion because he'd sold his own house and had nowhere to go.

Furthermore, the story said: "To get to his own bed, Grant has to stalk by the bed of the blonde beauty he married two years ago. When Miss Hutton remodeled her home on the Pacific Palisades, she thought it might be a romantic idea to install one entrance and only one to her husband's bedroom. This entrance is through her own bedroom. Grant either travels that route without speaking to his wife as he traverses her boudoir, or he puts a ladder to his window. The window must be forty feet high, and the boudoir cold like an igloo."

Reminded of the story years later, Grant claimed that the reporter must have been drunk or preparing an entry for the Burlington Liars Club. "There was an entrance off the library to my room and one off the patio," he said. "It's true that I used the entrance through Barbara's bedroom because that was the part of the house I used the most. Good God, why would I climb a ladder? Why would Barbara permit me? I wasn't in any position to climb ladders at any point in our association. She didn't lock me out of the house or anything so ridiculous."

Actually, it was Barbara Hutton who moved out first, leaving Hollywood for San Francisco to take refuge in her favorite suite at the Mark Hopkins Hotel. In October, Grant had second thoughts about the separation and paid her a surprise visit.

Elsa Maxwell said later that Grant begged Hutton to go out on the town for one last night of dancing like the old days and that she surrendered to his charms. In any case, the Grants issued a terse manifesto the next day: "We are reconciled. The truth of our misunderstanding and reunion is known only to us."

The couple returned to Los Angeles, where it soon became evident that the rules had been changed. Giving up the lease on

Westridge, they moved to a smaller house in Bel Air, that mountainous area overlooking Beverly Hills known as "a branch of heaven." There was not enough room for Hutton's devoted dragons, Ticki Tocquet and Sister Latimer, who had to stay in a hotel and travel back and forth to work every day. The couple could be alone when they most wanted to be alone. They stayed home, refused invitations, gave no parties.

But the Grants fought so much that there were frequent separations within the supposed reconciliation. On one such occasion, Grant packed his bags and moved into the guest cottage of his friends Rosalind Russell and Frederick Brisson. A couple of days later, Russell decided to play peacemaker and invited Hutton to dinner.

"Cary and Barbara wound up sleeping in Freddy's room in our house, and Freddy moved in with me," Rosalind Russell recalled. "Next morning, Freddy went back to his room to get a pair of socks and saw Barbara alone in bed. Then he went into his bathroom and there was Cary asleep on the floor. Stepping over him, Freddy picked up a toothbrush and came back to me. 'I think we've got trouble again,' he said."

The on-and-off-again reconciliation lasted four months. By February 1945, an Allied victory in Europe seemed imminent and Hutton started dreaming of resuming her vagabond prewar lifestyle, which hardly suited Cary Grant. Hutton also became jealous of Grant's friendship with a blond socialite named Betty Hensel, whom he had dated in the months between their first separation and reconciliation. Grant claimed the affair was over—Hensel had just become engaged to millionaire William Dodge—but Hutton didn't believe him.

In retaliation, she started a flirtation with Philip Reed, an actor who somewhat resembled Cary Grant and was another of Mae West's so-called "discoveries." When Grant found out about the relationship, he became "very difficult" and tried to ruin Reed's career by spreading damaging gossip about him, Reed later claimed.

"Cary hated my guts and thought I was breaking up his marriage, but it was already finished," Philip Reed said.

On February 25, Grant and Hutton separated again, jointly announcing that "We have decided we can be happier living apart." Since divorce was unmentioned, the Hollywood gossip mongers wondered if still another reconciliation might be forth-coming.

The suspense mounted as Grant started being seen around town again with Betty Hensel. When Hensel suddenly canceled her wedding to William Dodge, everybody assumed that Cary Grant was the reason.

Louella Parsons ran into Grant at a party at Lady Mendl's and asked him point-blank, "Are you going to marry Betty Hensel?" Looking embarrassed, Grant replied, "How can I say what I'll do in the next year? Right now I have no plans. I'm still a married man."

Just to spite Grant and to delay any plans he might have for marrying Hensel, Barbara Hutton took her time about applying for a divorce. Not until July 1945, five months after the last separation, did she file divorce papers through attorney Jerry Giesler, who was also handling her still unresolved custody dispute with Count Reventlow.

When the second-richest girl in America (Doris Duke was the richest) turned up in a dingy Los Angeles courtroom on August 30 to divorce her third husband, reporters couldn't resist pointing out that her slip was showing beneath her black silk suit. Cary Grant did not attend, but was represented by agent-manager Frank Vincent, who had served as best man at the wedding. When Hutton saw Vincent, she rushed over and embraced him with a joyful, "Oh, darling!"

Turning somber-faced and trembling slightly, Hutton mounted the witness stand to testify before Judge Thurmond Clarke. "Mr. Grant and I did not have the same friends," she said. "He did not like my home, and on more than one occasion when I had a dinner party and invited friends, he refused to come down to dinner because he was too bored.

"He didn't like them, and naturally he stayed upstairs. My friends would ask me where he was and I would have to make some excuse, which was very embarrassing. When he did come down, he obviously didn't look amused, and I could see it and they could see it. Naturally, that was embarrassing, too."

Prompted by Jerry Giesler to describe the effect of Grant's conduct, Hutton said, "It made me rather nervous. I couldn't eat or sleep. I had to get treatment from a physician."

The hearing took fifteen minutes. Neither party received a financial settlement nor requested one. But as a souvenir, Hutton gave Grant two oil paintings by Utrillo and Boudin that she had purchased during the marriage.

According to Frederick Brisson, Grant also kept about $125,000 worth of jewelry, watches and trinkets that Hutton had given him in their time together. "But knowing Barbara, she probably never asked for anything back," Brisson said.

"I shall never marry again," Barbara Hutton told reporters as she left the courtroom. Urged to elaborate on her testimony at the hearing, she said: "Cary never took me out when we were married. At night he liked to listen to the radio or paste clippings in his scrapbook. But I'm not implying that he's conceited. In fact, he was always running himself down. He used to say, 'I can't understand why someone like you would marry me.' "

For months afterward, Cary Grant dropped from the Hollywood social scene and avoided comment on the divorce. Years later, while Hutton was making news with another of her four subsequent marriages, he turned reminiscent with an interviewer: "I don't really know why the marriage went wrong. It could have been successful, but I don't know what happened. Barbara and I know each other better now than we ever did when we were married.

"Sometimes I think people expect too much out of marriage. They expect a paradise on earth. Each of us, then being somewhat younger than we are now, thought we had perfection. We still hopefully believe that some such thing exists."

To the suggestion that most American couples expect to stay married for the rest of their lives, Grant snapped, "Yes, and kill each other! But Barbara and I enjoyed our marriage, and I think we had a wonderful time. I learned many things and I'm grateful for everything I had. I trust Barbara enjoyed the marriage, too, but we just moved on. There's nothing very extraordinary about that, if people have the courage to do it."

Grant also said that "Barbara and I really saw very little of each other. I'm not sure that either of us really wanted to marry the other by the time we got around to it. But I'm sure that I would have been a better husband to her today. My hope was to get affection. I didn't know I had to give it, too. Our interests were not the same. I was more interested in my work than I should have been, I suppose."

With Cary Grant now batting zero for two in the Hollywood

matrimonial ball game, Louella Parsons breathlessly asked her readers, "With the crossroads of his marriage behind him, will Cary choose the lone trail or one that leads to romance?" There was no quick answer.

12

Postwar Blues

"Cary was in one hell of a state after his divorce from Barbara Hutton," said Frederick Brisson. "I never saw a man more broken up. He felt humiliated. I think he really believed himself to be the Cary Grant you see up there on the screen, that he should have been able to master any woman. Many of us warned him that no man could handle Barbara, that she'd eat him alive, but he wouldn't listen."

Although Grant had become depressed after the collapse of his first marriage to Virginia Cherrill, he now seemed in permanent despair. On the set, his fellow workers described him as moody and uncommunicative. Directors found him more finicky and apprehensive than ever. Leading ladies looked for excuses to avoid being cast opposite him.

Purchasing a small six-room house in the upper reaches of Beverly Hills, Grant followed the example of its previous owners, Howard Hughes and Katharine Hepburn, by rarely going out except to work. He spent his evenings reading books on mysticism, searching for something that would bring him inner peace or at least a reason for living.

By a twist of fate, Grant's divorce coincided with the end of World War II, which meant he had a double adjustment to make as Hollywood switched over to peacetime operations. With stars like Clark Gable, James Stewart, Tyrone Power, Henry Fonda, Robert Montgomery, David Niven and Robert Taylor returning from military service, Grant envisioned cutthroat competition for the really choice roles. He also expected radical changes in the movie industry itself once the Justice Department reopened its antitrust proceedings against the major studios, which had been suspended for the duration of the war.

Even before the divorce proceedings, Grant decided that work might be the best therapy for his discontent. In June 1945, he ended more than a year of self-imposed unemployment by accepting an offer from Warner Brothers to star in *Night and Day*, a musical based on the life of Cole Porter.

Not expecting to be taken seriously, the small, gnomelike Porter had jokingly suggested that Cary Grant should portray him on the screen. Nobody expressed any opposition, least of all Grant himself, who felt honored to be the personal choice of his favorite composer of popular music.

But Grant owed Columbia a commitment and couldn't sign for *Night and Day* without Harry Cohn's consent. Easier said than done, since Cohn and Jack Warner were power-mad egomaniacs who rarely strayed off their home turf, expecting others to come to them. Before he'd agree to loan Cary Grant, Cohn insisted that Warner had to come over for a breakfast meeting to discuss it.

Jack Warner popped a few blood vessels but finally went, a considerable victory for Cohn because Warner Brothers was the bigger and more powerful studio. As soon as Warner left, Cohn telephoned every columnist in Hollywood to tell them how he'd bested the mightier of the two moguls. Grant got so disgusted by being made the pawn in Cohn's caper that he never worked for him again.

Night and Day had been under development since 1943, when Irving Berlin told Jack Warner that the story of Cole Porter's courageous comeback from a crippling horseback-riding accident would be an inspiration for wartime casualties. Encouraged by the success of the George Gershwin biofilm *Rhapsody in Blue*, Warner proceeded to make a three-hundred-thousand-dollar deal with Porter, giving him the right to approve the script, cast and song selection.

Over a period of two years, seventeen writers tried to come up with an acceptable screenplay. Except for Porter's riding accident, how could they sustain dramatic interest in a life that was one triumph after another? As Orson Welles put it, "What will they use for a climax? The only suspense is: will he or won't he accumulate ten million dollars?"

In no way could the film deal with Porter's homosexuality or his marriage of convenience to a wealthy older woman. Neither the censors nor Cole Porter himself would allow it.

Porter and wife Linda, who selected Alexis Smith for her screen counterpart, closed up their apartment in New York's Waldorf Towers and settled in Beverly Hills for the duration of the filming. Cary Grant took the assignment very seriously, spending weeks with Porter to study his speech mannerisms and personal idiosyncrasies.

But it was impossible for Grant to make himself look anything like the elfin, monkey-faced Cole Porter. For physical resemblance, Fred Astaire might have been a better choice, but he wasn't even considered because of his close professional relationship with Porter.

Another major Broadway composer, Arthur Schwartz, produced *Night and Day,* with Porter's lifelong friend Monty Woolley serving as technical adviser and also portraying himself in the film. Porter and Woolley had been classmates at Yale and shared a passion for young black men, which, of course, was never mentioned in the script. But the relationship between Porter and Woolley had to be distorted in the film anyway because of the age discrepancy with Cary Grant. While Porter and Woolley were roughly the same age, Grant was a dozen years younger, so white-haired Woolley ended up as a Yale professor rather than an undergraduate!

Cole Porter wanted to hire all the original stars of his stage and film hits to re-create their numbers in *Night and Day,* but Jack Warner overruled him for fear of bankrupting the studio. Mary Martin and Eve Arden were the only Porter alumnae used, with Jane Wyman, Ginny Sims and lesser-known performers dividing up other Porter songs made famous by Fred Astaire, Ethel Merman, Libby Holman, Danny Kaye, Gertrude Lawrence, Bob Hope, Sophie Tucker, Jimmy Durante, et al.

Cary Grant usually had the right to approve directors, and he soon regretted that he didn't in the case of *Night and Day.* Jack Warner placed the film in the hands of the highly proficient but also much despised Michael Curtiz, of whom the swashbuckling

Errol Flynn once said, "He liked blood so much that he insisted the protective tips be taken off the swords."

The tyrannical, cobra-tongued Hungarian so infuriated Grant that he finally exploded when production concluded. "If I'm ever stupid enough to be caught working with you again, you'll know I'm either broke or I've lost my mind," Grant told the director.

Curtiz apparently bore no grudge against Grant for chewing him out in front of the entire company. Years later, he gave one of the best descriptions of Cary Grant's technique: "Some actors squeeze a line to death. Cary tickles it to life."

Whether the blame had to be placed on Curtiz, Porter or Grant himself, the credibility of Cary Grant as Cole Porter was destroyed from the first moment the forty-one-year-old actor appeared on screen as a carefree college student leading a chorus of equally mature-looking classmates in a rendition of Porter's early song "Bulldog."

A scene depicting the composition of the title song, "Night and Day," was a masterpiece of contrivance. Against exceptionally loud sound effects of the falling rain and ticking clock mentioned in the lyrics, Grant composed the song for Alexis Smith while accompanying himself at the piano. In further contrast to reality, the script depicted Cole Porter as a World War I soldier-hero who was crippled by an exploding bomb (his leg injury actually came when he fell from a horse in 1937).

In another key scene, Grant had to sing "You're the Top," the lyrics of which contained a reference to a famous rodent named Mickey Mouse. Adamantly opposed to giving free publicity to Walt Disney, Jack Warner demanded that the reference be changed to Warner Brothers' own cartoon star, Bugs Bunny.

Producer Arthur Schwartz had so much respect for Cole Porter's work that he had Cary Grant sing the original lyric, hoping that Jack Warner would forget all about it. But when Warner saw the rushes, he lost his temper, telling Schwartz: "I had a perfectly good line for you—'You're funny, like Bugs Bunny.'" Schwartz had to admit it wasn't bad, but Warner backed down when told it would cost seventy-five thousand dollars to call Grant back to do the scene over.

Cole Porter adored the film, but couldn't resist telling everyone "There isn't a word of truth in it." Although harshly treated by critics, *Night and Day* proved a huge commercial success, Cary

Grant's biggest up to that time. In a period when the average
movie ticket cost forty-one cents, Warner Brothers earned four
million dollars in rentals.

In October 1945, Grant started an association with David O.
Selznick, producer of *Gone With the Wind* and many other quality
films. Now concentrating more on packaging than producing, Selznick recruited Grant for three properties that he sold to RKO after
assembling the basic components of script, cast and director.
Selznick's name never appeared in the credits, but he received a
percentage of the earnings.

The Grant-Selznick affiliation began auspiciously with *Notorious,* which reunited Ingrid Bergman, Alfred Hitchcock and writer
Ben Hecht, Selznick's winning team from *Spellbound.* Cary Grant
played the role of an American intelligence officer hunting Nazi
fugitives in Brazil at the end of World War II. Enlisting Ingrid
Bergman as an undercover agent, he finds himself falling in love
with her against his better judgment after she seduces and marries
suspected Nazi Claude Rains.

Notorious touched off a lifelong friendship between Grant and
Bergman, although they were never romantically involved. He was
one of the few people to stick by her when she received worldwide
condemnation for leaving her husband and child for Italian director Roberto Rossellini in 1949.

Bergman had Cary Grant to thank for the one truly sexy performance of her career. In the famous hotel-room scene in *Notorious,* she left no doubt that she couldn't wait to hop into bed with
him. Although the censors monitored movie kisses with a stop-
watch in those days, Hitchcock cleverly exceeded the three-second
limit with one of the longest osculations on record.

As Ingrid Bergman described the process: "Cary and I just
kissed each other and talked, leaned away and kissed each other
again. Then the telephone came between us, then we moved to the
other side of the telephone. So it was a kiss which opened and
closed; but the censors couldn't and didn't cut the scene because
we never at any one point kissed for more than three seconds. We
did other things; we nibbled on each other's ears, and kissed a
cheek, so that it looked endless."

Although Grant started *Notorious* still bearing a grudge against
Hitchcock for giving preferential treatment to Joan Fontaine during the making of *Suspicion,* he quickly became an advocate of the

director's methods. One day, while having trouble in opening a door as the script required, Grant complained to Hitchcock that he couldn't manage it because he had to hold his hat in his hand at the same time. Hitchcock pondered a moment, then asked dryly, "Have you considered the possibility of transferring the hat to the other hand?"

While Grant tended to be a perfectionist, often demanding more retakes than were necessary, Hitchcock never had any major problems with him. Asked if Grant ever lost his temper, the director said, "No, he only becomes petulant."

Since the end of the war, Grant had been anxious to get back to England for a reunion with his mother, but work and international travel restrictions prevented it until April 1946. Although he hadn't seen Elsie Leach in seven years, they kept in touch as best they could throughout the war. He knew that she was doing as well as could be expected, given the food and housing shortages that plagued a nation digging itself out from the devastation of Nazi bombs and V-2 rockets.

Grant's mother was now sixty-eight, but he found her to be "extremely good company. Sometimes we laugh together until tears come into our eyes."

Alert to everything that happened in her son's life, Mrs. Leach impishly scolded him for divorcing Barbara Hutton before she had a chance to get a discount at the Bristol Woolworth store. Impressed by the Scottish terrier that appeared in *The Awful Truth* and *Bringing Up Baby*, she'd discovered a talented cocker spaniel that she wanted Grant to take back to Hollywood to use in his next movie.

Grant no sooner returned to California than RKO sent him to New York with Ingrid Bergman and Alfred Hitchcock to publicize the world premiere of *Notorious* at Radio City Music Hall. When the group was getting ready to return to Los Angeles, Grant received a telephone call from Howard Hughes, offering to fly them back in his private plane.

After they canceled their airline reservations, Hughes kept them waiting for three days, alternately setting departure times and then canceling because of mechanical problems. Mrs. Hitchcock lost patience and took the train, but the others decided to sweat it out.

Much to everybody's surprise, the departure finally took

place. Alfred Hitchcock later described the trip like a scenario for another Cary Grant–Ingrid Bergman movie he hoped to make some day: "I do not recall what sort of aeroplane Mr. Hughes had at the time; however, it was quite comfortable. He did all the flying himself, you know. I believe there was a captain aboard, but Hughes kept throwing him out of the cockpit.

"Well, we thought we were as good as home, but then we began to make stops. In St. Louis, I believe, for a change of clothes and to go to a nightclub. Then we were dropping in on some cabaret in Denver, or perhaps it was a restaurant in Nevada. It took, as I recall, almost two days to fly from New York to Los Angeles. Eventually, however, we did arrive."

And safely. Had they been flying with Howard Hughes a few days later, they might not have been so lucky. On July 7, 1946, Hughes was testing his streamlined, needle-nosed XF-11 military plane, capable of flying 400 mph. The aircraft developed engine trouble and Hughes found himself plunging toward the heart of Beverly Hills. Aiming to make an emergency landing on the golf course of the Los Angeles Country Club, he missed by one block and crashed into a house, which, luckily, was unoccupied at the time. Hughes was rescued from the wreckage by a marine sergeant who lived nearby and whom he rewarded with a lifetime stipend of two hundred dollars a month.

Working at the RKO lot when he heard about the accident, Grant rushed to the hospital where his friend had been taken. Doctors gave Hughes slight chance of living through the night, but he did, and the process of literally sewing him back together again began. Grant was one of the few visitors that the reclusive millionaire would permit, and he knew that Hughes was out of danger when he started sending for his two favorite girlfriends, Lana Turner and Ava Gardner.

Grant was occupied at the time with *The Bachelor and the Bobby-Soxer,* the second of his Selznick-packaged films. The script by future novelist Sidney Sheldon was originally called *Suddenly It's Spring.* Producer Dore Schary opposed the new title on the grounds that it suggested an unsavory sexual relationship between a teenager and an older man. But Selznick knew the drawing power of a provocative title and couldn't be talked out of it. If the public wanted to think they were going to see Cary Grant having an affair with Shirley Temple, that was their problem.

In 1940, United Artists wanted to cast Grant and Temple as father and daughter in F. Scott Fitzgerald's "Babylon Revisited," but the project died in the planning stage. That teaming might have worked better than in *The Bachelor and the Bobby-Soxer,* where middle-aged playboy Grant became the prize in a tug-of-war between Temple and older sister Myrna Loy.

Unintentionally, the romantic farce pointed up a problem that producers now had to confront in picking leading ladies for Cary Grant. He was obviously too old for eighteen-year-old Shirley Temple but also appeared younger than like-aged Myrna Loy. Time had proved much kinder to Grant than to his female contemporaries, most of whom had to switch from romantic leads to character parts if they wanted to go on working.

The Bachelor and the Bobby-Soxer helped to earn Grant a reputation for giving directors nervous breakdowns. This particular director, Irving Reis, tended to be indecisive about everything and couldn't function well under pressure from a perfectionist like Grant. A week after filming began, Reis collapsed and was ordered to bed for a complete rest.

In the meantime, producer Dore Schary, an old friend of Grant's from Broadway theatre days, took over the direction. When Reis recuperated, they established a system where Schary worked with the actors while Reis concentrated on the camera setups.

"This arrangement satisfied Cary, who found Reis too complicated a director," Dore Schary said. "Cary was a brilliant romantic comedy actor who was aware of what he could do best, how best to do it and who could help him achieve it."

While comedian Don Barclay, Grant's former vaudeville partner, was watching the filming of a picnic scene for *The Bachelor and the Bobby-Soxer,* another onlooker asked him, "Why do they do such humiliating things to Mr. Grant? Making him carry a potato on a spoon and taking those dreadful falls in the mud?"

"Madam," Don Barclay replied, "if you will watch the expression on Mr. Grant's face, you will see it is little short of beatific." Although Grant denied it, Barclay believed that he subconsciously preferred roles that took him back to his slapstick routines with the Pender troupe.

Nary a critic described *The Bachelor and the Bobby-Soxer* as vintage Cary Grant, but it was another box-office smash, his third in a

row after *Night and Day* and *Notorious*. As a result, he now com-
manded $300,000 a picture, plus a participation in the profits.
Probably the highest-paid film actor at the time, he was envied by
contemporaries like Clark Gable, Spencer Tracy and Errol Flynn,
who, being shackled to long-standing studio contracts, received
peanuts in comparison.

Frank Vincent, the agent responsible for much of Grant's success, died suddenly at age sixty-one while his client was in the
midst of making *The Bachelor and the Bobby-Soxer*. Seeing a way of
keeping an extra 10 percent of his fee for himself, Grant acted as
his own agent from that time on, assisted in contract negotiations
by lawyer Stanley Fox.

By January 1947, Howard Hughes had fully recovered from
his near-fatal accident and invited Grant on another flying trip.
Using a twin-engined B-23 bomber that Hughes had converted to
private use, they flew to New York so that Hughes could attend to
some business connected with his takeover of Trans World Airlines.

Afterward, flying westward again, Grant and Hughes disappeared. Their last radio contact was with the Indianapolis airport.
The plane was presumed lost.

The news media had a field day with the potential disaster,
bracketing Cary Grant and Howard Hughes with Will Rogers,
Carole Lombard, Leslie Howard and other Hollywood notables
killed in air accidents. The New York *Daily Mirror* reported its
telephone switchboard to be inundated with calls from Cary
Grant's female admirers, with few bothering to inquire about
Hughes's fate.

Needless to say, Grant and Hughes turned up safe and sound.
On the flight back to Los Angeles, weather conditions were so
perfect that they decided to head for Mexico. After spending the
night in Nogales, Arizona, they took off for Mexico City the next
morning without bothering to notify the air controllers of the
change in plans. It wasn't until they touched down for lunch and
Grant spotted a Spanish-language newspaper with the headline
SENORES GRANT Y HUGHES CREYENDO MUERTO that they knew they
were even missing!

A few weeks later, Grant became enmeshed in trouble of another kind when he went to work for the king of independent
producers, Samuel Goldwyn, in *The Bishop's Wife*. The problems

started when Jean Arthur dropped out of the title role, claiming to be pregnant. Goldwyn called up Arthur's husband, Frank Ross, and screamed, "You know what you did? You didn't just screw her —you screwed me!"

Before signing another star for the part, Goldwyn asked his director, William Seiter, "How would you like to work with Laurette Taylor?" Seiter said that he'd love to, except that Taylor had died the previous year. Goldwyn really meant Loretta Young.

Based on a novel by Robert Nathan, *The Bishop's Wife* was a romantic fantasy that required a special kind of casting for the pivotal role of an angel named Dudley. Convinced that no actor could play it except Cary Grant, Goldwyn delayed production six months in order to get him.

But as soon as filming started, Goldwyn began to regret being so patient. He thought that Grant's interpretation was far too ethereal and fey. Goldwyn wanted an angel with sex appeal, but Grant didn't agree.

"I won't be happy playing it that way," Grant said. "You want me to be happy, don't you, Mr. Goldwyn?"

"I don't give a damn whether you're happy or not," Goldwyn replied. "You're going to be here only a few weeks, and this picture will be out for a long time. I would rather you should be unhappy now and then we can all be happy later."

Goldwyn had a theory that when everyone was contented while making a picture, it usually turned out a stinker. After viewing the first week's rushes, he fired director William Seiter, threw out everything that Seiter shot, ordered sets rebuilt and started over. The decision cost Goldwyn an extra $900,000, including $100,000 in overtime that he had to pay Cary Grant while production shut down for six weeks.

When the new director, Henry Koster, took over, Goldwyn wanted Grant to change roles with David Niven, who had been playing the Episcopalian bishop married to Loretta Young. Grant refused and sulked all through the filming, making Koster's job even more difficult.

Grant's obsessive concern with details caused frequent delays. In a winter scene where he and Loretta Young had to enter a house and stomp snow from their boots, he suddenly stopped short and wanted to know why there was no frost on the windows. Production came to a complete halt while the frustrated set decorators scurried around to pacify him.

Grant considered his right profile his best side and preferred to be photographed that way. Since Loretta Young felt the same way about her profile, the director had a major problem when the script called for a love scene in which the two stars were required to face each other.

Henry Koster came up with what seemed to be the ideal solution. While Young looked out a window and exclaimed about the beauty of the sky that night, Grant stepped up behind her, put his hands on her shoulders, and whispered sweet nothings in her ear.

Everybody was satisfied except Samuel Goldwyn. When he saw the scene and realized the vanity behind it, he exploded. "From now on," he told Grant and Young, "if I only get half your face, you get only half your salary."

Loretta Young did not become a member of the Cary Grant fan club: "Each morning, I would arrive on the set in wardrobe and makeup, ready to go to work. But instead, Cary would start dissecting our scene with the director. It made me so nervous I would go into a scene all depressed and unsure. I finally said, 'Cary, please, I don't mind your doing this because I know you're trying to get a better film, but please don't do it around me.' He apologized to me, and never did it again—at least not in my presence."

Young also remembered a moment when she and Grant were watching some of the rushes with the director. "A huge close-up of Cary appeared on the screen," Young said. "He looked supremely handsome and I said, 'Oh, look at that beautiful cleft in Cary's chin!' 'Beautiful cleft nothing,' said Henry Koster, jokingly. 'That looks more like a baby's bottom!' Cary got furious and said, 'Well, that does it!' and slammed out of the projection room. He came back in five minutes, but he was still sulking."

When *The Bishop's Wife* was finally finished, the producer still thought it lacked the famous "Goldwyn touch." After several disappointing sneak previews, Goldwyn hired two of the best writers in the business, Billy Wilder and Charles Brackett, to do three new scenes that were shot and integrated into the picture. But the RKO release went on to flop at the box office anyway, even when Goldwyn tried to add spicy sex appeal by advertising it as "Cary and the Bishop's Wife."

In the summer of 1947, Grant went to England to visit his

mother and to confer with Sir Alexander Korda, whose independent company, London Films, had just signed a co-production deal
with 20th Century–Fox. Korda intended to star Grant in a romantic
swashbuckler based on Daphne du Maurier's *The King's General*, but
the project was later abandoned because of script and budgetary
problems.

Except for Betty Hensel, his usual companion when he went
out on the Hollywood nightclub circuit, Grant had formed no
serious female attachments in the two years since his divorce. But
that began to change one night in London when he and Alexander
Korda attended *Deep Are the Roots*, an imported Broadway hit about
racial prejudice, at Wyndham's Theatre.

Although Grant went mainly to see the performance of Faith
Brook, daughter of his actor-friend Clive Brook, he also came away
impressed by another actress in the cast. Her name was Betsy
Drake, an American making her stage debut, according to the
program notes.

With dark blond hair, lovely features and a silky voice, she
reminded Grant of the young Margaret Sullavan. "There's real
talent there," he told Alexander Korda, and then thought no more
about it.

A few weeks later, Grant sailed back to the United States on
the *Queen Mary*, accompanied by one of his closest friends, sixty-
six-year-old Frederick Lonsdale, a phenomenally successful British
playwright of the pre-World War II era and also a celebrated eccentric. Since the age of forty, Lonsdale had never been able to remain
in any one place for very long. Arriving to stay a week at someone's
house, he'd depart the same evening. He once left a New York-
bound liner at Cherbourg because he couldn't face the boredom of
the voyage.

Grant called him "maddening but irresistible," noting that
much of the fun of being Lonsdale's friend came from the suspense
over how long his visits would last.

For their August 1947 departure on the *Queen Mary*, Grant and
Lonsdale arrived at the customs shed at Southampton with two
Rolls-Royces. They traveled in one and the other contained their
luggage and hampers of food and wine from Harrods and Fortnum
& Mason.

Watching them was Betsy Drake, returning to New York following the expiration of her six-month work permit. "The boys

were feeling no pain. I wanted to enter into the fun. Make a joke, pop a cork. But Cary didn't notice me. I was just another passenger," she recalled.

The next day, Grant and Drake met for the first time. As usual, the *Queen Mary* had many celebrities on board, and Grant was hurrying to keep a tea date with fifteen-year-old Elizabeth Taylor and her mother. Grant later claimed that Betsy Drake tried to pick him up by jumping out of a phone booth and posing like a pinup girl with one hand on her hip. Drake insisted that the ship lurched and sent her flying just as Grant happened to be passing.

In any case, they collided and Grant immediately recognized Drake from *Deep Are the Roots,* even if he couldn't remember her name. Blushing with embarrassment, she marched right past him without saying a word.

The following morning, Grant was taking a stroll with another Hollywood-bound passenger, Merle Oberon, when he spotted Betsy Drake farther down the deck. Nudging Oberon, Grant said, "There she is. That's the girl."

Merle Oberon turned and looked. "Fine. Now go introduce yourself."

Grant smiled, took a step and then hesitated. "Look, it's like this, Merle. I don't want her to think I'm picking her up. Would you talk to her for me? Ask her to have lunch with us."

"But I don't know her," Oberon said. "I've never met her."

"That's all right. Go on. You're a woman," Grant insisted.

Merle Oberon couldn't believe it: Cary Grant, the debonair ladykiller, not only reluctant to talk to a girl but also afraid of being rejected. She almost laughed out loud, but thought better of it. Without further argument, she marched over to Betsy Drake and arranged the date.

When everybody met for lunch, Freddy Lonsdale also found himself strongly attracted to Betsy Drake. "If Freddy had been twenty years younger, I would certainly have lost Betsy to him," Grant said later.

It was easy to understand why the two men became entranced by the much younger woman. Twenty-three and a slender five feet six, she resembled Peter Pan, with short hair and sparkling blue eyes. She was highly intelligent and a self-confessed bookworm, with a seemingly encyclopedic knowledge of subjects like astronomy, hypnotism and yoga.

During lunch, she told them all about herself. Her grandfather had built the Drake Hotel in Chicago, but the family lost everything in the 1929 stock-market crash. Determined to be an actress, she paid for drama lessons by working as a switchboard operator and as a model for the Montgomery Ward mail-order catalog.

Cary Grant's courtship of Betsy Drake could hardly be called "whirlwind." When the *Queen Mary* docked, he flew straight on to Los Angeles to start a new film, while she remained in New York to enroll in acting classes and to look for another stage role. Drake also had some sort of relationship going on with a young actor named Stewart Hoover. Before leaving for London, she had shared an apartment with him in Greenwich Village. Nobody knew for certain whether they were married or just living together.

In October 1947, Grant started the third of his Selznick-originated RKO films, *Mr. Blandings Builds His Dream House,* based on Eric Hodgins's novel about the perils of a city family moving to suburbia.

Selznick immediately spotted the bestseller's potential as a vehicle for Grant and Myrna Loy, whom he envisioned developing into a romantic comedy team like Spencer Tracy and Katharine Hepburn. This time Grant and Loy worked together more effectively than in *The Bachelor and the Bobby-Soxer.* Acting and behaving like people their own age, they were quite convincing as parents of two adolescent daughters.

With the debonair Melvyn Douglas providing romantic complications, *Mr. Blandings Builds His Dream House* brought back memories of Grant's sophisticated comedies of the thirties. While not nearly as well written or directed, it was enormously popular among postwar audiences, who identified with the housing and readjustment problems depicted in the film.

Although Grant and David O. Selznick never made another film together, Grant's friendship with the producer came in handy when he persuaded Betsy Drake to move to Los Angeles at the beginning of 1948.

Perhaps Grant was influenced by Selznick's own obsession with furthering the career of his actress-wife, Jennifer Jones. At any rate, he convinced Selznick and Dore Schary, now the head of production at RKO, that Betsy Drake had the makings of a major movie star.

Amid great publicity and fanfare, Drake signed a contract in

which Selznick and RKO would share her services. The arrangement not only gave the unknown actress an immediate seal of
approval from two powerful Hollywood entities, but also concealed the fact that a certain well-known actor had personal de-
signs on her affections.

13

The Third Mrs. Grant

After meeting on the *Queen Mary,* Cary Grant and Betsy Drake had kept in frequent contact by telephone. As time went on, he started flying her to Los Angeles for weekend visits (not as generous as it might seem, since he prevailed on Howard Hughes to give him free tickets on TWA).

When Grant arranged Drake's movie deal, he wanted her to move into his house in Beverly Hills, but she refused to rush into an arrangement they might both regret later. Instead, she rented a tiny furnished apartment in Hollywood, which she paid for herself out of her salary of two hundred fifty dollars a week.

Neither Selznick nor RKO had any assignments for Drake, so Grant persuaded Dore Schary to let her appear opposite him in *Every Girl Should Be Married,* in a role originally intended for Barbara Bel Geddes. Drake resisted the idea. Acting opposite Cary Grant in her first movie not only seemed too severe a test of her abilities but was also likely to start talk that she only got the part because he fancied her.

But Grant said he didn't care what other people thought and promised to help her through any rough patches. As it turned out, he directed most of the film himself, even though Don Hartman received credit for it. Grant also supervised a rewrite of Drake's role, adding some of her personal quirks and mannerisms to make the job easier for her.

Every Girl Should Be Married was clearly a labor of love on Cary

Grant's part, with everyone, himself included, deliberately kept off center stage so that Betsy Drake could bask in the limelight. Grant encouraged her to imitate the young Katharine Hepburn in her role as a department-store clerk trying to trap a bachelor pediatrician into marriage.

The results received mixed reviews. *Newsweek* said that Drake's "frenetic charm and wind-blown naturalness are sometimes nerve-racking but more often thoroughly appealing." *Life* complained that Drake "has an inability to stand still for more than a second at a time."

Further plans for Grant and Drake to work together had to be tabled in the autumn of 1948, when Grant succumbed to nine years of persistent badgering from Howard Hawks to make another screwball comedy. Based on a true story called "I Was an Alien Spouse of Female Military Personnel Enroute to the United States Under Public Law 271 of the Congress," the script had its title changed to the zippier and more provocative *I Was a Male War Bride.*

Grant loved the idea of co-starring with brassy "Oomph Girl" Ann Sheridan, but the 20th Century–Fox production presented a major problem. Foreign location filming meant being separated from Betsy Drake for several months. He decided to take her along, regardless of what the gossip mongers might make of two unmarrieds traveling together.

I Was a Male War Bride was Cary Grant's first Hollywood film made outside the United States. With the advent of television and a postwar surge in international travel, movie audiences could no longer be fooled by studio replicas of the real thing. Location filming also meant cheaper labor costs and a chance to use up blocked earnings that American companies couldn't withdraw from certain countries under currency restrictions.

Grant's itinerary took him to Allied-occupied Germany for the exterior scenes and then to England to wrap things up at London's Shepperton Studios. With Betsy Drake along for company, Grant looked forward to the equivalent of a three-month paid vacation.

En route to Germany, Grant and Drake stopped in Paris to visit his great friend Lady Mendl, who had left Hollywood at the end of the war to reopen her adored Villa Trianon in Versailles. Built in 1750, the exquisitely restored château was one of the great showplaces of Europe. Grant wanted Drake to see it before the ailing nonagenarian died (which she did the following year).

Weighing about ninety pounds without her jewels, Lady Mendl was confined to bed with crippling arthritis. But one afternoon, she permitted Grant to take her in his arms and carry her downstairs to the parlor.

"Not being able to see the narrow winding steps, but only gingerly feel them beneath my feet, I was troubled for my precious cargo's safety," Grant recalled. "Yet Elsie chattered unconcernedly and gaily about her plans for redecorating and entertaining and *living*. Her motto as long as I had known her was 'Never explain, never complain.' Any words of philosophy from such a woman are worth consideration."

Arriving in Germany to begin *I Was a Male War Bride*, Grant assumed the role of a French army captain who marries an American WAC and discovers that he won't be permitted to enter the United States unless he goes as a "war bride." The script hewed to one basic joke, with Grant suffering indignity upon indignity as he gets snarled in military red tape.

Howard Hawks directed it almost as if he were making a silent movie, minimizing dialogue and stressing visual humor. When filming started in Heidelberg and Bremerhaven, Grant had a ball. Hawks gave him free rein of his talent for slapstick, letting him continue with a scene for as long as he thought he could milk laughs from it.

Grant insisted on doing most of his own stunts. In a scene that called for him to be thrown from the sidecar of a speeding motorcycle, he executed a neat barrel roll that he had learned as a Pender boy. In true Fairbanksian style, he also grappled with a rising railway gate and allowed himself to be flung from a ten-foot-high window. His greatest challenge came, however, while donning female drag to impersonate a WAC.

"The wig I wore was made from a horse's tail," Grant said. "It itched like hell. And I wasn't too happy about wearing a skirt because I've got legs like knotted rope. The funniest moment was when we were playing a scene by a pier and I stopped to pull up my stockings. When I looked up, there were all these sailors whistling at me."

Despite the physical demands of the script, Grant encountered no problems until production shifted to London in December 1948. In the midst of England's severest winter in years, Ann

Sheridan came down with pleurisy, causing a two-week halt in filming while she recuperated.

Then Grant started feeling unwell and thought he had influenza. But when he developed jaundice and lost forty pounds in a matter of weeks, doctors diagnosed a severe case of infectious hepatitis.

Although 20th Century–Fox kept the gravity of his illness secret at the time, Grant said later that he had nearly died. Years of heavy drinking had damaged his liver, so the infection was much harder to treat than in a healthy person.

Grant convalesced for two months in a furnished flat in London's Mayfair, his case complicated by his hypochondria and mistrust of all doctors. Years later, he said that he might have committed suicide if it hadn't been for Betsy Drake, who took care of him and calmed his fears.

When Grant was strong enough to travel again, Drake took him back to Los Angeles. In the meantime, Howard Hawks finished all that he could of *I Was a Male War Bride* in London and arranged for Grant's remaining scenes to be shot at the Fox studio in Hollywood.

In negotiating his deal for *I Was a Male War Bride*, Grant had exacted a promise from 20th Century–Fox to hire Betsy Drake for a film. When they returned from Europe, she worked opposite William Powell and Mark Stevens in *Dancing in the Dark*, a Technicolor musical titled after the Howard Dietz–Arthur Schwartz Evergreen.

No one was supposed to know, of course, that Grant had got Drake the job. Although gossip columns now linked them as lovers, Drake kept denying wedding rumors with statements like, "If I should marry before I've done at least two successful pictures on my own, no matter how good I might be, I would simply be known as Mrs. Cary Grant. I hope later to make another picture with Cary, but now I want to concentrate on working without him."

But the year-end holiday season of 1949 seemed to bring with it an epidemic of wedding fever. On December 20, Clark Gable ended seven years of widowerhood and took a fourth wife, Lady Sylvia Ashley. Five days later, on Christmas Day, Cary Grant concluded four years of bachelorhood by making Betsy Drake his third wife.

Grant and Drake selected Christmas for the ceremony because it was the one day that Howard Hughes felt reasonably certain that he could break away from business activities long enough to serve as best man.

To keep the wedding secret from the press, Grant and Drake drove to a back runway of Los Angeles Airport, where Hughes picked them up with one of his private planes and personally piloted them to Scottsdale, Arizona. Landing in the middle of the desert, they were picked up by a chauffeured limousine and taken to a ranch owned by realtor Sterling Hebbard, where the marriage was performed.

Conducted by a Methodist minister, the nuptials took ten minutes, but might have been shorter. In the middle of the proceedings, Howard Hughes dropped the wedding ring and everyone had to crawl around the floor searching for it.

Grant was forty-five years old, his bride twenty-six. After RKO's publicity department released news of the marriage, Hedda Hopper reminded her readership of a remark made by screenwriter Lenore Coffee: "When a man of forty falls in love with a girl of twenty, it isn't her youth he is seeking but his own."

Home for the Grants continued to be the six-room Beverly Hills house that he bought after his divorce from Barbara Hutton. Formerly owned by Howard Hughes, it still looked like the lair of a recluse, with sparse furnishings and motel-like decor. Grant kept promising to redecorate, but just as quickly talked himself out of it because of the expense and the prospect of workmen disrupting his privacy.

Since the Grants had been intimate companions for two years, a honeymoon trip seemed unnecessary. A few days after the wedding, Grant started the ominous-sounding *Crisis* for MGM. His friend Dore Schary was the studio's new head of production, after being fired from the same job at RKO by Howard Hughes.

Grant took the assignment mainly to oblige Schary, who intended to revitalize MGM by starting a fresh roster of stars and cleaning out the deadwood from the previous Louis B. Mayer regime. Although Grant liked the script that Schary offered him, his experience with *None But the Lonely Heart* made him skeptical. Would the public accept Cary Grant as a brain surgeon confronted with the moral dilemma of whether or not to operate on an evil Latin American dictator? But Schary thought that Grant needed a change from his usual comic roles, and he agreed.

Crisis was yet another film in which Grant launched the career

of a major director, in this case screenwriter Richard Brooks.
"Cary told me, 'If you can write it, I don't see why you can't direct
it. What you don't know, I certainly know,' " Brooks recalled.

But Grant's motives may have been more selfish than benevo-
lent. Working with a novice director, he had more control over a
film than he did with an experienced one. Also, Grant's fee of three
hundred thousand dollars a picture sometimes left no room in the
budget for hiring a higher-priced "name" director.

Set in a fictional country suggesting Juan Peron's Argentina,
Crisis had a minor love interest, with MGM contractee Paula Raymond thrown in for window dressing as Grant's wife. The lack of
romance was rare for a Cary Grant film and probably the main
reason why it flopped at the box office. His fans wanted to see him
as a lover and not as the conscience-stricken adversary of malevo-
lent Jose Ferrer.

While Grant made *Crisis*, Betsy Drake worked at Warner
Brothers in *Pretty Baby*, a comedy programmer with Dennis Morgan
and Zachary Scott. After that, the Grants almost disappeared from
sight, neither working again for over a year.

Grant had always cherished his privacy, and Drake did hers, so
they spent most of their time at home. "Betsy is the first wife I've
had who is also a friend," he said at the time. "Our marriage has
developed into a warm, relaxed companionship."

Frederick Brisson said, "Cary developed an extra dimension
after marrying Betsy. Up until that time, I don't think he ever
harbored a serious thought in his life, and the only thing he read
with much attention was scripts. Betsy opened up a whole new
world of ideas for Cary."

Drake's main interests were nature, metaphysics and Bud-
dhism. "I came home one day to find the house crawling with
books on spiders," Grant recalled. "I glanced through one by a
Frenchman named Henri Fabre, and I became fascinated by the
little fellows myself. Spent the rest of the day reading about them. I
discovered there was so much I wanted to learn. Reading was a
refreshing release from the idiocies of life, idiocies I knew only too
well."

At times, however, Drake's bookish ways irritated Grant. She
rarely returned from a shopping trip without twenty or thirty
books piled in the trunk of the car. Grant considered it an extravagance as well as an inconvenience. Whenever he wanted to sit

down in a chair or go to bed, he first had to shift an enormous pile of books.

"Sometimes I wonder why my husband hasn't murdered me and buried me in the cellar in the best Hitchcock tradition," Betsy Drake said. "He's a man of no hobbies and I'm a woman of many."

When Drake decided to learn photography, she filled the small house with equipment. After Grant stumbled over his wife's tripod for the eighteenth time, he said, "Betsy, you should have hobbies that don't take up so much space. I suggest that you learn to write on the head of a pin."

But when Drake tried her hand at writing short stories (presumably not on the head of a pin), she found Grant to be helpful and encouraging. "He's really an excellent critic," she said. "When he'd tell me what was wrong with a story, I first used to blow up and get mad. But as soon as I calmed down, I realized Cary was right. He's a perfectionist in writing as he is in acting."

Grant disapproved of Drake's culinary experiments. She couldn't even boil an egg when they first married. He loved to tell friends about the time he walked into the kitchen and found her examining a plucked turkey, trying to tell the front from the back.

While actor Stewart Granger was having lunch at the Grants' one day, Drake waved a cookbook in the air and boasted that she had only 108 more recipes to get through before she had it mastered. "But judging by the look Cary gave me, I don't think he was going to allow her to continue much longer," Granger said. The Grants had become close friends with Granger and his sweetheart, Jean Simmons, both of them recently arrived from England. When Granger said he wanted to buy Simmons an engagement ring, Grant told him, "Wait a minute, I'm sure I've got a diamond ring somewhere."

To Granger's amazement, Grant went to a safe and started pulling out all sorts of jewelry—pearls, gold cigarette cases and compacts, brooches, pendants, earrings, watches and finally a beautiful four-carat diamond ring. "Cary told me I could have it at a very reasonable price and generously suggested I could pay him back when I could," Granger said.

When Granger and Simmons decided to get married in December 1950, Grant took care of all the arrangements and persuaded Howard Hughes to loan them his private plane so that they could fly to Tucson, Arizona, for the ceremony. Later, Grant re-

gretted introducing Hughes to the Grangers. Hughes fell in love
with Jean Simmons and tried to break up the couple.

In January 1951, Mr. and Mrs. Cary Grant ended a year of
leisure by going back to work, separately at first and then as a team.
While Drake made the United Artists drama *The Second Woman*,
Grant signed with 20th Century–Fox for a Joseph L. Mankiewicz
project based on *Dr. Praetorius*, a well-known German play and
movie by Curt Goetz.

Having worked previously with Mankiewicz on *The Philadelphia
Story*, Grant hoped to hit a second jackpot. In the interim,
Mankiewicz had become Hollywood's ranking "genius" after win-
ning four Oscars for writing and directing *A Letter to Three Wives* and
All About Eve.

Mankiewicz wanted Anne Baxter to appear opposite Grant,
but pregnancy (she was married to actor John Hodiak) forced her
to resign the role. Cary Grant thought it would be a great opportunity for Betsy Drake, but studio head Darryl F. Zanuck selected
another Fox star, Jeanne Crain, on the strength of her performance
as a black girl passing for white in *Pinky*.

Zanuck ordered a new title for *Dr. Praetorius* because of the
box-office flop of *Crisis*, in which Grant also played a doctor.
Zanuck proposed "Let Nature Take Its Course," but Mankiewicz
finally won him over with *People Will Talk*.

Grant's role differed radically from the farcical figures that he
usually played in comedies. The story of a medical school professor who marries a student who's expecting another man's child was
considered very daring in the prudish 1950s.

Grant's delight in portraying such a noble but unpompous
character demonstrated itself throughout the film. Admirers of his
artistry usually cite the scene in which he conducts a student orchestra in the Brahms Academic Festival Overture as one of the
highlights of his career. The triumphant smile on Grant's face, the
slight trace of tears in his eyes as the music swells into the
"Gaudeamus Igitur" theme seem positively saintly.

Perhaps because Joseph Mankiewicz couldn't decide whether
People Will Talk should be comedy, drama or a satire on the medical
and teaching professions, the film became overburdened with dialogue and moved at a turtle's pace. Although it was generally
admired by critics, the public stayed away.

About the only benefit Cary Grant derived from it (apart from his three-hundred-thousand-dollar fee) was finally getting his hand and footprints immortalized in cement in the forecourt of Grauman's Chinese Theatre when *People Will Talk* premiered there in August 1951. By that time, Grant had been a Hollywood fixture for almost twenty years. A testimonial to his place in movie history seemed long overdue.

That summer, Grant and Betsy Drake signed with Warner Brothers for their second film together, *Room for One More.* Whether or not it reflected a personal desire to raise a family of their own, the couple selected the project for themselves after reading Anna Perrott Rose's book about her experiences as a foster parent to "disturbed" and handicapped children.

Feeling that none of Drake's previous films did justice to her talent, Grant hoped that this one would put her over. Everything centered on Drake as the kindhearted housewife who takes in stray youngsters that nobody else wants. Playing the husband, Grant was not so much her equal partner as the family buffoon, the target of the children's comical pranks.

Room for One More became a movie that people either loved or loathed, depending on how they felt about precocious children, six of which were on display. Grabbing most of the attention was Grant's personal "discovery," five-year-old George Winslow, whom he spotted in a television interview with Art Linkletter.

Winslow's startling *basso profundo* voice earned him the nickname "Foghorn." Besides sounding funny, he had a delightfully innocent attitude. Winslow's encounters with the cantankerous Cary Grant not only stole the picture, but also earned him numerous movie and TV roles before a normal voice change ended his career at age twelve.

Room for One More received some of the most diverse and unexpected reactions of any Cary Grant film. Judges at the Venice Film Festival gave it a special prize for "Positive treatment of social problems regarding childhood and adolescence." But the highbrow Manchester *Guardian* condemned it: "The behavior of American children and the attitude at once maudlin, indulgent and puerile, which American grown-ups (on the screen) adopt toward their young are subjects which simply should not be allowed to cross the Atlantic."

Released during the heyday of family sitcoms on television, *Room for One More* offered nothing different from the competition and proved only mildly successful at the box office. But Grant was delighted when Betsy Drake finally received some of the recognition he thought she deserved. "She's not quite like any other young star or starlet. She has a charming style all her own," said *Photoplay.* "Betsy Drake is superb as the young wife; pretty, intelligent and tenderly amusing," *Variety* noted.

Despite the acclaim, Betsy Drake didn't make another movie for five years. Now that she'd proved herself as an actress, she became more interested in developing other skills and interests, especially writing. Also, her husband discouraged her from seeking further acting assignments as he became increasingly pessimistic about his own career and the film business in general.

Grant's discontent really boiled down to the fact that most of his recent movies were box-office losers. Around that time, he developed his famous "Hollywood streetcar" theory, which came from a Charlie Chaplin comedy he had seen in his youth. As Grant remembered it, Chaplin boarded a trolley at the rear, eventually got kicked off at the front by the crush of all the passengers who got on after him, and then jumped on again at the rear, holding on for dear life.

In Grant's opinion, "The streetcar just goes around in circles, not going anywhere. There is room on it for just so many, and every once in a while, if you look back, you'll see that someone has fallen off to let a new passenger on. When Ty Power got on, it meant we left someone sprawled out on the street; and somebody had to fall off to make room for Greg Peck.

"Some fellows who get pushed off run around and climb back on as character actors. Adolph Menjou is one. Ronald Colman sits up with the motorman. And Gary Cooper is smart. He never gets up to give anybody a seat. After much confusion and waiting, I finally got a seat."

But by 1951, Grant saw himself as a standee again, "just hanging onto a strap and being jostled around."

Between 1948 and 1951, Grant made five films, but only *I Was a Male War Bride* became an unqualified hit. In March 1952, when he signed for another screwball collaboration with Howard Hawks, he said, "I've tried to get away from my usual type of roles, but they don't seem to be half as successful as my comedies. So why fight it? The public wants me in comedies and that's how they'll have me from now on."

The new Howard Hawks film started out as "Darling, I Am Growing Younger," but 20th Century–Fox changed it to *Monkey Business* after getting permission to use the title of a 1931 Marx Brothers comedy. In the "ain't life gland" plot, Grant played a research chemist who, through a series of mix-ups in the laboratory, believes that he's discovered a formula to make people younger. As in previous Howard Hawks comedies, Grant received free rein, cavorting with a chimpanzee, reverting to childhood to play games with George "Foghorn" Winslow, and taking a wild car ride with a platinum blonde named Marilyn Monroe.

Although she had a secondary role to leading lady Ginger Rogers, Monroe still managed to disrupt filming as a result of her personal problems of the time. Distraught over recent scandals about her nude calendar art and her mother's insanity, she became ill and had to be hospitalized soon after *Monkey Business* went into production.

Having caused a similar disruption when he came down with hepatitis on his last Hawks film, Grant agreed to shooting around Monroe until the studio could determine whether or not she had to be replaced. When it turned out that Monroe had appendicitis, doctors were able to freeze the appendix and postpone an operation long enough so that she could complete the few scenes she had in the picture.

In an interview, Grant described working with Monroe: "I found her a very interesting child. I was able to have several chats with her on the set and I thought her most attractive, very shy and very eager to learn her job. We discussed books and I mentioned a few she might want to read."

Grant's remarks about Monroe led to some frank comments about women in general: "At one time, I had very little regard for womanhood. As a matter of fact, it's only recently that I have been able to accept women as friends. I had an enlightening, let's say. I suddenly discovered that women are born with great wisdom and serenity. Men are taught to fight the world. But women are so much brighter and wiser. They have innate wisdom.

"It's something that's been dawning upon me for the past eight or ten years," he continued. "Perhaps as one grows older and therefore more observant, one is less apt to worry about one's own behavior. Now I can appreciate why my ex-wives divorced me. I was horrible, loathsome. They were absolutely right in divorcing me."

One of those ex-wives, Barbara Hutton, had just come back into his life in a peripheral way. Now divorced from her fourth husband, she asked Grant to help her find a place to live in Beverly Hills so that she could be near her son while he attended private school there. Grant arranged for Hutton to rent the home of his close friend Irene Mayer Selznick, who had become a successful stage producer in New York since divorcing David O. Selznick over his affair with Jennifer Jones.

By this time, sixteen-year-old Lance Reventlow had a much closer relationship with Cary and Betsy Grant than he did with either of his real parents. Although Lance received an allowance of a thousand dollars a month from his mother, the Grants couldn't help feeling sorry for him because he suffered from chronic asthma and lugged around a container of oxygen in case of emergency. Grant often invited him to be their houseguest and also arranged Lance's first dates, naturally with teenage starlets.

After *Monkey Business*, Grant kept to his pledge of taking only comedy roles by signing with MGM for *Dream Wife*. For quite some time, Grant had been eager to make a film with Deborah Kerr; though seventeen years his junior, she seemed closest in style and sophistication to his best leading ladies of the past. Grant wanted MGM to team them in Terence Rattigan's *O Mistress Mine*, one of Alfred Lunt and Lynn Fontanne's biggest stage hits, but the movie rights were unavailable.

Dore Schary and Sidney Sheldon, who previously had worked with Grant on *The Bachelor and the Bobby-Soxer*, finally sold him on starring with Kerr in an original comedy tailor-made to their talents. After one story conference, Grant also approved Schary's suggestion that Sidney Sheldon should direct the film as well as write it. (Years later, Grant kidded Sheldon that he was sorry he didn't commission a novel instead because it undoubtedly would have turned out better.)

If nothing else, *Dream Wife* showed why the movie business seemed on its last legs in 1952. Although television had dealt a catastrophic blow to theatre attendance, MGM still kept grinding out forty-four pictures a year, most of which never even had a chance for survival because there was no audience for them. Filmed in black-and-white instead of color, *Dream Wife* lacked even the main technical advantage that theatrical movies still had over television (CinemaScope, 3-D and stereophonic sound were yet to come).

Artistically speaking, *Dream Wife* couldn't compare with the prewar Cary Grant comedies that the public could now see at home free. The contrived plot found Grant as a bachelor diplomat who believes that a woman's place is in the home. Disgusted with fiancee Deborah Kerr's devotion to her career in the State Department, he jilts her for a belly-dancing Middle Eastern princess trained in the 1,001 ways of pleasing a man. All ends happily when the princess (Betta St. John) becomes emancipated and Grant begs Kerr for forgiveness.

Cary Grant was forty-eight when he made *Dream Wife*. For the first time on the screen, he looked haggard and even a bit embarrassed by the shoddiness of his surroundings. Soon after finishing the film in November 1952, he announced that he was taking a rest from acting and considering permanent retirement.

"It was the period of blue jeans, the dope addicts, the Method, and nobody cared about comedy at all," Grant recalled.

14

Sophie Somebody

Cary Grant's so-called "retirement" lasted eighteen months. In December 1952, he and Betsy Drake shuttered their Beverly Hills home and booked passage on a freighter bound for Hong Kong. In the first days of 1953, they turned up in Tokyo, where they visited Korean War evacuees in U.S. military hospitals before sailing to Singapore and other Far Eastern ports.

By spring, the Grants were back in California, dividing their time between Beverly Hills and Palm Springs, where he purchased a rambling Mexican-style house with a swimming pool and tennis courts.

The couple spent so much time by themselves that the fan magazines called the relationship "Hollywood's strangest marriage." Louella Parsons couldn't believe that two movie stars could lead such a peaceful, unglamorous life.

The Grants rarely turned up at premieres, parties, restaurants or nightclubs. Instead, they busied themselves with intellectual pursuits and self-improvement schemes that the Hollywood establishment considered weird and far-out, although they would be considered "normal" today.

The couple were among the first in celebrity circles to advocate the use of health foods and vitamin therapy, to which Grant attributed his youthful appearance.

"I'm sick and tired of being questioned about why I look young for my age and why I keep trim," Grant said. "Why should the idiots make so much of it? Why don't they emulate it, rather than gasp about it? Everyone wants to keep fit, so what do they do? They poison themselves with the wrong foods, they poison their lungs with smoking, they clog their pores with greasy makeup, they drink poison liquids. What can they expect?"

Hypnotism became one of the Grants' greatest enthusiasms after Betsy Drake read Leslie LeCron's *Hypnotism Today* and ran out to buy every other available book on the subject. One evening, Grant suggested that Drake use hypnotic influence to help him stop smoking.

"Your fingers are yellow, your breath stinks and you only smoke because you're insecure," she told him to repeat over and over again.

"I went to a sleep in a trance," Grant recalled, "and when I woke up, I felt perfectly splendid. But automatically, as usual, I reached over to the bed table for a cigarette. I lit it and was nauseated. I haven't smoked since or wanted to."

Grant also claimed that hypnotism cured him of a tendency to sneak an occasional shot of whiskey, forbidden since his bout with hepatitis. "We use hypnosis to release tensions, to relax mind and body," he said.

Cary Grant's daily life seemed no different from that of other retirees, except that he was forty-nine and not past sixty-five. In Palm Springs, the Grants went horseback riding at sunrise and again at sunset, swam, played tennis, read and pursued their hobbies.

"The days we like best are when it rains," Drake said. "We get up in the morning, put on blue jeans or shorts and sit around drinking coffee, discussing everything from God to the garment industry."

While Grant was famed for his highly polished style, Drake claimed that he went in for "good old-fashioned slapstick" at home, a carry-over from his vaudeville days. "He will fake a fall or go into a silly song and dance, and I'll laugh my head off," she said.

Although Grant professed to be retired, producers still sent him scripts and he turned down a few that he regretted later, including *Roman Holiday, Sabrina* and *Guys and Dolls.* But he nearly made *A Star Is Born*, developing a case of cold feet at the last minute.

Cary Grant and Judy Garland had been a mutual-admiration

society for years. He loved her vibrant performing style and she never kept it a secret that she had a crush on him. When Garland and producer-husband Sid Luft started planning the musical remake of the 1937 Janet Gaynor–Fredric March movie, Cary Grant seemed perfect casting for the charming matinee idol who becomes a pathetic alcoholic while watching his wife rise to overnight stardom.

Despite all of Garland and Luft's persuasive efforts, however, Grant couldn't decide whether he wanted to make the film or not. He knew that portraying an alcoholic convincingly was one of the most difficult assignments for an actor, because audiences tend to find such behavior comical. Since he already had an identification as a comedian, he feared that no matter how hard he tried, a broken-down, drunken Cary Grant would be greeted with hysterical laughter.

Still vacillating, Grant went to Garland and Luft's house one evening to confer with them and their director, his old friend George Cukor.

"Cary read his part aloud with me," Cukor remembered. "He was absolutely magnificent, dramatic and vulnerable beyond anything I'd ever seen him do. But when he finished, I was filled with a great, great sadness. I knew that Cary wouldn't do the role. He would never expose himself like that in public."

Nor did he. Around midnight, about an hour after Grant left, Betsy Drake turned up at the Lufts' front door, dressed in tennis shorts and sneakers.

"Lay off Cary!" she shouted at Garland and her husband. "You've got to let him go! He can't eat, he can't sleep! You're driving him out of his mind!"

The Lufts weren't sure whether Grant sent Drake or if she came of her own accord, but they agreed to her demand. After she left, Garland suggested James Mason: "He'll be a better drunk than Cary anyway." Whether he was or not, nobody will ever know, but Mason did win an Oscar nomination for his performance.

In December 1953, the press tried to drag Cary Grant from retirement long enough to comment on Barbara Hutton's sudden marriage—her fifth—to Porfirio Rubirosa, the notorious "Number One Foreign Co-respondent."

"With so many people talking, I think this is a fine time to keep my mouth shut," Grant said. Years later, however, he admitted sending Hutton a telegram in which he begged her not to marry Rubirosa because he already had an affair going with Zsa Zsa Gabor. But Hutton ignored all warnings and it cost her $2 million to get a divorce. She and Rubirosa separated after seventy-three days of connubial something-or-other.

In 1954, Cary Grant turned fifty. The year started ominously when right after the holidays he lost his great friend, sixty-six-year-old Dorothy di Frasso.

Decked out in a full-length mink coat and a $175,000 diamond necklace, the countess died from a heart attack in her train compartment while returning from the opening of Marlene Dietrich's new nightclub act in Las Vegas. Traveling companion Clifton Webb, who discovered the body, said that he was unsure whether Dietrich's performance or Di Frasso's upset over Barbara Hutton's recent marriage had caused the coronary.

On the day before the funeral service, after all the other mourners had left the mortuary, Cary and Betsy Drake stayed behind to keep vigil throughout the night. "Dorothy hated to be alone," Grant told reporters the next morning. "She was gay, blithe, full of laughter, and she loved to be surrounded by friends. We wanted to spend one last night with her."

Cary Grant also accompanied Di Frasso's casket back to New York for burial. At a gathering of her friends there, he recalled the countess's "haunting grief" over not having had the foresight to plant a time bomb in her Roman villa when it was used by Mussolini for a meeting with Hitler prior to World War II. If those really were her sentiments, they raise further doubt about her alleged service as an Axis spy.

Another of Grant's close friends, Alfred Hitchcock, finally convinced him to go back to filmmaking. Phoning Grant in Palm Springs one day, Hitchcock asked if he could drive down to see him about a project.

"Of course, we'd love to have you," Grant said, "but I should tell you that it won't do any good. I've made up my mind. My acting days are over."

During lunch beside the pool, Grant outlined all his reasons for retirement. Hitchcock listened patiently until Grant finished and then slowly told him about a movie he intended to make if he could only find the right cast. The plot concerned a reformed jewel thief who's hounded by the police because of a sudden outbreak of robberies that seem to fit his old method of operation. To prove his innocence, the man must track down the real burglar.

Having aroused Grant's interest, Hitchcock waddled out to his Rolls-Royce and came back carrying a script. Handing it to Grant, he said, "There isn't a thing wrong with you, old man, that a first-rate screenplay won't cure. I'd appreciate it if you'd read this as soon as possible." Looking at his watch, he announced that he had to get back to Los Angeles.

As Grant accompanied his fellow Britisher back to his car, he lapsed into a Cockney accent: "Alfred, me pal, I don't want ye to git yer hopes up."

Hitchcock dismissed the apologies. "Just give it an honest reading, my good man, and tell me what you think. *I* think you'd be perfectly splendid in the part."

Before driving off, Hitchcock said matter-of-factly, "One last thing. It might help you as you're reading. Grace Kelly has agreed to play the girl . . . and a good part of the picture will be shot on the Riviera."

Naturally, Hitchcock's mini-suspense ploy worked, and Grant signed for *To Catch a Thief.* Ironically, he ended his retirement by going back to work for Paramount Pictures, where his movie career had started nearly a quarter of a century earlier.

Now fifty years old, Grant started to worry over how he'd look in Paramount's new high-clarity VistaVision process. Before leaving for France, he spent a week going over wardrobe needs with costume designer Edith Head.

"Cary's taste is impeccable," Head said afterward. "I consider him not only the most beautiful but the most beautifully dressed man in the world. His is a discerning eye, a meticulous sense of detail. He has the greatest fashion sense of any actor I've ever worked with. He knows as much about women's clothes as he does about men's."

Head described the way that he worked out a color scheme for his clothes throughout the movie: "He found what Grace Kelly was wearing in each scene, then selected clothes to complement hers. 'She's wearing a pale blue bathing suit for the beach scene? Good, I'll wear plaid shorts. She's wearing a gray dress? How would it be if I wear a dark jacket and gray slacks?' "

Grant attributed his interest in clothes to Elias Leach's having been a presser in the garment trade. "My father first put into my

mind the idea of buying one good superior suit rather than a
number of inferior ones," he recalled. "Then even when it's
threadbare, people will know it was once good. He taught me the
feel of cloth and a liking for expensive shoes. I still wear suits made
twenty years ago and topcoats that are thirty years old."

Grant generally wore his own clothes on screen. For *To Catch a
Thief,* he took along eight suits, plus a duplicate of each in case of
mishaps. His suits were made in Hong Kong, as well as by Quintino
in Hollywood and Brooks Brothers in New York. He never used a
belt or suspenders; his trousers had a tab-type waistband that he
designed himself.

And he never wore garters. As Howard Hawks once said,
"How do his socks stay up? Cary Grant's socks wouldn't *dare* fall
down."

The beachfront Carlton Hotel in Cannes became home for the
Grants while he made *To Catch a Thief.* Grace Kelly also stayed
there, along with her lover, fashion designer Oleg Cassini, although Paramount tried to keep it secret to protect the virginal
image of its star property.

Legend has it that Kelly met her future husband, Prince Rainier of Monaco, during the filming, but that actually happened on a
visit to the Cannes Film Festival the following year. On this trip,
the nearest Grace Kelly got to Monaco's pink palace was on a
sightseeing excursion that she took with her makeup man on their
day off.

One weekend, Grant received a phone call from Barbara Hutton's great friend Aristotle Onassis, inviting him to bring Betsy
Drake and any friends that he wished to a luncheon party on his
yacht *Christina* in Monte Carlo Harbor. Grace Kelly tagged along
with the Grants, but out of shyness kept in the background. Since
she was nearsighted, she wore her customary hornrimmed glasses.
Nobody paid her any particular attention.

Onassis insisted on taking the Grants on a tour of his floating
palace. In the salon area, he proudly called their attention to the
bar stools, which were covered with the skin of a whale's penis.
Betsy Drake surprised even her husband when she quipped, "Do
you mean that's Moby's dick?"

As the party ended and everyone started to leave, Onassis
took Grant aside and invited him to return whenever he liked.
Nodding toward the bespectacled blonde who'd been following

the Grants around the whole time, Onassis said, "And, please, bring your secretary along, too." No one would have dreamed that she'd become princess of the realm two years later.

Filming *To Catch a Thief* became almost a vacation for Grant. Since he and Kelly had each made two movies with Hitchcock before, the director relaxed some of his strict rules and permitted a great deal of improvisation.

In a scene shot along the Corniche Drive high above the Mediterranean, they found themselves in a silly, playful mood and covered with chicken feathers. They began to invent dialogue as they went along, making sure to incorporate all the necessary plot points. Hitchcock did three complete takes and then chose the best bits from each for the final cut.

Hitchcock could also be a tyrant, Grant revealed: "We had a scene where I had to grab Grace's arms hard, while she was fighting me, and push her against a wall. We went through that scene eight or nine times, but Hitch still wanted it again. Grace went back behind the door where the scene took place and just by chance I happened to catch a glimpse of her massaging her wrists and grimacing in pain. But a moment later, she came out and did the scene again. She never complained to me or to Hitch about how much her arms were hurting."

Remembering his only working experience with Grace Kelly, Grant said that "She was sometimes criticized for always being cool and composed. It was the composure born of confidence, application, concentration and knowledge. She reduced acting to its simplest form. Grace made acting look easy, the way Joe Louis made boxing look easy—so simple. Sometimes you see an artist work and you say, 'Oh, I could do that.' It's only those who have worked the hardest and the longest who can make it look that simple."

After finishing *To Catch a Thief* in September 1954, Grant didn't make another movie for nearly two years, although not entirely by choice. He wanted to see how *To Catch a Thief* turned out before he decided whether to continue working or to retire permanently.

But unfortunately for Grant, Hitchcock became involved in hosting a weekly television series and took forever editing *To Catch a Thief,* which delayed the movie's release until the autumn of 1955. In the meantime, Grant lost patience and decided to sign for another film anyway, Stanley Kramer's *The Pride and the Passion,* only to have that postponed because of script and budgetary problems.

As often happens when two people are together twenty-four hours a day with nothing to occupy them but themselves, Grant's marriage to Betsy Drake was starting to show signs of strain. In December 1954, they celebrated their fifth anniversary—a new matrimonial record for Cary Grant—but common intellectual interests apparently weren't strong enough to overcome certain sexual problems.

Even with his closest friends, Grant shied away from discussing those difficulties beyond admitting that he no longer felt attracted to Drake the way he had when they first married. Rosalind Russell said they seemed more like brother and sister than husband and wife. *The National Enquirer* went quite a bit further by stating that "the real reason for the domestic bliss of Cary Grant is that he likes his boyfriends and she likes her girlfriends. That way neither gets jealous."

Rumors of homosexuality in the Grant household circulated for years, nourished by revelations that the couple had separate bedrooms and eventually separate dwellings.

"Finding marriage too confining, Cary asked Betsy to move into a rented house and they met periodically at his place or hers," said Sheilah Graham.

Although Grant made no films in 1955, he kept in the news by rejecting offers. Otto Preminger wanted him for *Bonjour Tristesse,* but vanity prevented him from playing the father of Audrey Hepburn, whom Preminger had in mind for the other lead (David Niven and Jean Seberg took over). Twentieth Century–Fox sought Grant for *Can-Can* and Columbia pursued him for a musical version of *It Happened One Night.* Grant said that if he did anything, it would be a remake of *His Girl Friday* with Grace Kelly, but the rights were unavailable.

Even Mae West wanted Cary Grant again. In May 1955, he attended the opening of her new nightclub act at Ciro's, where she performed with a chorus line of bikini-clad musclemen. When Grant went backstage afterward, West tried to talk him into appearing with her in a remake of *She Done Him Wrong.*

West claimed it would be a sensation: the first time in the history of the movies that two stars re-created their original roles.

Grant just humored her. The mere thought of sixty-four-year-old Mae West telling fifty-one-year-old Cary Grant to come up and see her sometime would frighten anyone!

Growing bored by professional inactivity, Grant agreed to go on a national publicity tour when *To Catch a Thief* was released in September 1955. It marked the first time that he would be placed in direct contact with the public since the bond rallies of World War II. To work up the courage for such an ordeal, he had to be hypnotized by Betsy Drake.

Paramount sent Grant all over the United States, making personal appearances, meeting theatre owners and giving press and radio interviews. His one restriction was that he wouldn't do television, where he had no control over the lighting or camera angles.

In New York, Grant drew the biggest crowds since the heyday of "live" stage shows when he appeared at the Paramount Theatre between opening-day performances of *To Catch a Thief.* He was visibly moved by the applause he received after telling the audience of the significance of the occasion. While Archie Leach struggled to make a name for himself on Broadway, he had killed many a spare hour sitting in those same seats. And Cary Grant's very first movie, *This Is the Night*, premiered at the Paramount, more years before (twenty-three) than he cared to tell.

How much Grant's personal showmanship contributed to the success of *To Catch a Thief* is impossible to calculate, but the film became his biggest hit of the decade. Women especially flocked to see its fabulous clothes and Riviera settings, as well as the much-talked-about love scene in which Hitchcock used exploding fireworks to symbolize sexual orgasm.

Critics weren't equally enthusiastic about *To Catch a Thief,* many describing it as an eye-pleasing but rather vapid romantic comedy that lacked the excitement and suspense they had come to expect from Alfred Hitchcock. But nearly everyone thought that Cary Grant gave his best performance in years. Perhaps it wasn't so much a performance as reconfirmation that he could still play "Cary Grant," with his luster not diminished by the passage of time but actually burnished to a warmer glow.

The success of *To Catch a Thief* should have meant a new beginning for Grant's career, but he goofed in selecting *The Pride and the Passion* as his next film. His experience there, professionally as well as personally, knocked him for a loop.

As a result of his commitment to *The Pride and the Passion*, Grant also lost a chance to do *The Bridge on the River Kwai*, which became one of the most lauded box-office blockbusters of the fifties. William Holden, who took the part Grant turned down, earned $3.5 million from his participation in the profits.

That it took eighteen months to get *The Pride and the Passion* implemented should have been warning enough of trouble ahead. Producer-director Stanley Kramer did his best work with nominally budgeted black-and-white movies like *High Noon, Champion, The Men, Home of the Brave* and *Member of the Wedding*. A four-million-dollar historical spectacle, to be filmed on location in English in a Spanish-speaking Fascist dictatorship, seemed an insurmountable task for God or even Cecil B. DeMille. But Kramer somehow convinced United Artists to finance the project.

C. S. Forester's Napoleonic Wars novel *The Gun*, dealing with a British attempt to capture a gigantic cannon from the Spanish before it falls into the hands of the French, provided the basis for *The Pride and the Passion*. Kramer originally planned to team Cary Grant with Marlon Brando, but the latter thought that the cannon would turn out to be the real star of the movie and he turned down the assignment.

The role finally went to Frank Sinatra, who had been on the comeback trail since winning an Oscar for his supporting role in *From Here to Eternity*. Sinatra's singing, however, created another vacancy in the cast, because Kramer wanted Ava Gardner for leading lady. Now separated from Sinatra after a tempestuous five-year marriage, she refused to make a movie with him.

Cary Grant's contract gave him the right to approve the female star of *The Pride and the Passion*. When Stanley Kramer told him that he wanted to hire an up-and-coming Italian actress named Sophia Loren, Grant exploded: "My God! You want me to play with this Sophie somebody, a cheesecake thing? Well, I can't and I won't!"

Grant phoned Arthur Krim, president of United Artists, to register his objection: "Kramer wants this girl in the picture. I want out!"

"Wait a minute, Cary, you haven't met her," Krim said. "We think she's going to be one of the biggest stars in the world. Go to Spain to start the picture and just meet her, that's all. If you don't like her, we'll try to find someone else."

Grant's first meeting with twenty-one-year-old Sophia Loren took place at a party in Madrid. Grant arrived an hour late, which made the always punctual Loren extremely angry. But when he finally strolled in, dimpled, debonair and mumbling apologetically, "Ah, yes, Miss Lorbrigida . . . er . . . Brigloren . . . I can't remember Italian names," she quickly fell under his spell.

As for Grant, he left the party floating on air. "My God, Stanley, you're right," he told the producer-director. "I can't understand my prejudices. This girl is magnificent. What is the matter with me?"

Thanks to Grant's sudden change of heart, United Artists signed Loren for the film at a fee of two hundred thousand dollars. Italian producer Carlo Ponti, who managed her career and was also her lover, couldn't believe their luck. He said later that he would have paid United Artists that sum just to get Loren established in Hollywood films.

"Windmillville" became Frank Sinatra's epithet for the plains region around Avila, Spain, where *The Pride and the Passion* was filmed. In April 1956, Cary Grant checked in with Betsy Drake after attending the wedding of Grace Kelly and Prince Rainier in Monaco. Sinatra brought along his lover of the moment, beautiful twenty-four-year-old jazz singer Peggy Connelly. Loren had a part-time companion in Carlo Ponti, who commuted back and forth to Rome, where he ran a production company in partnership with Dino DeLaurentiis.

Frank Sinatra quickly appointed himself the court jester, and started by giving Loren a few lessons in English. Soon she was saying things like "It was a fucking gas" and "How's your cock?" to everyone she met.

Loren started the film expecting to become smitten with Sinatra, a *paisano* whose romantic vocalizing she adored. But when she discovered that he had taken advantage of her naïveté by teaching her obscenities, she wasted no time in denouncing him as "A mean little guinea son of a bitch" in front of the entire company.

Repelled by Sinatra's behavior, Loren found herself being drawn more and more into Grant's company. "I was fascinated with him and his warmth, affection, intelligence, and his wonderfully dry, mischievous sense of humor," Loren remembered. "In the beginning he was very reserved with me, and if our talk turned to something sad or introspective, he would try to make a joke out of it to keep it from touching him.

"But more and more, he confided in me and trusted me. There were patches of self-doubt in him which he disclosed with reluctance. He was deeply disturbed over the fact that he had never had a really sustained relationship in his life. He talked about his early life in England, his struggles and the three women he had been married to. But when he got too close to his center, he would put up the mask he hid behind and turn to joking.

"At first I was puzzled by the way Cary hopped from one foot to the other," Loren continued, "but as I got to know him, I began to realize that he had an inner conflict of wanting to be open and honest and direct and yet not to make himself more vulnerable. Of course, one cannot have it both ways, and slowly as our relationship grew and his trust in me grew, he came to realize that trust and vulnerability went hand in hand. When his trust was strong enough, he no longer bothered with his mask."

Grant's tender feelings became apparent when he started sending Loren roses every day and telling visiting journalists, "Sophia is so sensuous that most men would long to tear the clothes off her on sight."

After work, Grant often whisked his leading lady off to romantic hilltop restaurants for midnight suppers. Betsy Drake seemed amazingly understanding. The only time that she told her husband to cool it was when the honeymooning Rainiers came to visit. The Grants had promised to take the newlyweds sightseeing and to the bullfights, which they did.

In July 1956, Drake got tired of hanging around doing nothing while her husband courted another woman. Before the press found out about the odd triangle and made a scandal out of it, she decided to go home to Beverly Hills. Packing her things, she drove to Gibraltar to catch the next ship bound for the United States, which just happened to be the Italian liner SS *Andrea Doria.*

On July 24, the *Andrea Doria* collided with the Swedish SS *Stockholm* in heavy fog about sixty miles from Nantucket Island, Massachusetts. Fifty-two people died when the *Andrea Doria* sank to the bottom of the ocean, but Betsy Drake was one of several hundred passengers rescued by another passing ship, the SS *Île de France.*

Although she escaped physical injury, Drake received emo-

tional scars that haunted her for years. She also lost the only copy
of a book that she'd been working on for two years, plus a pearl-
and-emerald necklace and matching earrings that Grant had given
her as a wedding present. The jewels, reportedly worth $125,000,
were stored in one of the ship's safes, but have yet to be found in
any of the attempts to salvage the sunken liner.

"I love her so much that, for once in my life, words fail me,"
Cary Grant said when the Associated Press called him for a statement about his wife's rescue.

What Grant really felt can only be guessed. But Tony Faramus,
a British butler who worked for him for years, swears that he once
heard Grant shouting at Drake, "I wish you'd gone down with the
ship. It might have saved us both a lot of problems."

Drake's decampment gave Grant freedom to pursue Sophia
Loren more aggressively. Dining by moonlight one evening while a
gypsy crooned in the background, Grant opened his heart. "He
told me that with every passing day, he was more sure that we
belonged together," Loren recalled, "that finally he had found in
me someone to whom he could totally relate. 'I trust you and love
you and want to marry you,' he said."

But such declarations only made Loren skeptical; they reminded her of scenes she'd seen in some of his old movies. She
adored him—what woman could resist Cary Grant?—yet she
sensed an instability and lack of maturity that she felt would make
him an unsatisfactory husband.

But an unsatisfactory husband might be better than no husband at all. Loren decided that she couldn't afford to reject Cary
Grant until she clarified her position with Carlo Ponti, whom she
really wanted to marry. Like his rival, Ponti also had a wife, but
Italian law forbade divorce. The real-life soap opera had too many
plot complications and too many characters to be resolved easily or
quickly.

"I told Cary that I didn't dare give an answer yet. That I still
needed time and I needed to go back to my own environment and
to be able to make up my mind away from the magic of those
Spanish nights," Loren said.

Meanwhile, Grant faced problems of another kind with Frank
Sinatra, who kept calling him "Mother Grant" around the set.
Although Sinatra claimed to be only poking fun at Grant's solici-
tude toward the cast and crew, Grant thought he had a more

malicious intent and felt deeply insulted. He finally lost all respect for Sinatra when the "Chairman of the Board" walked off the picture with seven weeks of production still remaining.

"Hot or cold, on Thursday I'm leaving the movie. So get a lawyer and sue me," Sinatra told Stanley Kramer. And off Sinatra went, homesick for his Rat Pack cronies and fed up with not even being able to reach them by phone because of the primitive state of telephone service in Franco's Spain.

After weeks of frantic negotiation, during which Kramer worked around Sinatra by having Cary Grant play his scenes to a clothes dummy, the fugitive star agreed to complete his portion if it were shot in Hollywood. That forced a further delay in finishing the movie because Grant and Loren were already booked for other projects and couldn't regroup with Sinatra for several months.

Returning to California, Grant found Betsy Drake experiencing psychological trauma over her experience on the *Andrea Doria.* "Betsy had simply stopped functioning, either as an actress or in any other field in which she had once been interested," said Rosalind Russell. "It was pathetic to see her wasting away like that."

Grant thought that work might be the best therapy for his wife, so he wangled her an acting job at 20th Century–Fox, where he had some bargaining clout because of a forthcoming commitment of his own. Drake's first movie in five years, *Will Success Spoil Rock Hunter?*, was a frenetic sex comedy starring Jayne Mansfield and Tony Randall. Drake walked through her role like a zombie and went back to searching for a more effective solution to her problems.

By this time, Cary Grant had given up all thoughts of retirement. In 1957, he made four films and also finished what remained of *The Pride and the Passion,* all adding up to his most active year since the 1930s.

In February, Grant started the first of two films for producer Jerry Wald, the chubby dynamo who reportedly inspired the character of Sammy Glick in Budd Schulberg's novel *What Makes Sammy Run?* Wald was launching a new long-term deal at Fox with *An Affair to Remember,* a remake of the 1939 Charles Boyer–Irene Dunne picture *Love Affair.*

Grant had reservations about taking over a role already identified with another of the screen's Great Lovers, but he liked the idea of working again with Leo McCarey, who directed him in *The Awful Truth* and also made the original *Love Affair*.

Jerry Wald clinched the deal by selecting Deborah Kerr for Grant's leading lady. The producer predicted an enormous success because Hollywood had a critical shortage of the stylish and sentimental romances that were so popular in the thirties. Wald believed that there were no longer enough actors around who could play them convincingly: "Today's actors either look good and talk lousy, or they look lousy and talk good."

While he made *An Affair to Remember*, Grant and Betsy Drake stepped up their experiments with hypnotism. The intention was to cure her trauma over the *Andrea Doria*, but the treatment seemed to work better on him than it did on her.

Deborah Kerr recalled arriving at the studio early one morning and finding Grant already eating his lunch from a hamper of health food that he brought from home. "That woman," Grant told Kerr. "She caught me sneaking a cigarette last night, so she hypnotized me so that I wouldn't smoke today. Now I can't stand the taste of a cigarette and I'm starved. It's awful to have a wife who literally hypnotizes her husband."

When Kerr said kiddingly that Drake would be starting on his stocks and bonds next, Grant said, shrugging, "Oh, she got those years ago."

Cinematographer Milton Krasner took Grant aside one day to tell him that a lump on his forehead made the filming of close-ups very difficult. The lump originated as the vestige of a minor accident in Grant's childhood. He had been unconsciously rubbing the spot all his life, causing it to swell to a size that now suggested malignancy. Doctors said that removing it would mean hospitalization plus four to six weeks' recuperation before he could face a camera again.

Grant didn't want to delay production of *An Affair to Remember*, so he told Jerry Wald to shoot around him while he took a few days off.

"I had Betsy hypnotize me before the operation," Grant recalled. "She emphasized that I had to stay calm and even enjoy the operation. I did just that. The surgeon used a local anaesthetic. He might have been cutting my hair for all I cared."

The forty-five-minute surgery was followed by an incredibly

quick recovery. Grant did not even have a scar to show. The growth proved to be benign.

Grant's nearly overnight recovery permitted him to start his next Jerry Wald film as soon as they finished *An Affair to Remember*. The new one was called *Kiss Them for Me*, based on a flop Broadway play adapted from *Shore Leave*, Frederick Wakeman's bestselling novel about a group of navy officers on leave during World War II.

Jerry Wald persuaded Grant to do the film by promising him Audrey Hepburn as leading lady. But Hepburn had other commitments and suggested that Wald hire her close friend Suzy Parker, who'd never acted in her life but ranked as the top American photographic model of the day.

When Wald sent Parker a telegram in New York asking her to come to Hollywood to test for a movie with Cary Grant, she thought someone was playing a practical joke and threw it away. Only when Audrey Hepburn telephoned her a week later to find out why she hadn't responded did Parker follow through and get the part.

As if one untrained and inexperienced actress weren't enough to lumber Cary Grant with, Jerry Wald chose Jayne Mansfield for another major role. Hoping that he could eventually star the top-heavy blonde in the life story of Jean Harlow, Wald thought that casting her opposite Grant would give her some class and stop Hollywood and the general public from treating her like a dirty joke.

But the pairing of Cary Grant and Jayne Mansfield didn't work, and only caused him endless embarrassment during the filming of *Kiss Them for Me*. Since Grant just happened to be the movie idol of her youth, Mansfield behaved like a lovesick autograph hunter, letting out swoons and pinching herself every few minutes to make sure that working with Cary Grant wasn't merely a dream.

Grant gave Mansfield a few lessons in deportment when she got involved in an incident with Sophia Loren, newly arrived in Hollywood to finish her scenes with Grant and Sinatra in *The Pride and the Passion*. At a party held to introduce Loren to the press, Mansfield arrived wearing a low-cut gown that barely concealed her nipples. As she leaned over to greet the seated guest of honor, one of her breasts popped out right in Loren's face.

Photos of Sophia Loren staring askance at Jayne Mansfield's

exposed breast hit scandal sheets all over the world. "Respect-able" newspapers that wouldn't print the photographs at least told the story. Mansfield's behavior created shock and indignation among the old standard-bearers of the movie industry. Cary Grant and Joan Crawford were the first to warn her that if she continued such tawdry headline-hunting tactics, she'd be run out of Holly-wood.

In July 1957, Cary Grant's first films to be released in two years—*The Pride and the Passion* and *An Affair to Remember*—reached theatre screens within days of each other. Launched with a massive advertising campaign, *The Pride and the Passion* did excellent busi-ness for the first week and then plummeted after adverse reviews and negative word-of-mouth.

Producer-director Stanley Kramer later blamed himself for the disaster: "Cary Grant never did well in costume drama. He was really a drawing-room character. But with one of my more blatant bursts of creative misjudgment, I cast him in a role and it was not for him. You know, in the tight military pants, the frilled shirt of the British officer."

Kramer compounded his mistake by putting Frank Sinatra into a wig with bangs and casting him as a leader of Spanish rebel peasants. "Frank looked like he was going to burst into 'Besame Mucho' at any moment," Kramer said.

The fiasco of *The Pride and the Passion* might have sent Cary Grant back into retirement if *An Affair to Remember* hadn't quickly wiped out any fear that his career might be over.

As Jerry Wald anticipated, the half comedy, half soap opera about two lovers who find each other again after years of separa-tion became one of the biggest hits of 1957, thanks largely to the deftness and charm of the Cary Grant–Deborah Kerr partnership.

"It was our most successful work together," Kerr said many years later. "To this day it's shown over and over again in the States and in England and on the Continent, as well as Australia. And hundreds and hundreds of people tell me how *many* times they have seen the movie, and how they wept at every viewing."

Meanwhile, Cary Grant's real-life infatuation with Sophia Loren headed toward an unhappy ending. Prior to starting *The Pride and the Passion,* Grant had made a development deal with Paramount for *Houseboat,* to be based on an original idea by Betsy Drake about a widower and three young children.

The Grants had intended *Houseboat* to be their third film together, but after what had happened in Spain, Grant impetuously arranged for Loren to replace Betsy Drake in the movie. Ten months later, he began to regret that decision when Loren reported for work with Carlo Ponti in tow.

"Cary's heart was broken," said Frederick Brisson. "Sophia and Ponti were sharing a bungalow at the Bel Air Hotel, practically in Cary's backyard. He couldn't understand how she could choose a fat, bald and unhandsome man like that over Cary Grant. His pride in his image hurt more than his ego."

Grant tried to have Loren removed from *Houseboat,* only to find that his contractual right to approve leading ladies was irrevocable once he'd exercised it.

"Cary obviously didn't want to have to go through the torment of being on the set with Sophia every day," said *Houseboat* director Melville Shavelson. "He had to take it out on somebody and I was the most convenient, although after the picture was over he apologized for giving me such a hard time.

"He objected to the photography, he objected to portions of the script, he objected to things which in normal situations he would not have minded at all. His problem was with Sophia. And that made the picture hard going for everybody."

Shavelson did an enormous amount of hand-holding. "Sophia often came to me crying, largely because of what was going on between her and Cary on the studio floor," the director said. "She made it clear so many times to him that Carlo Ponti was her man, but apparently Cary just couldn't understand that. He couldn't comprehend this father-fixation that Italian women have, this need for the care, the comfort and the guidance which Sophia certainly got from Carlo Ponti."

Grant grew even more miserable when Louella Parsons announced to the world that, through proxy, Carlo Ponti had obtained a divorce in Mexico and married Sophia Loren. The news surprised even the bride and groom. Ponti had started the proceedings weeks earlier, but his attorneys weren't nearly as fast in reporting the outcome as Louella Parsons, who had spies everywhere.

When Loren arrived at the studio that day, one look at Cary Grant told her that he knew everything. "I hope you will be very happy, Sophia," he said, kissing her coolly on the cheek.

The climax of *Houseboat* had yet to be filmed. Unhappily, reality and fantasy overlapped in the script. Cary Grant and Sophia Loren were to be married in a sumptuous church ceremony set to Mendelssohn's music.

Grant, who'd never won an Oscar, should have received at least a nomination for the way he masked his true feelings while he stood at the altar with Loren. Costumed by Edith Head in a long white gown of antique lace, she was the bride of his dreams. One can only guess how he felt as they took the sacred vows and came as close to being real-life husband and wife as they ever would.

"I cared very much for Cary and I was aware of how painful it was for him to play the scene with me, to have the minister pronounce us man and wife and take me in his arms and kiss me," Loren recalled. "It was painful for me, too, his make-believe bride. I could not help thinking of all those lovely times in Spain, of all the souvenirs I had in my memory. I'm very romantic and vulnerable, and I would cherish forever what Cary brought into my life."

Grant's personal ordeal continued long after he finished *Houseboat.* Filled with self-doubt and emotional insecurities, he was on the verge of total collapse when Betsy Drake came to the rescue. Finding herself making remarkable progress in an experimental program at the Psychiatric Institute of Beverly Hills, she persuaded her husband to join the group.

15

Rebirth

On his first visit to the Psychiatric Institute of Beverly Hills, Cary Grant underwent a complete examination and evaluation to make sure that he had no active psychoses or suicidal tendencies. Candidates who did were immediately rejected because they would be unable to deal with the terrifying unconscious material that often could be unleashed in the radical therapy being tested.

After being accepted, Grant attended several indoctrination sessions before actual treatment began. He learned all about the drug being used—lysergic acid diethylamide—more commonly called LSD. It was chemically related to mescaline, an alkaloid derived from cactus plants, which Indian tribes in Mexico and the Southwestern United States had used for centuries for its psychedelic effects.

The institute's directors, Dr. Arthur Chandler and Dr. Mortimer Hartman, believed that LSD could be beneficial in therapy because it acted as a psychic energizer, emptying the subconscious mind and intensifying emotions a hundred times. In large doses, LSD produced a dreamlike state in which the user hallucinated, saw a dream world in brilliant colors, and felt disassociated from reality.

In smaller, controlled doses of the type recommended by the institute, LSD allegedly broke down memory blocks and caused the patient to vividly relive past experiences as far back as gestation. This relieved emotional tension and could help the patient to

understand his problems much faster, Chandler and Hartman believed.

Grant also learned how to prepare himself for the treatments:
no sedatives, tranquilizers or analgesics for at least twenty-four
hours prior to each LSD session; no food for four hours preceding
each session (to increase the absorption rate of the drug, which
took from fifteen minutes to two hours to take effect).

Under no circumstances could Grant be left on his own after
an LSD session. He would be given a barbiturate such as Seconal
and then be taken home by his wife or some other responsible
individual who could remain with him for the rest of the day and
evening. He was forbidden to drive a car until the following day. As
a further precaution, before retiring for the night he had to telephone the therapist to report on any aftereffects. If he was feeling
too agitated to sleep, he had to take another capsule of Seconal.

Since Grant had already shepherded Betsy Drake through the
same routine, he adapted to it easily. The hardest part was finding
the time. Although only four or five hours were actually spent in
the therapist's office, an entire day had to be set aside to allow for
preparation and recuperation. For Grant, it usually had to be Saturday, which gave him an extra day to recuperate if he had to face
the cameras bright and early Monday morning.

Over a two-year period, Grant spent hundreds of hours on a
couch in a darkened room probing his psyche, stimulated by LSD
and the counseling of Dr. Hartman, whom he later called "My wise
Mahatma." Almost at once, Grant began to learn things about
himself that he had never known—or had never wanted to know.

"We come into this world with nothing on our tape. We are
computers, after all," Grant said in later years. "The content of
that tape is supplied by our mothers, mainly because our fathers
are off hunting or shooting or working. Now the mother can teach
only what she knows, and many of these patterns of behavior are
not good, but they're still passed on to the child. I came to the
conclusion that I had to be reborn, to wipe clean the tape.

"When I first started under LSD," he continued, "I found
myself turning and turning on the couch, and I said to the doctor,
'Why am I turning around on this sofa?' and he said 'Don't you
know why?' and I said I didn't have the vaguest idea, but I wondered when it was going to stop. 'When you stop it,' he answered.
Well, it was like a revelation to me, taking complete responsibility

for one's own actions. I thought 'I'm unscrewing myself.' That's why people use the phrase, 'all screwed up.' "

Grant said that "the first thing that happens is you don't want to look at what you are. Then the light breaks through; to use the cliché, you are enlightened. I discovered that I had created my own pattern, and I had to be responsible for it. I had to forgive my parents for what they didn't know and love them for what they did pass down—how to brush my teeth, how to comb my hair, how to be polite, that sort of thing. Things were being discharged."

Grant believed that he had gone through rebirth. "The experience was just like being born the first time; I imagined all the blood and urine, and I emerged with the flush of birth," he said. "It was absolute release. You are still able to feed yourself, of course, drive your car, that kind of thing, but you've lost a lot of the tension.

"It releases inhibition. You know, we are all unconsciously holding our anus. In one LSD dream I (bleeped) all over the rug and (bleeped) all over the floor. Another time I imagined myself as a giant penis launching off from Earth like a spaceship."

Describing the effect of LSD, Grant said that his mind seemed to leave his skull: "I passed through changing seas of horrifying and happy sights, through a montage of intense hate and love, a mosaic of past impressions assembling and reassembling; through terrifying depths of dark despair replaced by glorious heavenlike religious symbolisms."

Betsy Drake put it even more dramatically when she explained that "You learn to die under LSD. You face up to all the urges in you—love, sex, jealousy, the wish to kill. Freud is the road map."

Whether Freud would have sanctioned the use of LSD as a shortcut to reaching those truths is another question, but it seemed to be working for Cary Grant. His first reaction was "Oh, those wasted years; why didn't I do this sooner?"

Never one to speak frankly or openly about his private life, he suddenly shed his reticence: "I know now that in my earlier days I really despised myself. When you admit this, you are beginning to change. Introspection is the beginning of change."

At first, the treatments seemed to help Grant's marriage to Betsy Drake. Apart from their individual progress, the LSD therapy in itself gave them a mutual interest they hadn't had before.

But work caused some long separations. In December 1957,

when Grant went to London for three months to make *Indiscreet,*
Drake stayed behind in California, claiming that she couldn't bear
the harsh English winters. Grant didn't seem to mind, despite his
near fatal illness in London nine winters earlier.

Although *Kiss Them for Me* turned out to be a critical and box-
office fiasco, Grant came away from it with high regard for the
director, Stanley Donen. Forming an independent production
company called Grandon, they made a deal with Warner Brothers
to distribute their first effort, to be based on Norman Krasna's
Broadway stage hit, *Kind Sir.* The play, which starred Charles
Boyer and Mary Martin, was the sort of urbane comedy of manners
that Grant thought had become extinct. He snapped it up as a
vehicle for himself and either Deborah Kerr or Ingrid Bergman.

Ostracized by Hollywood since the Rossellini scandal, Bergman seemed an impossibility until she surprised everyone by winning an Academy Award for *Anastasia* in March 1957. When Cary
Grant walked on stage at the telecast and accepted the Oscar in
Bergman's absence, the audience responded so warmly and sup-
portively that he realized that he'd be a fool not to sign her for *Kind
Sir* before someone else hired her. Norman Krasna agreed to
change the title to *Indiscreet* as a one-adjective reminder of Grant
and Bergman's previous hit, *Notorious.*

While the American press and public seemed to have forgiven
Bergman for her "sins," she still felt reluctant to return to the
United States to work *(Anastasia* was made in England). Krasna,
who adapted his play for the screen, easily solved that problem by
switching the story's locale from New York to London.

Little was gained, however, by the change. Just before *Indiscreet* started production in England, another scandal erupted as
Bergman walked out on Rossellini after discovering that he was
involved with another woman.

When Bergman landed at London's Heathrow Airport from
Paris, where she'd been appearing in a play, 150 reporters and
photographers waited in ambush for her. Fortunately, Cary Grant
came along as well, to help her through the fray.

"Next to my wife, Ingrid is the most wonderful woman I
know," Grant told the crowd while waiting for her to come through
passport control.

When Bergman reached the area of the lounge that had been
roped off for an impromptu press conference, she found Grant

sitting on the top of a table. "Ingrid, wait till you hear my problems!" he shouted across the heads of the journalists.

"That broke the ice," Bergman remembered. "Everybody burst into laughter. Cary held them at bay in such a nice way. 'Come on, fellas, you can't ask a lady that! Ask me the same question and I'll give you an answer. So, you're not interested in my life? It's twice as colorful as Ingrid's.' "

Finally, Grant and Bergman escaped and headed for London in a beige-and-black Rolls-Royce with the license plate "CG 1."

Grant stayed with Bergman almost constantly for the next few days, taking her dining, sightseeing and on tours of the antique shops that she loved. Although she had arrived in London looking like any other distraught middle-aged woman in the midst of a marital collapse, Grant's coddling helped to turn her back into the exquisite Bergman of happier days by the time *Indiscreet* went before the cameras. Much to her delight, Grant the producer had ordered the most elegant wardrobe of any of her films, with gowns by Pierre Balmain, Lanvin-Castillo and Christian Dior.

Made twelve years after *Notorious,* Grant and Bergman's second teaming proved less auspicious than the first. Grant was now fifty-three, Bergman forty-two. Both seemed too mature for the romantic shenanigans about a confirmed bachelor who pretends to be married in order to keep his romance with a London stage star from getting too serious.

In her first real comedy role, Bergman showed herself to be neither a deft comedienne nor convincing as a Great Lady of the English theatre. But just the mere presence of Grant and Bergman in an ultra-chic Technicolor trifle was enough of an anachronism for 1958 to make *Indiscreet* a box-office hit.

When *Indiscreet* ended production in February 1958, Grant ruffled a few feathers back in Hollywood when he joined a weekend junket to Moscow organized by producer Sam Spiegel. Returning to London, Grant told a reporter at the airport, "I don't care what kind of government they have in Russia, I never felt so free in my life."

As soon as Grant's remark reached American superpatriot Hedda Hopper, she rushed into print with the suggestion that Cary Grant should go back to the Soviet Union and stay there.

Afraid of ending up on the Hollywood blacklist of alleged Communist revolutionaries and sympathizers, Grant tried to clarify his statement the next day. What he really meant was that he enjoyed being able to walk around Moscow without being stared at or badgered to sign autographs. Since his movies were completely unknown there, it was the first time in twenty-five years that happened to him.

But on this side of the Iron Curtain, Grant couldn't make a move without causing comment. When he returned to the United States on the *Île de France*, Louella Parsons gushingly described it as a sentimental gesture to thank the captain for his part in saving Betsy Drake from the sinking *Andrea Doria*.

While stopping over in New York, Grant became involved in the amusing "Affair of the English Muffins" that bolstered his reputation for being miserly and a bit overzealous about getting value for money.

For years, while using the Plaza Hotel as his New York headquarters, Grant had been in the habit of ordering the same breakfast, which always included two English muffins split in half and toasted. But on this particular morning, he lifted the cover off the muffin warmer and discovered it contained only three halves instead of the customary four.

Rushing to the telephone, he asked room service: "Can you tell me why I am charged for four halves of English muffins but am only sent three?"

Room service had no explanation; neither did the assistant manager nor the managing director of the hotel. So Cary Grant went straight to the top and telephoned the hotel's owner, Conrad Hilton, in Beverly Hills. His office informed Grant that Hilton was in Istanbul.

Determined to find out the answer to his question, he telephoned Hilton in Turkey. Hilton told Grant that a hotel efficiency expert had discovered that most people only ate three halves of their English muffins and that the fourth half was usually discarded. Consequently, the kitchen staff now put the fourth halves aside and used them for eggs benedict on the luncheon menu.

"I still felt it was wrong," Grant recalled. "After all, the menu had stated 'English muffins,' not 'a muffin and a half.' " The Plaza apparently agreed. From then on, Grant not only got two full muffins with his breakfast orders, but he also often talked to friends about forming an "English Muffin-Lovers Society." Every member would have to promise to report any hotel or restaurant that made dishonest use of the plural by listing "muffins" on the menu and then serving fewer than two.

In the summer of 1958, Grant received an offer to portray nymphet connoisseur Humbert Humbert in the film version of Vladimir Nabokov's *Lolita,* which then had a reputation as one of the most degenerate novels of modern times. The producer told Grant that the role was such a plum that only two actors in the world were worthy of it, himself and Laurence Olivier.

"Well, you've just lost one of us," Grant said. "I have too much respect for the movie industry to do a picture like that. Perhaps books can deal with such subjects because they have a select audience. But they have no place on the screen." (As a result of censorship problems, the movie wasn't made until four years later, with James Mason again playing a role that Grant had rejected.)

Grant needed no coaxing, however, when Alfred Hitchcock approached him about doing another picture together. Since Grant had netted about $750,000 from his profit participation in *To Catch a Thief,* he wasn't about to turn down another golden opportunity, especially when the director promised it would be "the Hitchcock picture to end all Hitchcock pictures."

Hitchcock had made a deal with MGM for a film based on Hammond Innes's adventure novel *The Wreck of the Mary Deare,* but he and scriptwriter Ernest Lehman found the material unpromising and wanted to be released. Without telling MGM, they started to create an original script incorporating various ideas that Hitchcock had been toying with for years but could never fit into any of his previous films.

One was a pursuit across the giant carved likenesses of American Presidents Washington, Jefferson, Lincoln and Theodore Roosevelt on Mount Rushmore in South Dakota. Another was a scene at the United Nations, where a delegate is quietly murdered in the midst of a discussion in the General Assembly, leaving a doodle on his notepad as the only clue.

Those two ideas came together in a cross-country-chase thriller starting at the UN and ending on Mount Rushmore. Since the action moved inland from New York, Hitchcock and Lehman titled the project "In a Northwesterly Direction."

When Hitchcock had enough of an outline in his mind, he met with the MGM production brass and told them that the scripting of

The Wreck of the Mary Deare would take longer than expected and that he wanted to make another film for them in the interim. With all his skill and charm, Hitchcock told the story to a point where he knew he'd grabbed their interest and then stopped abruptly, claiming to have an urgent appointment elsewhere. As he left, his listeners were panting for more and assured him that he had a deal.

As the writing continued, Hitchcock selected the title "The Man on Lincoln's Nose," in tribute to the Mount Rushmore sequence. One day when lyricist Sammy Cahn dropped by the office to demonstrate the title song that MGM had commissioned for the film, Hitchcock went bananas and decided it wouldn't do at all.

Kenneth MacKenna, head of MGM's story department, suggested *North by Northwest,* and while no one liked that much either, it stuck. Hitchcock later denied that the movie had anything to do with a line in Shakespeare's *Hamlet:* "I am but mad north-north-west; when the wind is southerly I know a hawk from a handsaw."

Hitchcock had made his last two pictures with James Stewart (*The Man Who Knew Too Much* and *Vertigo*) and intended to use him again in *North by Northwest.* But as the script developed, Hitchcock saw it more as a vehicle for Cary Grant than James Stewart. Hitchcock believed that Stewart would be too earnest and dramatic for what was shaping up as a spoof on all the spy thrillers ever filmed.

"I made *North by Northwest* with tongue in cheek," Hitchcock recalled. "To me, it was one big joke. When Cary Grant was on Mount Rushmore, I would have liked to put him inside Lincoln's nostril and let him have a sneezing fit."

In August 1958, Grant went to New York to begin the location scenes for *North by Northwest.* Based as usual at the Plaza Hotel, he soon discovered that recently widowed Elizabeth Taylor Hilton Wilding Todd was also staying there. Having waited years for just such an opportunity, Grant phoned Taylor for a date, but she gently turned him down with a girlish giggle.

Grant couldn't have known the scene at the other end of the line. Taylor was in bed with her new lover, Eddie Fisher, to whom she signaled to listen in on the extension phone while she talked to Grant. Fisher said later that "my male ego soared" when he heard Elizabeth Taylor rejecting Cary Grant so that she could be with him. One can only guess how Grant felt about being turned down, with or without the knowledge that Taylor had company.

The filming of *North by Northwest* became a complicated mixture of locations and studio work, sometimes within the same scene. The United Nations wouldn't permit a fictional movie to be photographed there, but Hitchcock cheated by shooting a few exteriors with concealed cameras. All the rest of the UN scenes, as well as the close-ups on Mount Rushmore, were done with mock-ups at MGM's Hollywood studio.

By this time, Grant and Hitchcock had been working together for so many years that they respected and trusted each other's judgment. One morning they were doing the first shot of the day in the lobby of the Plaza Hotel. Reporting to work from his suite there, Grant stepped off the elevator and, without saying a word to anyone, proceeded to do a run-through of the scene, which required him to walk through the crowd and take a phone call. Afterward, he strolled over to the camera station and looked through the viewfinder to make sure that he had stayed within the guidelines.

A puzzled onlooker remarked to Hitchcock, "You haven't even said good morning to Cary. How does he know what to do?"

Hitchcock shrugged: "Oh, he's been walking across this lobby for years. What can I tell him that he doesn't already know?"

Not everything went smoothly. When they got to the scene where a crop-dusting plane appears out of nowhere over a deserted cornfield and tries to kill him, Grant angrily told Hitchcock, "We've already done a third of the picture and I still can't make head or tail of it. I don't understand what's going on and I doubt if anyone else will."

But that was exactly how Hitchcock wanted Grant to feel. Most of the fun of *North by Northwest* came from things happening to the hero with such bewildering speed that he doesn't know what it's all about. If Grant had it explained to him in advance, the spontaneity of his performance would have been ruined.

Whether or not he realized it at the time, Grant reached the zenith of his career with *North by Northwest.* Now fifty-four, he had rarely looked more handsome. His superb physical condition allowed him to get away with playing the son of Jessie Royce Landis, who was actually ten months younger than he was!

And *North by Northwest* itself had everything that one could ever expect of a Cary Grant movie—polished and witty dialogue, a stunningly complementary cast that included Eva Marie Saint and

James Mason and more laughs and excitement than any three films Grant had made in the previous fifteen years.

Watching Cary Grant in full command of his talent in *North by Northwest*, one would never suspect the crisis in his personal life at the time of filming. In October 1958, he and Betsy Drake announced a separation after nearly nine years of marriage.

"After careful consideration and long discussion," they said in a joint statement, "we have decided to live apart. We have had and will always have a deep love and respect for each other, but, alas, our marriage has not brought us the happiness we fully expected and mutually desired. So since we have no children needful of our affection, it is consequently best that we separate for a while.

"We have purposely issued this public statement in order to forestall the usual misinformed gossip and conjecture. There are no plans for divorce, and we ask only that the press respect our statements as complete and our friends to be patient with and understanding of our decision."

Cary Grant said later that "I've never clearly resolved why Betsy and I parted. We lived together, not as easily and contentedly as some perhaps; yet it seemed to me, as far as one marriage can be compared with any other, compatibly happier than most.

"Betsy was good for me. Without imposition or demand, she patiently led me toward an appreciation for better books, better literature. Her cautious but steadily penetrative seeking in the labyrinths of the subconscious gradually provoked my interest. Just as she no doubt intended. The seeking is, of course, endless, but, I thankfully acknowledge, of constantly growing benefit."

Betsy Drake believed that the LSD therapy helped her to make "the painful decision" to leave her husband. "Before I'd reached this peace of mind," Drake said, "I think if anything had happened to Cary, I might have killed myself. I had a terrible premonition that something was going to happen when I boarded the *Andrea Doria*, but I thought it was going to be something that happened to Cary. When that first lurch of the ship came, I thought, 'Thank God, it's happened to me.' "

Discussing the marriage, Drake said, "It was lived on Cary's terms, really. It was terribly frustrating to be married to him because he's a very self-sufficient man. He has a secretary and a valet. When I learned to cook, I felt wonderful, for at least I was useful. Cary wanted to be free, yet he wanted me always on tap. He'd go ahead on movie locations. I'd be dying to go, but I'd wait weeks for that call that said 'Come at once.' "

Betsy Drake claimed that as she got better from the LSD treatments, "I got more impatient with Cary. I used to be such a nice girl, everyone thought, so well-bred, so retiring. No more. Now I blow up. One turning point was the night I dressed up for a party, and then Cary, as usual, got on the phone. I waited an hour. Finally, I walked in and swore at him. He was terribly shocked. 'Why, Betsy!' he said. 'I've never heard you use language like that!' "

According to Drake, "I left Cary, but psychically, he'd left me long ago. I was still in love with him, and I'm not ashamed to say so. But he's going through a tremendous change. Who knows? He may come back to me, or not marry again at all, or marry somebody quite different from me. He's dizzy! Enormously stimulating! Younger than many younger men I know."

The Grants' so-called "separation" became one of the strangest in Hollywood history. It lasted four years, but the couple were frequently together, which puzzled their friends even more than their experiments with psychiatry and hypnotism.

"Cary arrived at my house one Christmas and I asked him to spend the day with us. My kids were wild about him," Clifford Odets recalled. "But Cary declined. 'I'm going up to Betsy's house to spend a couple of days with her,' he said. And he had a bag packed for the visit. Her house wasn't more than twenty minutes' drive from his, but he wanted to move in."

One evening, Grant and Drake turned up at a movie premiere, he by himself and she with a much younger man. "Look, that's my wife. Isn't she beautiful?" Grant said to a reporter as he pointed to Drake, who was farther down the lobby. Asked if he wasn't bothered by the sight of his wife with another man, Grant replied, "She would be incapable of being unfaithful. None of my wives has been unfaithful, and neither have I. That has never been the problem."

Friends believed that Grant would never allow Drake to get a divorce because of California's community property laws. "Cary wasn't about to part with any of his hard-earned dough if he could help it," Frederick Brisson said. "But I'm sure he supported Betsy all the time they lived apart. There was a period of about five years when she didn't make a single movie, so she had to be getting money from somewhere."

The threat of a property settlement was undoubtedly on Grant's mind when he negotiated the most lucrative deal of his career with his next film, *Operation Petticoat*, which began shooting in January 1959.

Although the film was financed by Universal Pictures, the actor's Granart Company (distinct from his Grandon partnership with Stanley Donen) produced it and owned the negative, which reverted to Grant at the end of seven years to do with as he wanted. More important, Grant would get 75 percent of the net profits once the film returned its production costs.

When it was released later that year, *Operation Petticoat* became the biggest moneymaker in Universal's history. Grant himself earned two million dollars *prior* to foreign distribution and TV sales.

A World War II comedy about a submarine commander's attempts to make his severely damaged vessel seaworthy again, *Operation Petticoat* gave Grant another opportunity to advance the career of a promising director, in this case Blake Edwards, whose past experience had been in television and low-budget movies.

Grant also found a role in the film for Dina Merrill, heiress to the Post cereal fortune and his former cousin-in-law through her kinship to Barbara Hutton. Grant was one of the first to encourgage the former Nedenia Hutton in her determination to become an actress. In *Operation Petticoat,* she played a nurse named Barbara, which her cousin found terribly amusing when she saw the film.

Grant never denied that he owed part of the success of *Operation Petticoat* to the popularity of co-star Tony Curtis, who made the film directly after he performed in Billy Wilder's hit comedy *Some Like It Hot.* Curtis's deliberate borrowing of Cary Grant's speech and mannerisms throughout the Wilder film delighted audiences. Grant loved to tell people: "Tony Curtis can 'do' Cary Grant better than I can."

When they started working together, Curtis told Grant how he learned to mimic him so well. While Curtis had served in the Navy, Grant's *Gunga Din* was one of the few movies in his ship's library. Curtis saw it so many times that he knew Grant's role by heart at the end of the six-month voyage.

During production of *Operation Petticoat,* Grant decided to go public about his experiences with LSD. Up until then, even his closest friends didn't know about them, although they noticed a dramatic change in his behavior and attitudes.

While Grant was working on location in Key West, Florida, Universal's publicity department flew in some top reporters and columnists to interview him. Among the first to arrive were Joe Hyams, Hollywood correspondent for the New York *Herald Tribune*, and Lionel Crane, who represented the *Daily Mirror* in London.

Dressed in his navy uniform for the film, Grant posed for a picture with Joe Hyams on the set and then took him to his dressing room for the interview. When the usually reticent Grant started talking excitedly about his experiments with LSD, Hyams asked for and received permission to tape the conversation.

"I have been born again," Grant said. "I have just been through a psychiatric experience that has completely changed me. It was horrendous. I had to face things about myself which I never admitted, which I didn't know were there. Now I know that I hurt every woman I loved. I was an utter fake, a self-opinionated boor, a know-all who knew very little.

"Once you realize that you have all things inside you, love and hate alike, and you learn to accept them, then you can use your love to exhaust your hate," Grant continued. "That power is inside you, but it can be assimilated into your power to love. You can relax. Then you can do more than you ever dreamed you could do. I found I was hiding behind all kinds of defenses, hypocrisies and vanities. I had to get rid of them layer by layer. That moment when your conscious meets your subconscious is a helluva wrench. You feel the whole top of your head is lifting off."

With his eyes flashing brightly, Grant described his reactions immediately after the therapy. "First, I thought, 'Oh, those wasted years!' Second, I said, 'Oh, my God, humanity please come in!' For the first time in my life I was ready to meet people realistically. Each of us is dying for affection and we don't know how to go about getting it. Everything we do is affected by this longing. That's why I became an actor. I was longing for affection.

"I wanted people to like me, but I went about it the wrong way," Grant said. "Almost all of us do. Every man is conceited, but I know now in my earlier days I really despised myself. It's when you admit this that you're beginning to change. Introspection is the beginning of courage. I was always professing a knowledge I didn't have. If I didn't know about a subject, I would disdain it. I was very aggressive, but without the courage to be physically aggressive. I was a bad-tempered man, but I hid it."

Grant believed that everything had changed now. "My attitude towards women is completely different. I don't intend to foul-up any more lives. I could be a good husband now. I'm aware of my faults and I'm ready to accept responsibilities and exchange tolerances," he said.

Joe Hyams saw such a terrific story in Grant's disclosures that he wanted to know how soon he could run with it. "Not yet," Grant said, "but the time's coming and I'll let you know when I'm ready."

Grant went on to discuss other matters, including his habit of wearing women's nylon panties. He claimed they were easier to pack than men's underwear and that he could also wash them out himself, which saved on laundry bills when he traveled.

Afterward, Hyams bumped into Lionel Crane, who was en route to interview Grant himself and asked how the meeting went. Eager to protect a potential scoop, Hyams said he got "the usual stuff" and left it at that. But he suggested that Crane try to talk Grant into making a guest appearance at a journalism course that the two newsmen conducted at the University of California at Los Angeles. Crane did and Grant accepted.

A few weeks later, Cary Grant turned up at a UCLA classroom with his supper in a brown paper bag and begged permission to munch on his sandwiches and banana while the twenty-five journalism students interrogated him. When they ran out of questions, Grant volunteered information about his experiences with LSD. Joe Hyams was astonished to find Grant speaking so openly about matters that were supposed to be confidential.

When Hyams mentioned it to Lionel Crane, the latter expressed surprise: "Didn't you know? That's all old stuff. Cary told me all that in Key West, just after his interview with you, and I printed it." Crane showed Hyams his article, which contained nearly everything Grant told Hyams. The main difference was that Grant gave Crane permission to publish it, but only in England, which explained why Hyams hadn't seen it.

A few nights later, Hyams ran into Grant at an opening at the Huntington Hartford Theatre and asked permission to run his interview now that Crane had already done so in England. Grant agreed, provided that Hyams stuck to his statements in Crane's piece, which he approved prior to publication.

Realizing that he still would be first in the United States to report on Grant's use of LSD, Hyams matched up his quotes with those in Crane's story and wrote a three-part series. The New York *Herald Tribune* became very enthusiastic about it and launched an advance promotional blitz to boost circulation.

The day that the *Herald Tribune* announced plans to run the series, Grant called Hyams at home, demanding that publication be canceled. When the frantic Hyams told him it was too late, that the first installment had already gone to press, Grant said, "I can't help that. You better find a way to stop them or you'll be discredited. I'll tell the press that I haven't seen you at all."

"That's ridiculous, and you know it," Hyams said.

"It's your word against mine, and you know who they'll believe," Grant replied before hanging up.

Before Hyams could decide on his next move, the phone rang again. This time it was Grant's lawyer, Stanley Fox, repeating his client's order that the series be killed. Making matters worse, Fox said, "Cary tells me he hasn't seen you for two years, which means that you've made the whole series up or pirated it from another source."

When the series ran as scheduled, there were immediate reverberations. The Los Angeles *Times* bought it from the Herald Tribune syndicate but added a boxed disclaimer that "Cary Grant says that he has not seen Hyams for two years."

Louella Parsons reported that Grant called her twice to say that he hadn't met with Hyams and that all the quotes from him were unauthorized. "When I was a girl, things were different in the newspaper business," Parsons commented.

Joe Hyams soon found himself *persona non grata* around Hollywood. Publicists canceled interviews with their clients and even his friends started to doubt his veracity. His young son returned from school one day in tears, after being taunted by his classmates for having a liar for a father.

As *Time* and *Newsweek* jumped on the bandwagon, Hyams was dismayed to discover that everyone took Cary Grant's side and not his. "For the first time, I realized the tenuousness of my claim on the world in which I operated and how quickly the press, my friends included, turned on anyone in trouble," Hyams remembered.

To restore his credibility as a journalist, Hyams knew that

either he had to get Cary Grant to retract his statements or sue him. While consulting lawyers, Hyams discovered what seemed to be the reason why Grant had become so difficult. The *Herald Tribune* articles aborted a lucrative deal that Grant had been negotiating with *Look* Magazine to write about his LSD experiences.

In May 1959, Cary Grant had the dubious distinction of becoming the first movie star ever to be sued for slander by a columnist. In the past, the reverse situation had always applied. Joe Hyams's demand for five hundred thousand dollars in damages immediately made the Hollywood community wonder if he might be telling the truth after all.

Rather than be dragged into the case, Louella Parsons printed a retraction. A publicist at Universal suddenly came forward and provided Hyams with a copy of the photograph taken of him with Cary Grant in Key West. That, plus Hyams's tape of the conversation, gave him an open-and-shut case.

During the pretrial depositions, Grant's attorney asked Hyams hundreds of questions about the interview. During one of his answers, Hyams let it drop that he decided not to mention in his articles that Grant wore women's panties. Asked to explain that decision, Hyams said, "Truthfully, I was afraid it might be taken by some readers that Cary Grant was not completely masculine."

When it came time for Grant to be interrogated, Hyams's attorney didn't believe that the actor would appear: "He won't want to go through with it. They made it tough on you to discourage you, but now that it's their turn, they'll chicken out."

The guess proved correct. The day before Grant's deposition, his attorney proposed an out-of-court settlement. In exchange for Hyams's dropping the lawsuit, Grant agreed to collaborate with him in writing his life story. Hyams could keep all the income derived from its publication, which he hoped would be serialized in a magazine.

Although Hyams realized that Grant had outfoxed him— whatever money he received from the series would not be coming out of Grant's pocket—he accepted the settlement as a moral victory that cleared his journalistic reputation.

But Hyams had little hope that the articles would ever be written. He thought that Grant would try to find a way out, either by dodging interviews or by cooperating in a perfunctory fashion. Hyams turned out to be wrong, but it took him four years to find out.

16

Boom, Like a Cannon!

The "new," LSD-created Cary Grant received mixed reviews from his friends and associates. "What is Cary fooling around with that stuff for?" asked Mae West. "Why doesn't he just come up and see me sometime? I'll straighten him out."

Alfred Hitchcock said, "I sometimes think Cary is attracted to LSD because those letters in England stand for pounds, shillings and pence."

Sheilah Graham, envious of the wonders Grant described, claimed that he offered to arrange an LSD treatment for her with his doctor but that she chickened out.

Clifford Odets thought that "the changes in Cary as a result of the treatment have been extraordinary. He's bloomed. He's lost his reticence and shyness. The barricade has been swept away, it seems, and he's now free and spontaneous. He's got a freshness, an alertness, an awareness of things he had never known before. Why he's almost like a kid."

David Niven didn't seem in the least surprised by Grant's interest in LSD. "Cary's a spooky Celt really, not an Englishman at all," Niven said. "There must be some fey Welsh blood there someplace. He gets great crushes on people like the late Countess di Frasso, or ideas like hypnotism, then moves on. Cary has great depressions and then great heights when he seems about to take off for outer space."

Niven recalled a weekend that he and his wife spent at Grant's home in Palm Springs. "Cary would vanish, and we'd find him hanging from parallel bars, or doing push-ups, or in a trance on the floor mesmerizing his big toe," Niven said. "He does nothing by halves. He was an excellent swimmer, for example, but then he took lessons to become a *perfect* swimmer. He keeps great chunks of himself in reserve."

Causing gossip and astonishment was Cary Grant's open courtship of voluptuous, well-endowed young women who hardly resembled his post-debutantish companions of the past. At the 1959 Cannes Film Festival, Grant became enamored of another member of the Hollywood delegation, Kim Novak. The *paparazzi* had a field day as Grant and Novak kept turning up in public places behaving like a pair of lovebirds.

Nearer to home, Grant frequently went on the town with statuesque Sheika Mosier, an exotic dancer who worked in Las Vegas under the name Yellow Bird. Grant told Earl Wilson: "I like girls who are *all* girls."

Grant raised even more eyebrows with his relationship with twenty-three-year-old Luba Otasevic, a star basketball player in her native Yugoslavia before she escaped from the Iron Curtain country. Although the press described her as "a girl almost embarrassed by her physical opulence," Otasevic's main appeal for Cary Grant seemed to be her resemblance to Sophia Loren, for whom she'd once worked as a stand-in.

While friends thought that Otasevic fulfilled his frustrated feelings for Loren, Grant himself compared her to Betsy Drake. "She's just like Betsy used to be, the proud young actress never taking proper care of herself, proudly rejecting help. I used to be that way, too," Grant said.

Rosalind Russell said that "Cary is never happier than when he's fussing over somebody, even when he's in the most desperate trouble. But he can't be forced. He must help in his own way, in his own good time."

Beldon Katleman, a friend and Las Vegas hotel owner, believed that Grant was attracted to Otasevic and Mosier because "they did not go out with him simply because he was Cary Grant, the movie star. They liked Cary for himself. To look at them, you might think they were the typical 'beautiful but dumb broads,' but they were both simple girls with simple tastes."

Grant often complained that the press overexaggerated his

dating and that he didn't even know half the women that the gossip columnists linked him with. As he mentioned that to his chauffeur one day, the latter replied, "Never mind, Mr. Grant. Just think. It would be much worse if they printed that you were out with a different young *boy* every night."

In the spring of 1960, when Grant went to England to make *The Grass Is Greener,* he caused more surprise by bringing along Betsy Drake. When reporters saw them arriving together at Heathrow, they wanted to know if the Grants intended to make an announcement of their apparent reconciliation.

"Why should we?" Betsy Drake snapped. "We might not be together tomorrow. Cary might decide to go somewhere I don't want to go, or I might want to go somewhere he doesn't want to go. But as long as we enjoy doing things together, we'll be together, because we're in love."

Drake had no connection with *The Grass Is Greener,* the second of her husband's Grandon partnerships with Stanley Donen. Although Grant rejoiced in the huge profits of *Operation Petticoat,* the World War II service comedy wasn't really his cup of tea. He still dreamed of getting back to the beautiful clothes and gorgeous settings of drawing-room farce. While Universal thought that such sophisticated fare lacked mass appeal, the studio had no choice but to indulge its top box-office attraction when he purchased a new British play by Hugh and Margaret Williams, who had a long string of hits in the Noël Coward-Freddy Lonsdale tradition.

Aware that it was a chancy project to begin with, Grant took a more active part than usual in the production side of *The Grass Is Greener* to make it more commercial. He hand-picked Deborah Kerr, Jean Simmons and Robert Mitchum for his co-stars; persuaded Noël Coward to arrange a group of his best songs into a background score; and had the play "opened up" to show some of England's lush countryside and architectural treasures.

Ironically, Osterley Hall, which stood in as the stately home of Grant and Kerr in the film, had been the residence of his ex-wife Virginia Cherrill, while she was married to the Earl of Jersey. (Cherrill had since divorced him and returned to California with her third husband, Florian Martini, an aeronautical engineer and ex-World War II fighter pilot.)

Writer Richard Gehman, who watched some of the filming of *The Grass Is Greener,* said that Grant behaved "more like a man in his mid-twenties than one in his mid-fifties. He was all over the place as he worked, bounding from the camera to the set and back to a lectern that stood at one side holding his script. He'd stand at the lectern, his head bent and supported by his hand, concentrating for a moment or two; then he'd go into action again."

In the course of half an hour, Gehman saw Grant consult with director Stanley Donen, show Jean Simmons the proper way to exit a scene, order a piece of scenery replaced, arrange an interview schedule with the unit publicist, examine some new costumes brought in by the wardrobe mistress and make seventeen tele- phone calls.

But that was Cary Grant the producer. Deborah Kerr, who by that time had made three films with him, later described the acting side. "I have never known a man to apply himself so seriously and so ruthlessly to the job at hand," Kerr said. "It was only because he could take his job so seriously that he was such a fine comedy actor. You would have to get up very early in the morning to steal a scene from him. I never did. But he played fair. Comedy is a cutthroat game and many Hollywood actors play it rough, expecting you to take care of yourself. But Cary never cheated.

"I learned so much from him," Kerr remembered. "He was an absolute genius at comedy timing. He believed in being always what it was his audience expected him to be, and that was why he achieved such enormous success."

Grant's frenetic activity on both sides of the camera did not leave him limp with exhaustion, as might have been expected in a man of fifty-six years. "It's true that Cary was tense after he fin- ished each scene," Richard Gehman said, "but to work off the tension he simply unknotted his tie, grabbed a cup of tea and went out for a brief walk. He kept that pace all day long, but at quitting time he didn't seem tired. He rested on the way back to London in his chauffeur-driven eighteen-thousand-dollar Rolls-Royce, in a reclining seat he had put in himself. By the time he got home, he was refreshed and ready for a pleasant evening with his wife."

The Rolls-Royce, plus a nearly identical twin that he owned back in Beverly Hills, contradicted the image of Cary Grant as a tightwad. "I believe in spending," Grant told Gehman. "If you have it, why hang onto it? I believe in spreading it around—for your friends, for yourself."

While Grant made *The Grass Is Greener*, he often spent weekends in Bristol visiting his eighty-two-year-old mother. Like her son, she seemed in remarkable condition for her age, still spry enough to run and jump onto the back of a bus if it failed to stop for her. Prior to his LSD experience, Grant had been reticent about his relationship with his mother, but he loved to talk about her now.

"She shops tenaciously for small antiques," Grant said, "and local dealers have learned either to put up the price in advance so that they can pull it down later, or if they're lucky enough to see her coming, pull down the shutters and close the doors, to protect themselves from the impact of her charms and the honesty of her age. She does her own marketing and every bit of her own housework, and whenever it is suggested that she get someone to help her, she avers she can do it better herself, that she doesn't want anyone around telling her what to do, and that the very fact of the occupation keeps her going. All of which is undoubtedly true."

Because of her psychiatric history, Grant did not want reporters pestering Elsie Leach, so he had an understanding with the Bristol press that if they left her alone, he would always cooperate by giving interviews or posing for pictures whenever he visited. That didn't prevent an enterprising American journalist from trying to interview her by phone when Universal paid for his trip to London to cover the filming of *The Grass Is Greener*.

Although trained by Grant not to accept such calls, Elsie Leach couldn't resist giving an answer when the reporter asked her if she was proud of her son's success. "Yes," she said, "but then he should be proud of me, as I brought him into the world." When Grant found out that his mother had been contacted, he was furious and ordered the reporter sent home before he could finish his assignment.

After Grant completed *The Grass Is Greener*, he went on a short holiday to Europe with Betsy Drake and then returned to Hollywood to work with Stanley Donen on the cutting and editing of the film. By the time it was released during the Christmas–New Year's season of 1960–61, he had put a year into its production and marketing, but the results were extremely disappointing.

The Grass Is Greener may be the only Cary Grant film that was so boring that a critic spent most of his review commenting on the star's shoes. "He turns up newly shod in almost every scene, and his wing tips, Scotch brogues, moccasins, pumps and velvet slippers all display the soft glow, the trim fit over the instep, and the tasteful slimness to be found only on the extremities of a gentleman who frequents the best bespoke booteries," said Roger Angell in *The New Yorker*.

Faced by unenthusiastic reviews and even worse business, Grant had to admit that the age of the polite drawing-room comedy had ended. He never attempted to make another one.

Instead, Grant turned to a genre unique unto itself—the Doris Day–Rock Hudson bedroom romp. Two of them, *Pillow Talk* and *Lover Come Back,* had been enormous successes for Universal, but Doris Day's husband and business manager Marty Melcher, became obsessively irritated at suggestions that the Day-Hudson *team* drew the crowds. To prove that his wife didn't need a steady teammate, he dropped Rock Hudson from plans for Day's next movie and started negotiations with Cary Grant.

Confronted with the heavy losses of *The Grass Is Greener,* Grant was more than willing to take on what seemed a sure thing, but he drove a hard bargain. *That Touch of Mink* became a three-way production between Grant's Granley Company, Day-Melcher's Arwin Productions and writer-producer Stanley Shapiro's Nob Hill Productions. The contract set so many precedents for shared ownership of a movie that it is still used as a model today.

As more than one critic pointed out later, the main difference between *That Touch of Mink* and the two Doris Day–Rock Hudson films was that Cary Grant played Cary Grant's part. In other words, the Day-Hudson films were copied from some of the prewar comedies Grant had made with the likes of Katharine Hepburn and Irene Dunne, but spiced up with suggestive dialogue and situations that were now permitted under a more liberal censorship code.

Grant played a wealthy bachelor, a sort of Red Baron of the boudoir, with Doris Day as her usual innocent small-town-girl-in-the-big-city. It was the traditional cat-and-mouse game, but the players, at ages fifty-seven and thirty-seven, were getting a bit long in the tooth for their seducer-versus-virgin roles.

Although it broke box-office records, *That Touch of Mink* failed in trying to make a delightful team of Cary Grant and Doris Day. While the twenty-year age difference didn't help, there was none of the chemistry that made Day and Rock Hudson look as if they were really having fun and not playacting.

Doris Day later explained why. "Of all the people I performed with, I got to know Cary Grant least of all. He is a completely private person, totally reserved, and there is no way into him," Day said. "Our relationship was amicable but devoid of give-and-take. For somebody who is as open and right out there as I am, it was hard at first to adjust to Cary's inwardness. Not that he wasn't friendly and polite—he certainly was. But distant. Very distant."

But Day praised Grant for his professionalism, naming him as the most exacting actor she ever worked with. "He concerned himself with every little detail: clothes, sets, production values, the works," Day said. "He helped choose my costumes and watched over the hairdresser when my hair was being done because he wanted me to look very special. He made me *feel* very special, too."

Day remembered a scene that took place in the library of a Manhattan townhouse. On the morning of filming, Grant arrived with cartons of things from his own library at home and proceeded to decorate the set with them.

"Not only did it make the set more attractive, but when Cary played the scene his own belongings made him feel right at home. It gave his performance that peculiarly natural, suave quality that is a hallmark of his pictures," Day said.

Like Loretta Young and other profile-conscious actresses, Doris Day had "a little conflict" with Grant over the lighting and camera angles. "In setting up for our first close-up, it developed that we both preferred to be photographed from the right profile," Day said. "I prefer the right side of my face because it is more open and less cheeky than the left. Almost all movie performers have such preferences. Of course, both actors in a scene cannot be photographed from the same profile, but our awkward impasse was quickly dispelled by Cary's graciously foregoing his preference."

Although far from being one of Cary Grant's best efforts, *That Touch of Mink* solidified his place in movie history as the star with the most films to play New York's Radio City Music Hall, the six-thousand-seat theatre that the industry considered the world's number one showcase.

At its opening in July 1962, *That Touch of Mink* became Grant's twenty-fifth film to be shown there. The management presented him with a sterling silver trophy as the Music Hall's "all-time box-office champion." Starting with *Sylvia Scarlett* in 1936, those twenty-five movies ran a total of ninety-nine weeks. Grant's nearest rivals were Ginger Rogers, with twenty-three films and fifty-five weeks, and Greer Garson, with eleven films and seventy-nine weeks. The next most popular male star was Fred Astaire, with sixteen films and sixty weeks.

By the time it finished its Music Hall run, *That Touch of Mink* had also became the theatre's all-time moneymaker, grossing $1.85 million in ten weeks. The record stood for five years until *Barefoot in the Park* brought in $2.1 million, but in twelve weeks and at higher admission prices.

While a large part of America flocked to see Cary Grant make love to Doris Day, his real-life partnership with Betsy Drake finally came to an end. In August 1962, Drake petitioned the California Supreme Court for a divorce, charging mental cruelty.

Drake said that her husband "preferred watching television to talking to me. He appeared to be bored with me. I became lonely, unhappy, miserable and went into psychoanalysis. He told me he didn't want to be married. He showed no interest in any of my friends."

Grant, as usual, did not appear in court. After the hearing, Drake told reporters, "I was always in love with Cary—and still am."

Details of the financial settlement were kept secret, but columnist Dorothy Kilgallen quoted an unimpeachable source that Drake would receive a million dollars plus a share of Grant's future earnings from some of the films he made while they were married.

Friends of the couple wondered if the miserly Grant would have been so generous. But there is evidence of at least one Cary Grant movie in which Drake had an interest. In 1968, her attorney petitioned Paramount for an accounting of Grant's income from *To Catch a Thief* since 1962 (the year of the divorce), claiming that Grant assigned half of those moneys to Drake.

Betsy Drake never married again. She eventually gave up acting and began a new career as a psychodrama therapist and teacher, working at various hospitals and universities in Los Angeles. In 1971, she also wrote a well-reviewed juvenile book, *Children, You Are Very Little.*

The divorce was Cary Grant's idea, even though he allowed Drake the traditional face-saving courtesy of being the one to file for it. Grant had found a new love interest in a twenty-five-year-old

Grant and leading lady Katharine Hepburn made a delightfully zany duo in *Bringing Up Baby*, 1938. (Culver Pictures, Inc.)

Cary Grant, Victor McLaglen, and Douglas Fairbanks, Jr., in *Gunga Din*, 1939. (The Museum of Modern Art/Film Stills Archives)

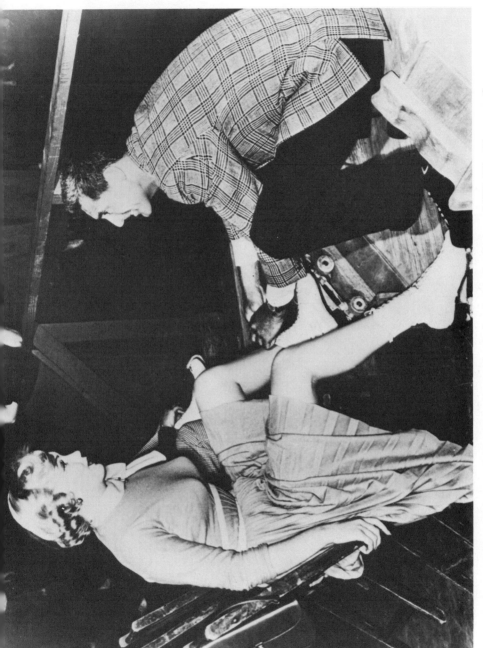

Marilyn Monroe and Cary Grant starred together in *Monkey Business*, 1952. (The Museum of Modern Art/Film Stills Archives)

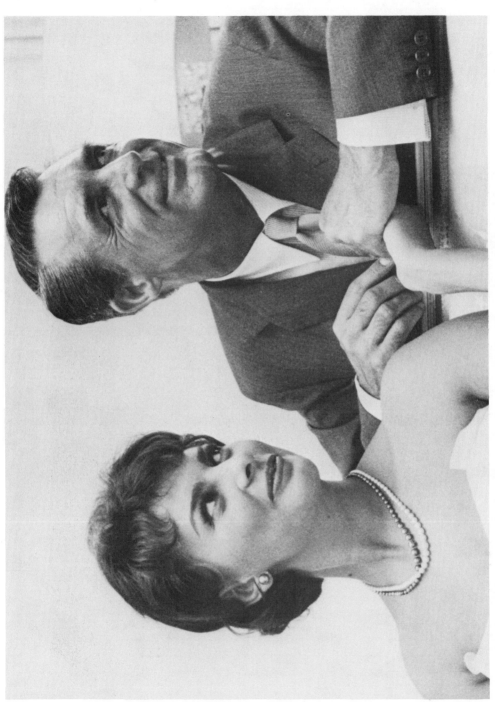

Sophia Loren's dazzling beauty left Grant starstruck during the filming of *The Pride and the Passion*, 1957, and *Houseboat*, 1958. (UPI/Bettmann Newsphotos)

Cary Grant with one of his favorite leading ladies, Ingrid Bergman, in *Indiscreet*, 1958. (Culver Pictures, Inc.)

Grant on the run in Hitchcock's thriller *North by Northwest*, 1959. (Culver Pictures, Inc.)

In December 1981, Cary Grant was honored as a Kennedy Center award winner. Shown (left to right) are Helen Hayes, Count Basie, Cary Grant and President and Mrs. Reagan. In the second row on the left is Grant's daughter, Jennifer. (UPI/Bettmann Newsphotos)

Frank Sinatra presents Cary Grant with a special achievement award at the Forty-second Annual Academy Award presentation, April 1970. (UPI/Bettmann Newsphotos)

Former actress Grace Kelly, who had co-starred with Grant in 1955 in *To Catch a Thief,* talks here with him after the fund-raising Motion Picture, Television Relief Gala, June 1971. (UPI/Bettmann Newsphotos)

actress named Dyan Cannon. While he had no immediate plans to make her the fourth Mrs. Grant, he wanted to be legally free in case he changed his mind.

Born in Tacoma, Washington, the half-Jewish, half-Baptist Samille Diane Friessen owed her professional name to Jerry Wald. While testing the unknown actress for a role in one of his pictures, he took one look at her remarkable physical assets and said, "You need a name that's explosive—Boom! . . . Bang! . . . Cannon!"

Although Grant worked for Wald at the time, he apparently didn't become aware of Cannon's existence until 1961, when he saw her on the short-lived TV series "Malibu Run." He became so excited that he tracked down her agent, Adaline Fiddler, and summoned her to his office. Claiming that he wanted to hire her client for a film, he spent three hours asking about Cannon's acting experience, family upbringing, her philosophy of life, etc.

Afterward, Fiddler telephoned Dyan Cannon in Rome, where she was vacationing with a girlfriend. "Cary Grant wants to see you about a picture. Can you come back?"

"Is he paying the way?" Cannon asked. When Fiddler said she didn't think so, that it was just an audition, Cannon answered, "Then I'll see him when I get back."

"Dyan," the agent said, "you're not only going to do this picture with Cary Grant, you're going to fall in love with him, and you're going to marry him."

"You are out of your mind!" Cannon declared, and continued with her vacation.

When Cannon returned to Hollywood, she went to meet Grant at his office at Universal City. "I wasn't hypnotized, but I was enchanted by Cary," she recalled. "I was charmed in the true sense of the word. We talked for a couple of hours. It was a marvelous conversation. I was completely smitten with him, and with his ideas. We talked about the movie he wanted me for, about our theories and philosophies. We talked about me and my family. About the essence of perfume oils. About everything."

Grant and Cannon began keeping company in 1962. "It was a private affair," she said. "Neither of us ever talked to other people about our relationship. Neither of us ever gave interviews. It wasn't an agreement between us to keep quiet. It was just our nature."

There were times when the couple broke off the affair and

then started anew, irresistibly drawn back together. The longest separation started in October 1962, when Grant had to go to Europe to make *Charade* and Cannon signed to do a play that would mark her Broadway debut.

Before leaving for Paris, Grant spent a few weeks in New York with Cannon while she rehearsed *The Fun Couple,* in which she appeared with Jane Fonda and Bradford Dillman. Grant also accompanied Cannon to Philadelphia for the opening of the play's tryout run. After attending the first performance, he predicted the play wouldn't last a week and tried to persuade Cannon to go to Europe with him instead.

Deeply hurt, Cannon sent Grant packing, only to find his prognosis correct. *The Fun Couple* ran for only three performances when it reached New York. Not eager to make up with Grant, Cannot found another job in the national touring company of Frank Loesser's hit musical *How to Succeed in Business Without Really Trying.*

Before leaving for Europe, Grant finally finished collaborating with Joe Hyams on the autobiographical piece that he owed him in settlement of their dispute. After several months of tape-recorded interviews with Grant, Hyams boiled them down into a series of three articles, which he then submitted to him for approval. Grant held on to them so long that Hyams had to threaten another lawsuit before he got them back.

Hyams sold the series to the *Ladies' Home Journal* for a whopping $125,000, all of which went to him as compensation for dropping his slander suit against Grant. The latter had no idea the articles were worth so much and blew his stack when he found out.

A few days later, Hyams received a phone call from Grant's lawyer, Stanley Fox, suggesting that Grant should receive something for the time he devoted to interviews and to editing and rewriting portions of the manuscript.

When Hyams asked Fox what Grant would consider fair payment, the lawyer answered, "Enough, say, for a new Rolls-Royce."

Hyams gasped, knowing that a new Rolls then cost about $22,000. "I'll have to think about it," he said. Then he called his own attorney and told him about the conversation.

"You're crazy to give Cary a dime," his lawyer said. "According to the contract, you're entitled to all the income from the article."

But when Hyams mulled it over, he felt that Grant had a point. "Certainly, after our lawsuit was settled, Cary had been more than fair to me in the amount of cooperation he gave me, even if it took an inordinately long time."

Hyams called Fox back and agreed to give Grant the money for the Rolls-Royce. He still had enough left over to pay off all his outstanding debts and take his family on a European vacation.

Meanwhile, Grant had started making *Charade* with Audrey Hepburn in Paris. The third of his collaborations with Stanley Donen, the Univeral release marked a double milestone in Grant's career: his seventieth movie and the thirtieth anniversary of his entry into films.

During an interview, Grant credited the longevity of his career to "Adaptability. Life is much more informal and casual today than it was when I did my first picture. We punched harder, used broader gestures, and more mannerisms then. To be contemporary, one has to mirror the tempo and bent of the time. You watch. You listen. And you reflect what you see and hear. It's fatal to freeze at any point in a career. Standing still means that the parade passes by. An actor must meet the shifting demands of audiences or else."

Although Grant had long wanted to work with Audrey Hepburn, the twenty-five-year age difference made him leery. Earlier, he had backed out of *Sabrina* and *Love in the Afternoon* for that reason (Humphrey Bogart and Gary Cooper, respectively, replaced him). He also rejected making *My Fair Lady* with Hepburn, although more out of respect to Rex Harrison, who had created the role of Henry Higgins on Broadway. "Not only will I not do it," Grant told Jack Warner, "but if you don't hire Rex, I won't even go to see it."

But Stanley Donen and writer Peter Stone were able to persuade Grant to do *Charade* with Hepburn by facing the age problem squarely and making it a running joke between the two stars throughout the film. Grant occasionally uttered lines like "At my age, who wants to hear the word 'serious'?" whenever Hepburn started getting romantic notions about him.

And Audrey Hepburn's doelike eyes gazed on Grant with such longing that it was plain their ages didn't matter. When she asked Grant, "Do you know what's wrong with you?" she immediately supplied her own answer. "Nothing!"

Charade deliberately evoked memories of an Alfred Hitchcock thriller, with Grant continually changing his identity and at one point dropping clues that suggest he might even be the killer. The love story was underplayed throughout, with only one passionate kiss between Grant and Hepburn in the entire film.

Most of the lovemaking was portrayed humorously. Teasing Grant about his dimple, Hepburn asked him, "How do you shave in there?" Grant's answer—"Very carefully!"—might have been even funnier if he'd been permitted to use Peter Stone's original line, "Like porcupines make love. Very carefully!" But Production Code censors considered it too risqué for 1962 audiences.

Cary Grant turned fifty-nine while making *Charade*, and he was starting to look his age. Critic Pauline Kael commented later: "It was obvious that he was being lighted very carefully and kept in three-quarter shots, and that his face was rounder and a little puffy. And although lampblack may have shielded the neck, one could tell that it was being shielded. But we saw him in Audrey Hepburn's terms: Cary Grant at his most elegant. He didn't need the show-stopping handsomeness of his youth; his style, though it was based on his handsomeness, had transcended it."

Following completion of *Charade*, Grant returned to California in the spring of 1963 and resumed his relationship with Dyan Cannon.

Courtship needed the assistance of a travel agent, since Cannon lived out of a suitcase most of the time, touring with the road company of *How to Succeed in Business*. But Cannon bragged later that Grant managed to visit her in every one of the cities that she worked in during the eighteen months she remained with the show.

Neither of them seemed concerned about the thirty-three-year age difference. "We only discussed it because other people would be constantly bringing it up," Cannon said.

She wondered how Grant kept up the pace that he did: "I'd be worn out and he'd still be going. This is a man who's very young in many ways. Young in spirit. Young in mind. Younger in mind than he's ever been before."

As Grant and Cannon started to become a public item, Grant didn't seem to mind that Cannon spoke freely to the press. In the past, Grant's wives and sweethearts were ultra-reticent about their relationships with him. Cannon proved to be the exact opposite, which indicated that Grant was beginning to loosen up a bit himself, or he never would have tolerated it.

"I think that I'm Cary's sister, his girlfriend, his mother, his everything. And I think he is the same way to me," Cannon told Louella Parsons.

Unlike Betsy Drake, Cannon didn't mind that Grant preferred watching TV to going out. "There's not a thing wrong with that," she said. "There's everything good with that, because for Cary Grant to go out in public can be very tiring. There's so little privacy."

Cannon's remarks suggested that it was fast becoming a Pygmalion-Galatea relationship. When they first met, Grant complained that she wore too much perfume: "Are you trying to keep men away from you?" After that, she went home and diluted all her perfume with water.

Grant also told Cannon how to dress. "I don't think he mentioned my clothes until I'd known him for about eight months," she remembered. "Then, in the middle of a date one evening, he said, 'You know, I saw a little dress down the street that would look very cute on you.' He described it to me, and I realized at once it was something entirely different from what I was wearing. 'You don't dress like you are,' Cary said. 'You dress too old, or too young. Why don't you look for the middle road? Why don't you dress the way you look, the way you are?' "

Cannon became a willing pupil. "Cary has helped me in every area," she said at the time. "This is a man who's lived a great many years, and I listen to him. Much of what he says works for me. Some doesn't, but for the most part I go along. But Cary doesn't preach —that would probably annoy me. He'll go on at great length about things that have happened in his own life. I haven't lived that long, but long enough to know there's a great deal to learn from anyone who has."

In January 1964, Cary Grant turned sixty. Asked if he had any plans to retire, he said, "I'm getting to the stage where I have to be very careful about love scenes with young actresses. The public doesn't like to see an older man making love to a young girl. It offends them. I'm well aware that I can't go on playing romantic parts much longer. After all, I'm quite an old fellow to some young people. But to be honest with you, I don't know what I will do. Maybe I will quit."

Deep down, he knew that he wouldn't. For the second consecutive year, the Theatre Owners of America had voted him the number one male box-office star. The smash business of *Charade* indicated that he could go on holding that position indefinitely. To walk away from his career at the peak of popularity and while making more money than ever in his lifetime would have been impossible for the man reputed to still have the second dollar he ever earned. "Cary used the first one to buy a wallet," went a longstanding Hollywood joke.

Grant decided to compromise by making a film that broke new ground for him and yet retained some elements of his past successes. In a story by S. W. Barnett called "A Place of Dragons," he found an idea that he turned over to Peter Stone, scriptwriter of *Charade,* to develop into his next project for Universal.

The result was *Father Goose,* a comedy depicting the misadventures of a crotchety hermit living on a tiny island in the South Pacific at the outbreak of World War II. Pressed into service as an intelligence agent for the Australian Navy, he finds himself sheltering a teacher and a gaggle of schoolgirls fleeing the Japanese.

Grant claimed to have a great affinity for his role as the stubbled, grizzled and semi-alcoholic beachcomber. "I'm closer to him than to any man I've ever played," he said. "As precise as I've always been about my attire and appearance, there has been that hidden desire, a subconscious urge, to go around like that, unshaven, untidy. I'm not a lover, really. I don't drink, but I'm sometimes grumpy, and have that hard shell of defense, seemingly impenetrable, but which can be softened at the right time by the right person."

For the role of the schoolteacher, Grant could have chosen a mature actress like Deborah Kerr, but he decided to use a younger one to appeal to a wider audience. When he telephoned Leslie Caron to offer her the part, she accepted instantly, without bothering to ask what the script was about.

"This was going to be heavenly, I thought, being in a slick, sophisticated comedy with the best of them all," Caron recalled. "I had been a waif or *jeune fille* too long. This was my big chance to be elegant, *très chic.* I began picturing myself in stunning creations by Yves St. Laurent." She had a rude awakening upon discovering that most of the action took place in a hut in the jungle and that her wardrobe consisted of a few shabby dresses.

Although it required extensive location work (with Jamaica doubling for the South Pacific) and didn't start production until April 1964, Grant and director Ralph Nelson finished *Father Goose* in time for it to be that year's Christmas attraction at Radio City Music Hall. It promptly broke the all-time opening-week box-office record set by Grant's *Charade* the previous year. It was extremely shrewd planning on Grant's part, indicative of why he had earned a reputation as the best actor-businessman in Hollywood.

Grant once described his personal method of making movies: "I am the producer, or should I say executive producer, since I hire a producer for the actual floor work. I can direct, learned during the war when good directors were in service making morale films. I was compelled to help out with many of those films I made at RKO and Columbia.

"But I wouldn't direct my own production," Grant said, "so I get the best director I can find, usually my first choice without having to go down a list. I obtain the services of an excellent scriptwriter and request his presence on the set in order to be on the scene if changes for the better are necessary.

"I'm not a writer or a director; I'm an improver. I work along with the film editor and I have the last word on the editing. Naturally, I choose the story and cast. I have my own offices. Just a secretary and lawyers. No agent. No overhead. Universal—or another company, I change periodically—puts up the money. They take a distribution fee, but after their investment is repaid, I own the picture. I learned that from the master himself; Chaplin always owned his pictures."

With *Father Goose* proving to be another big moneymaker, Grant seemed more interested in romancing Dyan Cannon than he did in making another film immediately. In the spring of 1965, gossip columnists thought they heard wedding bells not too far off when Grant took Cannon to Bristol to meet Elsie Leach.

"Cary's mother is a tremendous influence on him," Cannon said after the visit. "She's going on ninety, but she has a very strong personality. She was very pleasant to me, but kept calling me Betsy."

Cannon also took Grant to meet her family in Seattle. Her parents at first disapproved because of the age difference, but Grant's charm quickly won them over.

Grant and Cannon finally decided to get married when they

thought they knew everything about each other that they wanted to know. "I had researched him as far as I was capable, and he re-searched me as far as he was capable," Cannon said. "He didn't really propose. It was like there were no more movies we wanted to see playing at the drive-ins, so why not get married? It was not like any Cary Grant film, with that flash romance."

Wedding plans had to be temporarily set aside when Grant's great friend David O. Selznick died of a heart attack in June 1965, at the age of sixty-three. Only two years younger than Selznick, Grant sensed something of his own mortality in the passing. He also felt that he owed Selznick a tremendous debt, not only for the successful films they made together, but also as a role model in his own production activities.

At the funeral service, Grant read a tribute written by another Selznick friend, CBS chairman William Paley: "I cannot help but think that our world will never be the same—nor will heaven. And, if we are lucky enough to get there, too, David will see that all arrangements are made."

The following month, on July 22, Cary Grant and Dyan Cannon were married. Although Grant's weddings to Barbara Hutton and Betsy Drake had been kept private to avoid problems with the press, this one was even more top secret.

The world didn't learn of Cary Grant's fourth marriage until the eleventh day of the honeymoon. Even then the details were sketchy. The couple obtained a license in Goldfield, Nevada, but the civil ceremony was held in Las Vegas, probably at one of several hotels owned by Grant's perennial marriage adviser, Howard Hughes.

On July 30, Grant and Cannon checked into the Royal Hotel in Bristol, ostensibly to visit his mother, who had recently moved into the Chesterfield Nursing Home. Grant took the hotel's Churchill Suite and Cannon had a separate room down the hall, an arrange-ment that suggested they intended to keep their marriage a secret for as long as possible.

But Grant suddenly changed his mind in the midst of a conver-sation with Roderick Mann of the *Sunday Express,* who had traveled up from London to interview him about the British premiere of *Father Goose.*

"I'm only telling you now because you asked me," Grant said about his new marital status. "So many people have been hinting that we were thinking about marriage, were about to marry, or were actually married—but nobody really came right out and asked. We kept it a secret because marriage is a very private affair, and I prefer to do things quietly, without fanfare or intrusion. In fact, I have not even told my mother yet. That is why we are in Bristol."

Mann's publication of the news unleashed the kind of six-ring circus that Grant had always tried to avoid in the past. Dozens of reporters and photographers representing publications from all over the world started descending on Bristol to cover the story of the much-married sexagenarian and his eye-poppingly voluptuous fourth wife, who was young enough to be his daughter, if not granddaughter.

In a state of panic, Grant called Universal's publicity department in London: "You've got to get us out of here!"

"Why don't you give a mass interview and let them take photos. Then they'll leave you alone," it was suggested.

"I won't do that," Grant snapped. "I heard one of the sons of bitches say that if he could get a good shot of the two of us together, he'd make enough out of it to buy a new car. If anyone gets a car out of it, it'll be me!"

Matters heated up when a reporter went to the nursing home where Elsie Leach resided, only to discover that the newlyweds had already been there and left. "When are they coming to see me again?" asked the bewildered Mrs. Leach. "Cary promised they would."

After an incident in which a photographer raced up a back staircase trying to get to their floor before they did to waylay them as they stepped off the elevator, the couple started to plan an escape.

Their first attempt failed. Grant instructed the hotel management to relay the news that they'd checked out. Since the press had all the exits and entrances covered, nobody believed it. There was such an uproar that the police had to be called to restore order.

The next day, Grant's chauffeur, Tony Faramus, strolled into the hotel bar and became remarkably cooperative as reporters clustered around firing questions at him. Suddenly, a hotel bellboy appeared and handed Faramus a telegram which he opened, read and then passed around as evidence that the Grants had definitely checked out.

Dispatched from London under Cary Grant's name, the cable instructed Faramus to pack everything in the Rolls-Royce and drive slowly and cautiously back to the capital. When Faramus pulled away an hour later, the press conceded defeat and decamped as well.

Later, it turned out that the Grants had never left the hotel. They finally sneaked out in the dead of night and took a hired car to a friend's home outside London, arriving there at five in the morning. Their host, Gerald Abrahams, head of Aquascutum clothiers, kept the couple's whereabouts secret, and they stayed with him for two weeks without further bother from the press.

Afterward, the honeymooners flew back to Los Angeles so that Grant could get ready for a new film. Although they didn't know it at the time, it was the last film that Cary Grant would ever make.

17

Make Room for Daddy

After making five consecutive films for Universal Pictures, Cary Grant decided that he needed a change. Besides feeling that he could get more money elsewhere, he could no longer tolerate the sightseeing tours that Universal conducted through its huge studio in North Hollywood. Grant occupied a centrally located office-bungalow on the lot, and he thought that the tours were an invasion of his privacy.

But he resented even more not sharing in the three-dollar admission charge that people paid to "stare at us like animals in the zoo." Grant complained, "I can hear the guides say 'This is Cary Grant's car,' and 'This is where Cary Grant sunbathes.' " To avoid the hordes of tourists in the commissary, he began taking lunchtime picnics in the hills above the studio, only to be almost run over by a tour bus.

While negotiating with other studios, Grant unintentionally cost a friend a job by signing with Columbia Pictures for *Walk, Don't Run*. Producer Sol Siegel had been getting ready to offer the film to Spencer Tracy, but when Grant showed interest, Siegel opted for him as the bigger box-office draw of the two.

Ironically, the film was a remake of a George Stevens comedy called *The More the Merrier*, which Grant had turned down in 1943. Now he would play not the original role offered him, but one created by elderly character actor Charles Coburn (who had won an Oscar for his performance).

Although it would be easy to say that time had finally caught up with Cary Grant, years had to be shaved off the role because he looked so fit and robust. Scriptwriter Sol Saks also altered the plot to make Grant's part the lead. The original setting of the wartime housing shortage in Washington, D.C. was updated to a similarly crowded Tokyo during the 1964 Olympic Games.

While the title *Walk, Don't Run* had a literal reference to an Olympic walking race through the streets of Tokyo, it also became a metaphor for Cary Grant's determination, at age sixty-one, to change his screen image. He took himself out of the running as a romantic lead and saw himself ambling along in the future as a jolly wise uncle or lovable "Mr. Fix-It." Here he played a traveling business executive who acts as Cupid to a younger man and woman when the three strangers are forced to share one tiny apartment.

As had become his practice, Grant got involved in all areas of the production of *Walk, Don't Run.* For the roles played in *The More the Merrier* by Jean Arthur and Joel McCrea, he picked two actors whom he considered among the best of the up-and-coming stars, Samantha Eggar and Jim Hutton (whose career ended tragically in 1979 when he died of cancer at age forty-five).

Grant also became one of the first in Hollywood to give a chance to black composer-arranger Quincy Jones by commissioning him to write the musical score for *Walk, Don't Run.* The lyrics for two of Jones's featured songs, "Happy Feet" and "Stay With Me," were written by Peggy Lee, a great friend of Grant's and his favorite singer.

Walk, Don't Run was one Cary Grant film, however, where he merely approved the director instead of selecting him. Charles Walters had worked successfully with Sol Siegel before on *High Society,* the musical remake of *The Philadelphia Story,* so Grant saw no reason to break up a winning combination.

While Grant was making plans for the location trip to Japan, his wife told him that she thought she might be pregnant. Stunned, he said, "You have to find out."

When doctors confirmed it, the Grants celebrated by going to a night baseball game. Apart from watching television, Grant's favorite recreation was rooting for the Los Angeles Dodgers from his season box.

"But I will say that on that night, we paid less attention than usual to what was happening on the field. We were euphoric," Dyan Cannon recalled.

Remembering how the press went wild when fifty-nine-year-old Clark Gable revealed that he was becoming a father for the first time, Grant carefully avoided making an announcement for as long as he could. But fatherhood was the last thing that anyone expected of Cary Grant. When he left for Japan without taking his wife along, rumors started that the three-month marriage had gone *kaput.*

But Grant knew that the secret couldn't be kept indefinitely. Once he found himself out of reach of the Hollywood gossip-mill, he asked his lawyer, Stanley Fox, to discreetly leak the news.

As he feared, newspapers treated the announcement with front-page sensationalism, running banner headlines like CARY'S FOURTH EXPECTS FIRST and CARY GRANT PROVES IT'S NEVER TOO LATE. The stories rehashed his previous childless marriages and raised the unanswerable question of why Dyan Cannon had succeeded where Virginia Cherrill, Barbara Hutton and Betsy Drake had failed.

There were also the inevitable comparisons to Clark Gable, who had the misfortune to die of a heart attack before his son was born. At sixty-two, Grant took on the crown as Hollywood's oldest first-time father even before the big event took place!

After reporters were finally able to contact him in Tokyo, Grant would only comment that "becoming a father will be the most important role in my life." But Jim Hutton, his co-star in *Walk, Don't Run,* later described Grant's mood at the time.

"I have two children myself," Hutton said, "so naturally Cary and I talked a great deal about fatherhood. To safeguard Dyan's health, Cary thought it best she stay home in the States. He seemed lonely and confused. He would seek me out and talk for hours about what he wanted for his child and what he felt he could do for it. He told me that he hoped to have many children. He also said this might be his last picture, because becoming a father was more important than anything he had ever done."

Grant confessed to Hutton, "Before Dyan became pregnant, I really only had *me* to take care of. I felt free and footloose. And yet, fatherhood will make me freer than I've ever been, because at last I want the responsibility."

When Jennifer Grant was born on February 26, 1966, Bob

Hope couldn't resist jesting that the baby should have followed the advice of her daddy's latest movie, *Walk, Don't Run.* Jennifer arrived two months prematurely, weighing only 4.5 pounds.

Grant had returned from Japan by that time. To make room for the baby, the couple left his Beverly Hills house in the care of valet-chauffeur Tony Faramus and moved to a much larger one in Benedict Canyon, which Grant rented for two thousand dollars a month from the recently separated Gordon and Sheila MacRae.

Dyan Cannon first started feeling labor pains at four in the morning. Grant drove her to St. Joseph's Hospital in Burbank and stayed with her throughout the day. But doctors wouldn't let him into the delivery room to watch the birth when it occurred later that evening.

Jennifer was put in an incubator, but proved healthy and strong. After it was all over, Grant said, "I'm the world's worst worrier. Dyan had the baby and I did the worrying."

"She's the most beautiful baby in the world," he said as he took phone calls from reporters. "She's the most winsome, captivating girl I've ever known, and I've known quite a few girls.

"I've waited all my life, hoping for children, and when you've waited for such a long time, you hope like mad that everything will work out all right. In my case, I knew the birth of my baby was the chance of a dream coming true. It's never too late to become a parent."

Grant didn't think that his advanced age would prevent him from being a good parent: "I reckon I'm about ready for it. You're older, but you're able to understand a child better because you know yourself better. To everything disadvantageous, there is an advantage. One, I am materially able to take care of the child. Two, I'm older and therefore wiser, although perhaps that's too egotistical. I think I'm fitted to teach her spiritual values with more conviction."

He admitted, however, that "I may not be able to exert myself strenuously in playing children's roughhouse games or in bouncing a little girl on my knee. I think it's nice for a father to be able to play football with a son, but I'm not sure you should be playing football anyway. You can get your brains knocked out. But I can ride with my children and swim with them. Tennis I don't even play now. That's too exerting for me."

Grant sounded as though he were well on the way toward

founding a dynasty. "I hope to raise many children. Now we have a daughter and it's marvelous. But we want dozens—as many as possible. I can now financially afford to give them a good education and a healthful life. I think it's pretty difficult for children today. We are biologically ready to have children at twelve, but can't afford it until perhaps twenty-seven. I think this great rift is perhaps responsible for much of the juvenile delinquency—the inhibition of the life force."

The new mother said nothing for publication. Perhaps nobody asked her. Grant spoke almost like a single parent, seldom acknowledging Cannon's existence except with an occasional "we" instead of "I."

When wife and daughter were ready to leave the hospital, Grant announced that he was taking a year off to devote all his time to his family. While he didn't want that interpreted as a prelude to permanent retirement, he conceded that he could no longer play romantic leads.

"By now, my choice of subjects is very limited," he said. "I may wind up playing some old retired banker in a wheelchair. I want to go on and on, like Sir C. Aubrey Smith."

Grant really wanted to see how *Walk, Don't Run* turned out before he made any final decisions about his career. If that had been a hit, he undoubtedly would have been encouraged to do more films, even if they were only remakes of old Charles Coburn or Lionel Barrymore vehicles.

But *Walk, Don't Run* fared poorly, with the public and critics alike (*Time* couldn't resist calling it "Pedestrian!"). Grant felt humiliated when Radio City Music Hall declined to play it. Because of his track record there, he thought his films should be booked automatically. But he had to be content with the fact that he would remain the Music Hall's all-time box-office champion (by this time with twenty-seven pictures and 113 weeks' playing time).

In that same year, *Fame* magazine announced its "All-Time Top Ranking Money-Making Stars," based on records kept by Quigley trade publications since 1932. Cary Grant ranked ninth in a list that started with John Wayne, followed by Bing Crosby, Gary Cooper, Clark Gable, Bob Hope, Doris Day, Rock Hudson and Betty Grable. Just behind Grant in tenth position were Abbott and Costello.

Grant blamed his relatively weak showing on the fact that

some of his early successes were made for Columbia and RKO, which lacked the voting clout that the larger studios had. He didn't make his first appearance in the annual Top Ten Quigley polls until 1944, when he was number nine. He then fell off until 1948 and 1949, when he made the number eight and number six spots, respectively. He disappeared from the Top Ten list for ten years, then reappeared in 1959 in the number two slot, thanks to the success of *North by Northwest.* He held a high place every year after that through 1966.

The only poll that Grant seemed interested in winning now was "Father of the Year." Jennifer Grant had become the single most important thing in his life. He took weekly progress photographs and bought a tape recorder to capture Jennifer's every goo and gurgle.

Although any proud father might have done the same, it seemed a bit farcical in the case of Cary Grant. Who would have expected Mr. Elegance to come out with statements like "A hundred diapers a week at this age is the minimum!"

Having learned it from living with Barbara Hutton, Grant became almost paranoid about a possible kidnapping attempt on his daughter. To put potential abductors off the scent, he planted items with Hedda and Louella that he'd moved to a heavily guarded estate in La Jolla, near San Diego.

The Grants almost never went out, and visitors were limited to a few close acquaintances. All were sworn to secrecy about disclosing any information about Jennifer Grant. "I could answer all your questions about what the baby looks like and everything else, but I won't. It's forbidden," Frederick Brisson told an inquisitive reporter.

When Jennifer had turned four months old and weighed in at eleven pounds, Grant finally gave into pressure from the news media and permitted a few trusted photographer friends to come to the house for a photo session. Apparently, not even Grant's mother had seen a picture of her granddaughter yet. When the Bristol Press showed her a telephoto, Elsie Leach said, "She's lovely, and she looks just like Cary."

But others thought Jennifer had a closer resemblance to Dyan Cannon, with the same eyes, nose and light brunette coloring. Grant had the last word on the subject, however, when he said, "I hear that girls are supposed to look like their fathers, so maybe

Jennifer will end up looking like me, although sometimes I look terrible. But just now she looks like both of us."

In July 1966, the Grants took Jennifer to Bristol to meet her paternal grandmother, although Columbia Pictures paid for the trip in exchange for Grant publicizing the British premiere of *Walk, Don't Run.* To keep it a private family excursion, Grant booked passage under an assumed name on the *SS Oriana,* which sailed from San Pedro, California, through the Panama Canal to Lisbon, Le Havre and Southampton.

Before they departed, the Grants quarreled over his refusal to take along a supply of baby formula sufficient for the whole trip. "The cows in England are as good as they are in this country," Grant said. Cannon later claimed that Jennifer became sick as a result.

When the Grants arrived at the dock at San Pedro, someone had tipped off the press and they were greeted by a mob of reporters and photographers. Fending them off became a nightmare as the Grants tried to board with Jennifer and thirty-six pieces of luggage.

Arriving in their cabin, Grant blamed it all on Cannon for bringing too many things and proceeded to empty her suitcases of clothes and shoes (she had brought along fifty pairs) he said she didn't need. Cannon broke down in tears as Grant assembled a whole carload of items for the chauffeur to take back with him to the house in Benedict Canyon.

The transatlantic crossing ended happily, at least for Grant. "Presenting Jennifer to my mother was the proudest moment of my life," he recalled. Now eighty-nine, Elsie Leach studied her granddaughter carefully and through the veil of memory told him, "She looks exactly like you did when you were a baby."

Embarrassed by the way the press had treated the Grants on their honeymoon the previous year, the Bristol municipal officials held a luncheon in his honor. After listening to several speeches that lauded him as Bristol's favorite son, Grant expressed thanks and then made a few off-the-cuff remarks that seemed strangely inappropriate to the occasion.

"Our divorce laws are more relaxed now and women are in competition with men," Grant said. "Marriage is on the way out. I don't think it will exist in another hundred years."

Grant didn't have the courage to admit that his own marriage was on the rocks. His wife could no longer tolerate the Pygmalion-and-Galatea relationship that had developed between them. She had begun to sink into a condition of psychological subservience to her husband. Her moods were governed by his moods, which seesawed from great elation to deep depression.

"I lost my individuality completely after I married Cary," Cannon recalled. "I was so in love, so eager to please. I allowed it to happen to me, but it wasn't helped at all by Cary. He was always the dominant one. If you want to be a piece of lox, that's okay. But I didn't want it to be. It just happened."

To save herself from slipping into psychological obscurity, Cannon suggested that she resume her acting career. "But I didn't bring it up often, because I really had the feeling Cary didn't want it, and I found myself just living to try to please, to keep going," she said.

In October 1966, Grant took Cannon to the twenty-fifth wedding anniversary party of his friends Rosalind Russell and Freddy Brisson. Limited to only twenty-five couples, the swank affair was hosted by Frank Sinatra and wife Mia Farrow at the Sands Hotel in Las Vegas. Grant, who'd been best man at the Brissons' wedding, hoped that their successful marriage would show Cannon how happy they could be themselves if only they tried a little harder.

But if there were any lesson to be learned, Cannon failed to pick up on it. Rosalind Russell said later, "Cary did nothing but cry all evening about his problems."

In one of his more conciliatory moods, Grant came up with the idea of casting Cannon as his leading lady in "The Old Man and Me," an original script that he optioned from Isobel Lennart, a top screenwriter of the time. Shopping around for a deal, Grant told studio executives that he would do the film on one condition: "That you sign Dyan, without a screen test. You must take my word for it that she'll be good."

Not even Cary Grant could make such a demand. The project never got off the ground.

In December 1966, Cannon decided that she couldn't endure living with Grant any longer and took Jennifer with her to stay with her parents in Seattle. The marriage had lasted seventeen months. Since neither Grant nor Cannon announced any intention of filing for a divorce, Hollywood guessed that it would be his usual cliffhanger, with a reconciliation or two before the inevitable final cancellation.

But Grant had never had a wife as feisty or outspoken as this one, and it would be a long, painful tug-of-war played out in full view of the public. Heartbroken over having his daughter taken from him, Grant refused to comment on the situation. But friends said he was trying every means possible to get Jennifer back.

After a few weeks in Seattle, Cannon returned to Los Angeles with Jennifer and rented a small apartment near Malibu Beach. Refusing to communicate with Grant or to allow him to see Jennifer, she also started visiting a psychiatrist. "I knew I had to have outside help—to help my insides," she recalled.

But Cannon apparently wasn't all that mentally unbalanced. Although Grant tried to get evidence to prove that she was an unfit mother so that he could get custody of Jennifer, he never succeeded.

After a while, Cannon's money ran out and she started taking Grant's phone calls. The frantic father begged her to move closer to town so that Jennifer would be more accessible and he could see her every day. When Cannon agreed to his request, Grant began grumbling about the rent and also refused to pay for a nurse, although he said it wasn't out of stinginess. He believed that every baby, and especially *his* baby, should have the loving care that only a mother could give.

Early in 1967, Grant and Cannon started having frequent sixty-dollar-an-hour sessions with a marriage counselor, Dr. Andrew Salter, in an attempt to restore harmony to their relationship. Salter later sued Grant for seven thousand dollars in unpaid bills. Grant counterclaimed that Salter's counseling not only failed to correct and ameliorate the couple's estrangement but in fact made it worse.

But by the summer of 1967, the Grants appeared to have reached a reconciliation as they traveled together to Las Vegas for a Danny Kaye opening, and took eighteen-month-old Jennifer to Dodger Stadium for her first ball game. It seemed like a reprise of Grant's separation from Betsy Drake, except that now a child was involved.

As much as Grant wanted to be a family unit again, Cannon insisted on separate dwellings. "I still love Cary very much, and he still loves me. But it's nice to be free for a while," she said.

Although personal problems occupied most of his time, Grant hadn't given up the idea of making another movie. He joined forces with producer-director Mervyn LeRoy to portray "Buffalo Bill" Cody in an all-star extravaganza called *Cowboys and Indians*, but nothing ever came of the project. Ditto for a Howard Hawks collaboration on *Don Quixote*, with Grant in the title role and Mexican comedian Cantinflas as Sancho Panza.

Grant never stopped being inundated with offers. One of the most improbable came from stage producer Harold J. Kennedy, who wanted him to act in summer stock. Much to Kennedy's surprise, Grant said he'd like to do it just for the pleasure of working before a live audience again. But he refused to appear under his own name because of all the hullabaloo it would attract. Grant conceded that was impossible. Even in the smallest town, word would get out after the first performance, no matter what pseudonym he used.

In August 1967, Grant wished that he had left for the hinterlands when Dyan Cannon filed for divorce in Los Angeles Supreme Court, charging that he'd treated her "in a cruel and inhuman manner." It was the beginning of nearly a year of events and disclosures that created a new public image of Cary Grant as an LSD-created Dr. Jekyll and Mr. Hyde.

The divorce action started sedately, with no hint of the blockbusters to come. Cannon asked for "reasonable support," stating that monthly expenses for Jennifer and herself amounted to $5,470 a month. She estimated Grant's financial worth at $10 million, with an annual income of $500,000. In contrast, she claimed that her sole income was $400 a year from TV residuals.

While the case was being prepared, Cannon accepted an offer to do a Broadway play called *The Ninety Day Mistress*. Whether she mentioned that title to the judge is unknown, but she convinced the court that she was a "fit and proper" person to take Jennifer out of the state with her while working in New York.

When Cannon left Los Angeles with Jennifer to begin rehearsals, Grant turned up unexpectedly at the airport with a reservation on the same flight. "Just to make sure the baby is all right," he said.

Cannon managed to control her annoyance, but was finally exasperated when she discovered that Grant had also booked himself into the Croydon Hotel, where she occupied a suite with the baby and a private nurse. She ordered Grant to move elsewhere, so he went to stay with his friend Bob Taplinger, a public relations executive who owned an East Side town house.

When *The Ninety Day Mistress* opened at the Biltmore Theatre on November 6, Cary Grant turned up in the audience and also escorted Dyan Cannon to the producer's party afterward, managing to plant a few kisses on her cheek for the benefit of photographers. In the following weeks, he just happened to turn up whenever Cannon went to a restaurant or nightclub.

Although *The Ninety Day Mistress* received negative reviews and closed after twenty-four performances, Cannon received excellent personal notices and decided to remain in New York in the hope of being offered another play. Grant stayed on as well. He had no urgent business in Hollywood and no rent to pay as Bob Taplinger's house guest.

Through Taplinger, Grant learned that Cannon was having a luncheon interview with his longtime friend, columnist Sheilah Graham. Grant telephoned Graham that morning and begged her to intercede for him.

"I want my wife back, I want my daughter back. You can help me. I'll do anything she wants," Grant said.

"She wants to resume her career and to live in New York," Graham replied.

"I know," Grant said. "Poor baby. If she'll come back to me, I'll buy her the finest house in Manhattan. I'll co-star with her. With me, she can be the greatest star in the business. But now, poor baby, it's hit or miss. I realize I've made mistakes with Dyan, but I'll give her all the odds. I won't fight. She can have everything she wants.

"Dyan's a strange girl," Grant continued. "She believes I only understand rejection. She told me, 'You're only attracted to me when I reject you.' She has an attraction-rejection problem. I don't know why, but she has built up this kind of anger against me."

Sheilah Graham said that from all that she'd heard, Cannon seemed like "a tough babe."

"No, not tough," Grant corrected her. "The tougher they seem to be, the weaker they are. Dyan is strong. That's why I married her. I chose her for her strength, but instead of joining her strength with mine, she has used it against me. Emotionally, she's a child. I can understand it because I used to be like her."

When Graham asked Grant how she could help, he said, "Tell

Dyan she's making a big mistake. But don't say I'm unhappy, it adds to her power. Perhaps you shouldn't say I said it, it will only make her reject me more. Say it was Bob Taplinger."

Graham followed Grant's instructions, but, as she commented later, "Dyan is a clever girl and I could see from the way she smiled and raised her eyebrows that she knew I had talked to Cary." That afternoon, Graham called to tell him that she was unable to change Cannon's attitude.

"I didn't really think you could," Grant said, adding that since his last chat with Graham, there had been another argument with Cannon over some pictures of himself and Jennifer that appeared in that day's newspapers.

"When I telephoned to find out when I could see the baby again, Dyan got hysterical and shouted 'You'll never see her again if I can help it! I don't want crooks to see what my daughter looks like,' " Grant said. "I'd never go there now. It's the worst thing I could do."

Grant explained the cause of the new dispute. While showing Jennifer the sights of Manhattan from a chauffeured limousine, they stopped to eat at La Groceria in Greenwich Village. Spotting an opportunity to get some publicity for his restaurant, the owner called the *Daily News,* which dispatched a photographer.

"I do everything to prevent publicity of this kind," Grant told Sheilah Graham. "When I'd call for Jennifer at the hotel, I'd stop the car half a block away. I'd make the chauffeur take off his cap and he'd bring Jennifer out. You can imagine the furor if I'd gone into the hotel myself and walked out with my daughter. There would have been photographers and press all over the place."

Graham warned Grant that his handling of the situation was all wrong: "Go away. Leave Dyan alone. Make her think you don't care and she'll come running back on the double."

"I know," Grant replied miserably, "but I can't help myself. She'd be worried if she thought I was interested in another woman. She'd believe I'd rejected her. Perhaps you could put something in your column, me and another woman? I'm going to have more children. If not with Dyan, I'll marry another young woman and have as many children and grandchildren as I can."

With Christmas approaching, Grant's obsession with family problems took an odd turn when he made his debut as a recording artist. Goddard Lieberson of Columbia Records had been badgering him for years to make a Christmas album of readings from traditional holiday material, but he didn't become interested until his young daughter gave him a reason and inspiration.

With his friend Peggy Lee as lyricist and composer, Grant came up with "Christmas Lullaby." "I'm quite nutty about Peggy and I think many of her lyrics are profound, strangely profound. She has a unique choice of words," he said.

Under contract to a rival label, Lee couldn't perform on the disc, but she sat beside Grant in the recording studio and held his hand while he recited the lullaby: "Angels bless you, little one . . . my little one, sleep well . . . loving you the way I do, oh, my dear little one, sleep well . . . Merry Christmas!"

For the flip side of the 45 rpm single, Grant recited another Peggy Lee song, "Here's to You," comprised of different holiday toasts for health and happiness from countries around the world. The novelty of Cary Grant in a Christmas setting made for a seasonal hit, and the record still gets played on radio stations at that time of year. At Grant's request, all profits were donated to the Motion Picture Relief Fund.

For that Christmas of 1967, Cannon reluctantly complied with Grant's request that they make one last attempt at saving the marriage by spending the holidays together. But it didn't work out and Cannon refused to withdraw the divorce action. Not one to give in easily, Grant spent the first months of 1968 flying back and forth between Los Angeles and New York, still hoping to effect a reconciliation.

When the Los Angeles Superior Court set March 20 as the date for the divorce hearing, Grant saw no reason to remain in New York any longer. On March 12, before he left to catch a late-night flight out of Kennedy Airport, his longtime host Bob Taplinger held a small dinner party to cheer him up and offer moral support in the forthcoming litigation.

Afterward, one of the guests insisted on lending Grant his chauffeured limousine to take him to the airport. Gratia von Furstenberg, an associate in Taplinger's public relations firm, went along to keep Grant company.

It was a cold, rainy night. Not long after the limousine reached the Long Island Expressway, a truck coming from the opposite direction skidded and dislodged a spare-wheel assembly that flew across the highway divider and slammed into Grant's car.

In the moments that followed the crash, it looked as though Cary Grant had played his final scene. Bleeding profusely from the nose, he could hardly breathe and became convinced that he was dying.

Together with the other two blood-splattered occupants of the nearly totaled Cadillac, Grant was lifted into an ambulance bound for St. John's Hospital in Elmhurst, Queens. Halfway there, the ambulance roared through a flood caused by a backed-up sewer and stalled the engine. Already on the verge of hysteria, Grant started screaming for help as the driver tried vainly to restart the engine.

Finally, Grant and Gratia von Furstenberg were transferred to a police car and taken to the hospital, while their chauffeur, Troy Lindahl, elected to remain in the ambulance. He arrived at the hospital only minutes after the others did.

Grant thought he had a broken nose, but X-rays showed no damage beyond severely bruised cartilege. Whenever Grant breathed, he had pain, but X-rays indicated no rib fractures either. His face was cut and swollen, and he suffered from shock, but that seemed to be the extent of his injuries. The other two casualties were not as lucky. Gratia von Furstenberg had a broken collarbone and a right leg fractured in three places. Troy Lindahl's right kneecap was broken.

After being treated for their injuries, Grant and the chauffeur were heavily sedated and placed in a semiprivate room for the night, with a security guard posted outside the door. The next day, Grant was offered a room by himself but he preferred to continue sharing one with Lindahl so that he'd have someone to talk to. Of course, it also meant a savings on his hospital bill. When an attendant asked him if he had Blue Cross, Grant replied, "What's that?"

With Cary Grant under its roof, the hospital had to cope with more problems than it could handle, including one with the star himself. He thought that he knew more than the doctors did, and often disagreed with their procedures. Finally, an angry head physician told him that unless his attitude improved, he'd have to find another hospital. With quite enough troubles already, Grant managed a weak, "Okay, Doc."

As soon as word got out that Cary Grant was a patient, the hospital received thousands of cards, letters and telegrams addressed to him from all over the world. Women bombarded the telephone switchboard trying to get to talk with him. To reach Grant, friends had to ask for "Count Bezok," a code name he'd used for years.

"I feel like a Grade B movie," Grant confessed to a visitor. One of the first to arrive was Dyan Cannon, causing reporters to speculate on a reconciliation. But Cannon only came to determine whether the divorce hearing would have to be postponed. Grant agreed with her that it would be best to let it go on as scheduled. She and Jennifer flew to Los Angeles later that day.

Grant still had trouble breathing, and the pain was getting worse. After a specialist was called in for a second opinion, additional X rays showed two fractured ribs.

Although Grant had expected to be in the hospital for about a week, the stay stretched into seventeen days. He took it stoically. At least it kept him well protected from the fallout over his wife's explosive testimony at the divorce hearing, which depicted Cary Grant as a deranged "apostle of LSD."

18

A Divorce to Remember

On the day of the divorce hearing, Cary Grant cut himself off from the outside world, refusing to accept phone calls, disconnecting the TV and radio in his hospital room, and demanding extra sedatives to insure a night of restful sleep. Not until the next morning did he see the scandal-drenched coverage in the New York tabloids and let loose with an anguished "Oh, my God!"

According to Dyan Cannon's half-hour testimony, life with Cary Grant was more like a horror movie than the light romantic comedy she had expected. She swore under oath that Grant took weekly LSD trips in which he often beat her, accused her of infidelities and swore to "break her like a pony" to turn her into the sort of wife he wanted.

In her sixth month of pregnancy, Cannon said, Grant turned her into a sobbing wreck by claiming that her doctor was on the make for her and that he charged outrageous fees because she happened to be Mrs. Cary Grant. On several occasions, Grant humiliated her by yelling and screaming at her while they were out in public, she claimed.

On an evening that she intended to go out with some of her girlfriends, Grant forbade her to leave the house, Cannon testified. He took the keys to their three cars and barricaded himself in her dressing room, where he proceeded to sit down and read a book of poetry. She related that Grant then started to hit her, laughing all the while and calling the servants to witness her humiliation.

When Cannon threatened to summon the police, Grant allegedly talked her out of it with the warning that the press would descend on them *en masse* if she did. Instead, she called her friend and agent Adaline Fiddler. Cannon said that Grant grabbed the receiver and yelled into it, "Addie, stay out of my marriage. I'm going to break this girl. She's not going to leave until I break her."

After leaving Jennifer in the care of the servants, Cannon climbed the fence that surrounded the house and found refuge with friends, she told the court.

On another evening, Cannon said, Grant "freaked out" while they were watching the Academy Awards telecast in their bedroom. "He became violent and out of control. He jumped up and down on the bed and carried on. He yelled that everyone on the awards show had had their faces lifted, and he was spilling wine on the bed. This lasted a couple of hours—as long as the awards were on," she said.

Cannon admitted that Grant once persuaded her to take LSD before they were married, but that thereafter she had refused to join him in using the mind-expanding chemical. "He once told me I was on the verge of a nervous breakdown and he hoped I would have it so that the 'new me' would be a wonderful one. And he said that the 'new me' would be created through LSD," she stated.

Cannon said that her only reason for revealing Grant's LSD experience and philosophy was to justify her petition for their daughter's custody. "Mr. Grant is an unfit father because of his instability," she said, insisting that he should only be allowed to see his daughter in the presence of a registered nurse. She did not want Jennifer staying overnight in his house.

When Cannon finished her lurid testimony, Grant's attorney called two "expert" witnesses to discredit her claims. They were psychiatrists who had examined Grant the previous autumn, when the suit was instituted.

While not denying that Grant had frequently used LSD, Dr. Judd Marmor said that he found no reason to believe that it had harmed him or caused lingering negative effects. "Mr. Grant tends to be an emotional individual, but I have often seen that in actors," Marmor said.

The doctor further testified that Grant told him that LSD had "deepened his sense of compassion for people, deepened his understanding of himself, and helped cure his shyness and anxiety in dealing with other people."

Marmor said that Grant confessed to him that he once spanked Cannon for what he described to the psychiatrist as "reasonable and adequate causes." On that occasion, Cannon intended to go to a discotheque with friends, wearing a miniskirt and heavy makeup that Grant objected to.

"He pleaded with her that it wouldn't be right for his wife to go out alone and looking like that, and tempers flared on both sides," Marmor said. "There was an explosion on his part, and he spanked her."

Dr. Sidney Pomer, the other psychiatrist who testified in Grant's defense, said that he found no evidence of "irrationality, erratic behavior or incoherence" when he examined him.

During the second day of the trial, two of Dyan Cannon's friends testified. Agent Adaline Fiddler related the phone conversation in which Grant had told her: "I'm going to break this girl. I'm going to break her like a pony."

Describing the evening when Cannon phoned her, Fiddler said, "Dyan was frightened to death. She called my residence three times that night and I heard Mr. Grant screaming in the background. The baby was screaming, too."

Mary Gries, wife of director Tom Gries, also came to Cannon's defense by telling the court that Grant had said, "This girl is heading for a nervous breakdown and I hope she has it. That's the only way I can make her into the wife I want."

Grant had prepared some written testimony to be read in court that day. But when he saw the first day's press coverage, he decided that there already had been enough mudslinging and ordered his testimony to be withheld.

"Once the female has used the male for procreation, she turns on him and literally devours him," he told Bob Taplinger.

Although Cannon got her divorce, it didn't turn out to be the total victory she wanted. In fact, except for the damage to his reputation, Grant came out the winner, if there can be one in such a situation.

Cannon received a financial settlement considerably under what Grant had been prepared to give her in lieu of going to court. The judge ordered him to pay $2,000 monthly for child support, plus thirty-six months of alimony that would start at $2,250 and gradually decrease to $1,000 in the last of the three years.

What made Grant even happier was that he'd done better with regard to visitation rights than he had dared hope for—sixty days a year plus the right to keep Jennifer with him overnight.

If Grant worried about his tarnished image, he didn't show it when he checked out of St. John's Hospital a week later. Hospital personnel lined the main corridor, cheering and applauding as he stopped to shake hands with the executive director, a Catholic nun. Three years later, he returned to appear at a benefit to raise funds for the hospital's expansion program.

Grant refused to discuss his divorce with the crowd of reporters and photographers that had gathered. He said that his only plans for the moment were to "keep breathing in and out." Later that day, he flew back to Los Angeles in a private jet lent to him by George Barrie, president of the Rayette-Fabergé cosmetics and toiletries company.

Grant had first met Barrie, an ex-jazz saxophonist, when the latter called him to complain about a magazine interview in which he condemned the use of hairspray: "Why do women put that disgusting gook on their hair? Try to run your fingers through hair mucked up with that stuff and it removes your skin." Grant grew to admire Barrie for his acumen in turning a small hair-spray business into an international conglomerate, and they became good friends.

In 1967, Barrie appointed Grant a "creative consultant" to Rayette-Fabergé. While Barrie hoped to glamorize Fabergé's image through a Cary Grant connection, he also did it to give his friend an active interest while he sweated out the divorce action. During the last year of the Grants' estrangement, Grant attended sales conventions and visited Fabergé plants in the United States, England and Europe.

After the sensational disclosures of the divorce hearing, Barrie and Bob Taplinger helped Grant to get back on his feet. Fearful that the double shock of the scandal and the auto accident might send him into permanent hibernation from the world, they urged him to take a more active role in Fabergé. From the standpoint of public relations, a new image of Cary Grant as a solid, serious business executive could help to eradicate memories of the lurid headlines of his recent past.

In May 1968, Grant was elected a member of Fabergé's board

of directors. After the press announcement, the company's shares shot up several points on the New York Stock Exchange. George Barrie denied it was a publicity stunt, emphasizing that Grant would take an active role in management and not just sit in on board meetings.

Grant received a consultant's salary of $15,000 a year, plus an additional two hundred dollars for each board meeting that he attended. Not much on the face of it, but there were considerable fringe benefits, including a rent-paid luxury apartment in New York, unlimited travel expenses and the use of the company's private fleet of jet planes and helicopters. Reportedly, Grant also received a block of Fabergé stock, plus options for more.

"I'm doing this because I enjoy it and it's stimulating," Grant said at the time. "It isn't too different from films. We both make a product, can it and distribute it. My corporate duties will be to call attention to the products and tour the world on a good-will basis."

As a top-priority project, Grant hoped to oversee the development of a fragrance that could be used by both men and women. "Why are flowers only for women?" he asked. "They're for men, too. I think there ought to be more unity of the sexes. Why are there 'his and hers' towels, twin beds, and car gearshifts that separate people? Why shouldn't men use the same hairspray, the same cologne, as women, just as they're using the same soap and deodorants? The separation of the sexes is so manifest. Why shouldn't we develop things we can all enjoy?"

Grant said that he had no intention of giving up his movie career, but that he wouldn't consider any project that prevented him from spending time with daughter Jennifer. "She's the greatest production I was ever associated with," he boasted, expressing regret that he came to parenthood so late in life. "Had I known what it means and feels like, I would have a huge ranch and a hundred children by now."

With the Fabergé jets at his disposal, Grant frequently used them to visit his daughter while her mother worked in summer stock. Despite predictions to the contrary, the divorce publicity did not help Dyan Cannon's career. The only work that she could find was in regional theatres.

Although Cannon believed that her ex-husband had secretly spread a "Don't hire!" warning through all his showbiz contacts, it turned out otherwise. She had him to thank for her first major movie role, in *Bob & Carol & Ted & Alice*, produced by Grant's close friend Mike Frankovich. Grant had only one motive for helping: it ensured that Jennifer would be near him in Los Angeles while her mother worked there.

But Cannon had emotional problems and *Bob & Carol & Ted & Alice* was the only movie she made for almost two years. Grant grew increasingly concerned for Jennifer's welfare when he discovered that Cannon had become heavily dependent on drugs and alcohol.

In August 1969, eighteen months after the divorce, Grant went to court to prevent Cannon from taking Jennifer to stay with her maternal grandparents in Seattle. Grant claimed that Cannon intended to "dump" Jennifer there so that she could have more time for her addictions.

Cannon denied the charge, but the judge ruled in Grant's favor by insisting that Jennifer must remain in Los Angeles. Grant also won a motion to have his visiting rights extended from sixty to ninety days a year.

On the eve of Jennifer's fourth birthday in February 1970, Grant spoke about his relationship with his daughter. "We have a great rapport between us," he said. "Usually when she won't take her afternoon nap, I lie down with her and we both fall off. It's so heartwarming and restful, even if she kicks me in the head once in a while. She rubs it and says, 'Daddy, I'm making it well.' On another occasion, I fell asleep and snored so loudly it awakened her and she shook me and said, 'Stop it, Daddy!'

"I've been tape recording everything she does with me," he continued, "and I've also shot a great deal of film footage of her so she'll know, when she grows up, how deeply her father loved his little girl. Jennifer's a jealous female, too. One day we were together when I met Deborah Kerr and we kissed hello. This shook her up. She said to Deborah, 'You keep away from my daddy!' "

In March 1970, it suddenly looked as though Cary Grant might be the father of two daughters. A former ladyfriend, thirty-three-year-old Cynthia Bouron, slapped him with a lawsuit, claiming that he was the father of a seven-week-old girl whom she had registered at birth as Stephanie Andrea Grant. Bouron said that Grant had taken her out several times and then had brought her back to his house to spend the night.

At least part of Bouron's allegations were true. But Grant doubted that he had sired a child in the process. He told a friend that although they had had some sexual contact, they had never engaged in intercourse.

Grant immediately filed a countersuit to stop Bouron from calling him the baby's father until the paternity suit was settled, by which time he hoped to prove his innocence. The petition said: "This order is essential to preserve Mr. Grant's personal status and reputation in the community. Unless Miss Bouron is so restrained, she will continue to represent or publish that Mr. Grant is the father, to his humiliation, embarrassment and damage."

The scandal could not have come at a worse time for Grant. The Academy of Motion Picture Arts and Sciences had voted him an honorary Oscar that would be presented during the Academy Awards ceremony in April. Already worried that the paternity case might jeopardize his visitation rights with Jennifer, he did not wish to appear before his peers and a worldwide television audience with such a cloud of suspicion hanging over him. If Bob Hope or some other prankster made a crack, he would never live it down.

Just a few days before the telecast, however, everything worked out in Grant's favor. To support his position that he had not fathered Bouron's child, he took blood and sperm tests. Bouron, however, failed to appear with the baby for their scheduled tests. When mother and child did not turn up for two subsequent appointments set by the court, the judge dismissed the case.

Grant was exonerated, although it never became clear whether Bouron had been after money or was just mentally unbalanced. A private detective hired by Grant discovered that she had a reputation as a "Tiajuana hooker" and that the disputed baby was half black. (Three years later, someone bludgeoned Bouron to death in North Hollywood. The murder was never solved.)

With his hair now white, Cary Grant looked a bit like Cary Grant made up for an old man's role when he sauntered onto the stage of the Dorothy Chandler Pavilion in Los Angeles on April 7, 1970, to accept his honorary Oscar from Frank Sinatra. It was a walk that Grant had long ago given up hope of ever taking. His unhappiness over never winning one of the coveted gold-plated statuettes had become part of Hollywood legend.

Grant had been nominated twice for the Best Actor award, for *Penny Serenade* in 1941 and for *None but the Lonely Heart* three years later. He also claimed to hold an all-time record for being in films that won Oscars for his co-workers: Leo McCarey, Best Director for *The Awful Truth;* James Stewart, Best Supporting Actor, *The Philadelphia Story;* Joan Fontaine, Best Actress, *Suspicion;* Ethel Barrymore, Best Supporting Actress, *None but the Lonely Heart;* Sidney Sheldon, Best Screenplay, *The Bachelor and the Bobby-Soxer;* Gordon Sawyer, Best Sound Engineer, *The Bishop's Wife.*

Screenplay writer Peter Stone probably summed it up better than anyone when he accepted *his* Oscar for *Father Goose* and expressed a special debt of gratitude to Grant, "who keeps winning these things for other people."

Perhaps the reason the Academy passed over Grant so many times was that Hollywood underestimated his talent. "Light comedy has little chance for an Oscar," he once said. "When I say I won't win one, I mean now or any other year. You have to play dope fiends to get noticed these days. But what's more difficult— whomping someone in the belly or making them laugh? Any amateur can black out a tooth, stick on a beard and pretend he's something he isn't. The tough thing, the final thing, is to be yourself. *That* takes doing."

What finally caused the Motion Picture Academy to honor Grant can only be guessed at, since the behind-the-scenes politicking is always kept secret. But Grant's sixty-six years and the likelihood that he would never make any more movies undoubtedly entered into it. Also, Grant rarely appeared on television, so getting him on the show was a real coup. His presence would evoke some of the legendary Hollywood glamour that had been sorely missing from the annual event in recent years.

Before Frank Sinatra gave Grant the award, film clips traced the actor's career through his leading ladies, showing him in scenes with Mae West, Jean Harlow, Katharine Hepburn, Jean Arthur, Irene Dunne, Ingrid Bergman, Grace Kelly, Eva Marie Saint and Audrey Hepburn. The effect on the three thousand people in the theatre was electrifying. Many had forgotten just how wonderful Cary Grant had been or how many different eras his career spanned.

The celebrity-packed crowd proved that it, too, had idols, giving Grant a thunderous standing ovation. The television viewer could almost feel a physical transfer of affection.

Frank Sinatra waited patiently for the cheering to subside, then said, "No one has brought more pleasure to more people for so many years than Cary has, and nobody has done so many things as well. Cary has so much skill that he makes it all look easy."

Sinatra read the inscription on the base of the statuette: "To Cary Grant, for his unique mastery of the art of screen acting, with the respect and affection of his colleagues."

Half crying and half laughing at himself for doing so, Grant was too overcome by emotion to deliver much of an acceptance speech. He began thanking directors and writers he'd worked with over the years, not apologizing for taking the time to mention fourteen by name but asking, "Why not? This is a collaborative medium. We all need each other." He ended by remarking that "Probably no greater honor can come to a man than the respect of his colleagues."

Still hurting over the publicity from the Cynthia Bouron incident, Grant tried to get away as fast as possible to avoid reporters. While hurrying to his Rolls-Royce in the underground parking lot, he heard running footsteps behind him. Turning around, he saw Gregory Peck waving something in the air. Grant had forgotten to pick up his Oscar!

19

Silver Fox

Cary Grant's 1970 Oscar marked an unofficial turning point in his life. The award coincided with the start of a new decade, the first since the thirties that would bring no new Cary Grant movies. But his popularity and fame remained constant, thanks to continual revivals of his old films and to his much-publicized affiliation with Fabergé. He had become an institution, but a remarkably spry and youthful one for sixty-six.

Grant now divided his time between Los Angeles and New York, where Fabergé had its headquarters. Ironically, he began that new phase of his life where Archie Leach had started out exactly fifty years before. But now he occupied the same luxury suite in the Warwick Hotel that had been the love nest of Marion Davies and William Randolph Hearst at a time when he was residing in cheap theatrical boardinghouses.

People were startled to hear Cary Grant discussing perfumes instead of movies, but he often pointed out the similarities: "We researched 'Brut' just as you would research a screenplay. Then we ask ourselves where the raw essence can be found, which would be like finding locations for a movie, and how to get the quantities—the prints—in case we've got a hit.

"Perfumes are dramatic," Grant said. "You start a fragrance with a working title. For instance, 'Midnight in Rome.' No good! Then someone from another department comes in and suggests 'Kiku' and you sense it's just right. We did the same thing before we titled the movie *Operation Petticoat.* In this business, of course, my reviews come out in the shopping columns. Part of my job also is traveling around to the department stores, meeting executives and salespeople. I guess you'd call them personal appearances. I like to think it helps."

According to Fabergé president George Barrie, it helped very much. "When we purchased Fabergé seven years ago," Barrie said in 1970, "the company was doing $11 million in business. Last year it did about $140 million. I attribute some of that to Mr. G."

Grant had an office in the Fabergé town house, half a block from the Warwick Hotel, one of the few liabilities of the job. Since the town house was too near to ride to, it meant he had to duck autograph hunters whenever he walked back and forth. Also, he couldn't stand the street smells. "They stink," Grant said. "If I had my way, I'd spray the streets of New York with Fabergé!"

Grant functioned more like a senior statesman than pitchman. He never endorsed specific products, nor did he appear in advertisements or radio-TV commercials. When he went to department stores, he met the people who worked there and not the customers.

After causing a riot in the cosmetics department of Filene's in Boston, Grant made it a strict policy never to visit a store with advance publicity. "I don't like to do it because it stops department business and it's lost revenue for the store," he said. Some retailers disagreed. Neiman-Marcus in Dallas guaranteed it could sell a million dollars in Fabergé products in one day if Grant would appear there, but he declined.

The former "apostle of LSD" now advocated the use of new fragrances like "Xanadu," which promised "a whole new experience that starts with an X!" Sometimes Grant's former and current enthusiasms became intertwined. In London in 1971, loud disco music and psychedelic lighting effects from a "Xanadu" promotion going on in the next room inspired Grant to take a mind trip in the middle of an interview with the Manchester *Guardian.*

He suddenly started talking about a coming apocalypse, mentioning "an amalgamation of all knowledge" and a missile that would put male and female astronauts on the moon for the sole purpose of procreation. Then they and their offspring would forsake the planet earth and make it a kind of sun that would give life to the moon as the sun now does to the earth. The idea first came to him years before while taking LSD, he said.

Grant went on to express the view that life was cyclical, that everything happened before, that it would happen again, and that the Grand Canyon was where it all started. "The atomic missile bases are around there," he said. "I've flown over there many times. It's always struck me, and I see it more and more. The apocalypse will be in the same place again."

Asked if that would be the end of the earth, Grant said, "Well, it's the beginning of life somewhere else. Just as we give life to our progeny. I give life to my daughter, but I die off. She continues. She's my only ticket to eternity."

Grant invariably brought conversations around to his daughter, making it plain that his only really happy moments were those they spent together. "Jennifer is my life today," he said. "I plan around her, where she is, when I may have her. I'm not at all proud of my marriage record, but I have wanted a family for years. I finally have one in this child. I will do what I can for her."

What advice would he give her as he watched her grow? "I want Jennifer to give one man love and confidence and help," Grant said. "It has taken me years to learn that. I was playing a different game entirely. My wives and I were never one. We were competing. I will advise Jennifer to love someone and to be loved. Anything else she may get in her life is a bonus."

Causing endless complications in Grant's relationship with Jennifer was the state of war that existed between him and Dyan Cannon. They were constantly at loggerheads over custody rights and Jennifer's upbringing, usually landing in court when they could not settle their differences amicably.

Cannon was no longer the submissive, easily dominated person she'd been before the divorce. As her ex-husband had done with LSD, she claimed to have been "born again" through a psychiatric discipline known as Primal Therapy, in which she isolated herself in a padded room and screamed and pounded the walls until her tensions and hostilities were released. Her success with the technique eventually enabled her to resume her acting career. In 1971, she made four movies.

"It hasn't been easy getting over someone like Cary," Cannon said. "He's a highly aware man and he's affected my whole life. I've been told that a lot of men wouldn't dream of asking me out just because they know they can't compete with him. I was the heavy in our divorce, of course. Afterwards, people told me I'd never work again. I'd attacked America's sweetheart and I'd have to pay the price."

Cannon said that she lost a major role in a Broadway play because, as the producer told her, "Women just won't come to see you. You're the girl who treated Cary Grant badly."

Since Cannon traveled a great deal in her work, the necessity to obtain court permission before she could take Jennifer along became a major issue between the divorced parents. Whenever Cannon did get consent, Grant contended that it cut into the time he would have with Jennifer if she remained in California. He tried to get permanent custody, but the most that the court would give him was an occasional extra week or two.

Grant also couldn't understand why he had to pay Cannon her usual $1,500 a month child support during times Jennifer stayed with him. He wanted those periods cut to seven hundred fifty dollars a month, with the balance put into a special fund for Jennifer's education.

In April 1972, a Superior Court judge ruled that Jennifer had to stay with Grant in Los Angeles to continue her schooling while Cannon went to New York to make a film. But Grant was ordered to take Jennifer to visit her mother on two weekends, and also to let her see the three dogs that Cannon left in the care of friends.

Cannon passed up an assignment in England because the court wouldn't permit her to take Jennifer out of the United States. But she liked the script of *The Last of Sheila* too much to reject that offer and reluctantly left Jennifer with Grant while she went to France. Grant finally had to take Jennifer there anyway when she became homesick for her mother.

Later, Grant rented a house on Malibu Beach just two hundred feet away from the one occupied by Cannon and Jennifer. Claiming that his only reason for being there was to spy on them, Cannon filed a court order to have him evicted. "He stood in front of his house, on the beach, with binoculars trained on me and my guests," she said in the petition.

Grant counterclaimed that he rented the house not to torment Cannon but to make it easier for Jennifer to visit him every day. He didn't have to move. The judge ruled in his favor, but decreed that "each party is restrained from annoying, molesting or harassing the other."

Cannon also complained that Grant kept a separate wardrobe

for Jennifer and made her change all her clothes whenever she visited him because he didn't approve of her mother's choice of apparel. Cannon said that the practice had caused "conflicts" in Jennifer's mind.

The judge felt the matter was outside his jurisdiction, but did rule on two other controversial issues. In the case of her education, Jennifer had to attend Buckley, a well-established private school chosen by Grant, and not the unconventional, "advanced" one advocated by Cannon.

Grant wanted permanent custody of Jennifer's passport so that Cannon wouldn't be able to take her out of the country without his prior knowledge or consent. Cannon, of course, demanded it for the same reason. The court decided that Grant could keep the document in even-numbered years and Cannon in the odd-numbered. Neither could refuse to turn over the passport if the court gave one of them permission to travel with Jennifer at a time when it was in the other's possession.

The battles between Grant and Cannon were reminiscent of the ones he had witnessed between Barbara Hutton and Count Reventlow over their son. Ironically, a tragic ending to that conflict came just as Grant was experiencing similar difficulties. In July 1972, Lance Reventlow died in a plane crash at age thirty-six.

Since Grant had been like a second father to Lance, the death deeply affected him. Together with Lance's first wife, Jill St. John, he flew to Aspen, Colorado, in one of the Fabergé planes for the funeral service. After a requiem mass played by a rock orchestra, the widow, ex-Disney mouseketeer Cheryl Holdridge, scattered Lance's ashes to the wind off a mountainside. Barbara Hutton did not attend, having been estranged from her playboy son since giving him $25 million dollars on his twenty-first birthday.

Meanwhile, another major figure in Cary Grant's life was still going strong. By the time he visited his mother in Bristol in the summer of 1972, she had turned ninety-four, although she claimed to be only ninety-one.

Grant loved to tell the story of taking her for a ride in the country one afternoon. As they were driving along, Mrs. Leach turned to him and said, "Darling, you should do something about your hair."

"Why, what's wrong with it?" he asked.

"It's so white, dear. You should dye it. Everybody's doing it these days."

"Well, I'm not. Why should I?"

"If you must know, dear, because it makes *me* look old," Elsie Leach replied.

Although Grant had provided for his mother since she came out of Fishponds in the mid-1930s, she never let him feel any satisfaction over helping her. "Even in her later years, she refused to acknowledge that I was supporting her," Grant said. "One time —it was before it became ecologically improper to do so—I took her some fur coats. I remember she said, 'What do you want from me now?' and I said 'It's just because I love you,' and she said something like, 'Oh, you . . .' She wouldn't accept it."

Elsie Leach died in January 1973, at the age of ninety-five. Grant flew to Bristol as soon as he received the news, but in his customary manner he kept the details of the death and the funeral secret until it was too late for the press to make a fuss.

Even a grand old lady couldn't live forever, and Grant seemed resigned to the death. For all her lost years in the asylum, Elsie Leach still spent many more contented and comfortable ones thanks to her son's devotion and generosity.

Perhaps Grant was right when he said that life tended to repeat itself. Like his mother, he had also gotten a second start in life through his unexpected fatherhood, and Elsie's longevity offered him the hope that he, too, might live long enough to see his grandchildren.

Although Grant was very conscious of his age, he still rejected ceremonial homage to his elderliness. *Time* magazine once wanted to verify his age for a story and sent him a telegram that said: HOW OLD CARY GRANT? He immediately wired back: OLD CARY GRANT FINE. HOW YOU?

A few days before his seventieth birthday in January 1974, Grant took steps to avoid a worldwide outpouring of testimonials and eulogies. In an open letter published in *Daily Variety*, he stated that he was giving no birthday interviews. Being seventy, he said, was a thing totally without significance—to the world, to the movies or to himself.

As he entered his eighth decade, Grant continued to be active. Financier and Las Vegas kingpin Kirk Kerkorian appointed him to the board of directors of Western Airlines. He also became a board director and minority shareholder in an Irish real estate project called Shannonside, which proposed to build homes for affluent Irish-Americans seeking retirement in the Auld Sod. In addition, he worked in support of the World Wildlife Fund and Variety Clubs International, which aided various charities for crippled and underprivileged children.

Grant also kept busy with legal wrangling. Claiming that 20th Century-Fox used a clip of him from *Monkey Business* in a Marilyn Monroe documentary without his permission, he sued for a million dollars, but received ten dollars in an out-of-court settlement.

In 1973, Grant sued *Esquire* magazine for cutting his head from a twenty-five-year-old photograph and superimposing it on a model in a male fashion layout. Grant claimed the use of his likeness suggested an endorsement of the sweater worn by the model. Again he settled out of court, reportedly for a lifetime subscription to *Esquire*.

In the frigid December of 1974, Grant flew to New York and back to Los Angeles in the same day so that he could participate in the dedication of the Bristol Basin, a piece of Manhattan supporting the FDR Drive that was created from tons of World War II blitz rubble brought over from Bristol as ship ballast.

His dark California suntan, accentuated by his white hair and light camel's hair topcoat, made Grant look incredibly robust as he explained his sad personal reason for attending the public ceremony. "My Uncle Jack and his wife, Rose, and their children lived in a Georgian house in Bristol, which was their only protection against a blockbuster of a bomb which hit their street directly," he said in a short speech.

"When I returned to the site after the war, I composed a prayer. I hoped that humanity would conduct itself hereafter so that this kind of thing would never happen again. I add my hope today that it still will not."

In between all his other activities, Grant found time for a couple of new romantic relationships. While visiting a producer friend's office one day, he became attracted to a sultry-looking young woman sitting in the waiting room. "Who are you? Are you an actress?" he asked.

Twenty-year-old Vicki Morgan answered no, but that she wanted to be. Grant offered to help and invited her to have coffee or lunch with him sometime. An affair developed, but slowly, because Grant was extremely wary of getting involved with unknown starlets after the Cynthia Bouron scandal.

Whether or not Grant knew that Vicki Morgan also had an affair going on with department store tycoon Alfred Bloomingdale, he frequently invited her up to his house over a period of several months. Eventually, it became clear that they had nothing in common except a passing mutual infatuation.

Morgan told friends that Grant had been charming, but that she preferred the kinky and more exciting Bloomingdale, whom she later sued for palimony when that affair ended. Ironically, like Cynthia Bouron, Morgan also wound up being bludgeoned to death, by roommate Marvin Pancoast in 1983.

Grant formed a more lasting relationship with twenty-six-year-old Maureen Donaldson, an English free-lance reporter-photographer whom he met while attending a film festival in Sun Valley, Idaho. Once married to rock singer Dee Donaldson, she first came to the United States as a children's nanny, which explained part of her appeal for Grant. He was quite helpless dealing with the ordinary problems of an eleven-year-old daughter, but Donaldson came to his rescue on many an occasion.

Since she tended to dress like a hippie, Grant refused to take Donaldson places until she let him buy her some elegant clothes. One night they went to a formal dinner where Donaldson found herself seated next to football star Joe Namath, spokesman for Fabergé's "Brut." Noticing her British accent, Namath asked what brought her to Los Angeles. Jokingly or not, Donaldson replied, "Oh, I'm a tart. Cary Grant brought me."

Grant's affair with Donaldson lasted about four years. Every few months, she told gossip columnists that they were on the verge of getting married, but Grant just as quickly denied her statements. "I've been married four times. I'm obviously a failure at marriage. What went wrong? Who knows? Anyway, I'm not going to try again," he said on numerous occasions.

Since Grant had often turned down movie roles that required him to play the lover of much younger women, he seemed to be a bit embarrassed by his preference for them in real life. He usually tried to make a joke of it by quoting his friend George Burns: "At my age, it is increasingly more difficult to find any older ones."

Perhaps he was being overly sensitive. Such relationships were much more acceptable in the 1970s than in previous decades. His dalliance with Donaldson attracted little criticism from either the press or the public.

One of the reasons, of course, was that Cary Grant did not look like an old man. Even with the white hair, he could pass for mid-fifties, still moving with the quickness and poise of an acrobat. While he mentioned his age repeatedly, he offered it more as a boast than as an acknowledgment of really being a septuagenarian.

"Death?" he said when asked for his views on the subject. "Of course I think about it. But I don't want to dwell on it. I must say, I don't want to attract it too soon. When I was young, I thought they'd have the thing licked by the time I got to this age. I think the thing you think about when you're my age is how you're going to do it and whether you'll behave well. My mother lived to 95, and I want to live to at least 105 to see what happens. And I want to see my grandchildren."

Age still showed no signs of slowing him down. In 1975, Grant was elected to the board of directors of Metro-Goldwyn-Mayer, thanks to his credits as an actor-businessman and also to his close friendship with controlling stockholder Kirk Kerkorian. Since Fabergé now had a movie division of its own with Brut Productions, Grant's ties to the industry were as strong as ever. But he tried to stay in an advisory position, rather than getting directly involved in the actual production process.

At Fabergé, Grant had joined forces with British designer Mary Quant to develop a cosmetic kit for men, which would include such items as liquid makeup, two-tone face powder, eye shadow, mascara and lip gloss. The concept was considered daring even in the sexually liberated 1970s, but Grant had been toying with the idea since his early acting days.

Grant's endorsement of makeup for men revived some of the old rumors of homosexual tendencies. Many gays interpreted it as an old queen finally coming out of the closet to reveal "her" true nature. Whether it was or not, Grant would be the last one to say. The nearest he ever came to commenting on such rumors was in 1977, when writer Warren Hoge asked him about them during an interview for the New York *Times*.

Grant answered evasively, sounding as though he'd been prepared for just such a moment for years: "When I was a young and popular star, I'd meet a girl with a man and maybe she'd say something nice about me and the guy would say, 'Yeah, but I hear he's really a fag.' It's ridiculous, but they say it about all of us. Now in fact, that guy is doing me a favor. Number one, he's expressed an insecurity about the girl. Number two, he has provoked curiosity about me in her. Number three, that girl zeroes in on my bed to see for herself, and the result is that the guy has created the exact situation he wanted to avoid.

"Now on the other hand," Grant continued, "I know I have a happy husband and wife when a guy comes up to me and says, 'My wife just loves you,' and then I give her a little embrace and tell the guy kiddingly, 'Do forgive us.' Or a guy will come up to me and say 'See that girl over there? Please go over and whisper something to her or kiss her on the neck or put your arms around her.' Well, I'll do it because I know the guy trusts and loves that girl."

Grant stuck more to the point when questioned about his fabled wealth and miserliness. He described speculation about a twenty-five-million-dollar personal fortune as "nonsense" and "too much, by far." Besides, he noted, "One cannot really assess one's worth. That's hard for the fellow on salary to appreciate, but in business one only deals in paper."

To prove he wasn't a cheapskate, Grant said, "You could start by looking at my charity donations. Now, perhaps I've offended some people I wouldn't loan money to; they tend to be voluble. It's true I don't lead the life of a Frank Sinatra. But someone should ask the doormen and waiters I deal with. I pay my bills immediately, and a lot of big spenders don't. The fact that I have been reported to have so much money doesn't help either."

In March 1977, Cary Grant admirers held their breath as morning news programs issued a bulletin that the seventy-three-year-old megastar had entered a Santa Monica hospital for emergency surgery. Solicitude turned to amusement, however, when it turned out to be just for the repair of a groinal hernia and that Grant had stipulated some strange rules to the hospital authorities.

Registered under the name of Cary Robbins, he insisted that his true identity could not be revealed, nor could any surgery be performed on him in the presence of women. No female doctor, nurse, or attendant was to be allowed the chance to gaze upon his undraped body in the operating room. Whether it was just modesty or an inferiority complex can only be guessed at. Back in his hospital room, however, he permitted women to take care of him as long as they stepped outside when doctors came to examine him.

Grant caused more titters in 1977 when he lost steady companion Maureen Donaldson to a much younger movie heartthrob named Warren Beatty. It happened as the result of Beatty's attempt to coax Grant out of retirement by offering him a leading role in *Heaven Can Wait.*

Following a formula pioneered by Grant, Beatty was producing, co-directing and starring in a remake of the 1941 comedy-fantasy *Here Comes Mr. Jordan.* He wanted Grant for the part originally played by Claude Rains, that of a heavenly envoy who gives the dead hero a second chance at life. (James Mason finally got the assignment, marking at least the third time he had ended up with a Cary Grant reject.)

When Warren Beatty dropped by his house to discuss *Heaven Can Wait,* Grant said he wasn't interested. The fact that Dyan Cannon had already signed for another role in the film didn't seem to have any bearing on his decision. He told Beatty that life was short and that he didn't want to waste any of his remaining years in pursuits that no longer excited or amused him.

Beatty took the rejection graciously, which is more than might be said for his behavior after Grant asked Maureen Donaldson to walk the visitor back to his car. En route, Beatty asked Donaldson for a date. One tryst led to an affair, with Donaldson soon waving Grant cheerio and moving into Beatty's apartment at the Beverly Wilshire Hotel.

Whether it was maliciously intended or not, stealing a lover from Cary Grant must have been a challenge that a womanizer like Warren Beatty couldn't resist. The damage to Grant's pride also must have been considerable, especially after Maureen Donaldson told a gossip columnist that "the age difference was proving too much for Cary and me to handle."

Grant had a replacement for Donaldson waiting in the wings. The previous year, while attending a Fabergé trade show at the Royal Lancaster Hotel in London, he had become interested in a twenty-five-year-old brunette named Barbara Harris, who did public relations work for the hotel. Assigned to be Grant's publicist, she insisted on taking him around to appointments in her Mini automobile.

"My knees were up to my chin," he recalled. He could have

been chauffeured around in a Rolls-Royce, but he preferred to be with Barbara, whose refreshing unpretentiousness enchanted him.

"She introduced me to her friends and took me to little pubs with thatched roofs where we'd sit in a corner and Barbara would go up to the bar and order pints of mild and bitter for both of us," Grant said. He also became impressed by her devotion to her parents, who ran a dairy farm in Devon. The couple had once been in the colonial service in Tanganyika, where Barbara was born and grew up.

The romance developed slowly, since Barbara Harris was reluctant to leave England. Grant only saw her during business trips, so just her family and a few friends knew about it. The veil of secrecy was nearly broken, however, in February 1977, when Grant took Harris to Bristol to show her some of his childhood haunts and a fire broke out in their hotel.

It was early morning. When personnel started evacuating the guests, Cary Grant couldn't be found. But in the midst of the commotion, he and Harris suddenly turned up, having just returned from a late dinner with friends. To spare Harris embarrassment, Grant refused to identify her to reporters covering the scene. She ended up in front-page stories as "Cary Grant's mystery companion."

In 1978, after they'd known each other for two years, Grant finally persuaded Harris to quit her job and move to Los Angeles as his "lady-in-residence."

"I was absolutely terrified by the forty-seven-year age difference between us," Barbara Harris recalled. "Before I went, I thought—at great length—about the possibility of one day being without him. But I decided to go through with it because, otherwise, you don't enjoy the time you do have, which is extremely precious."

Once she made the move, she found her qualms disappeared instantly. "I've never thought of Cary as being older than I am," she said. "I think of us as being the same age because he has a wonderful, facile mind. In many ways he is far more alive than I because he's so interested and vibrant."

For the sake of appearances, Grant referred to Harris as his secretary, but it became obvious that the relationship went much deeper than that. As they started to be seen around Hollywood together, often with Jennifer in tow, the inevitable marriage rumors circulated, but were just as quickly denied.

"Cary is an old-fashioned man. He wants Jennifer and Barbara to get to know each other before he makes any decision that might be regretted later," a friend told Rona Barrett, probably at Grant's instigation.

Meanwhile, two of Grant's previous attempts at marriage and romance came back to haunt him. Sophia Loren published her autobiography, written in collaboration with A. E. Hotchner, in which she told the story of her experiences with Grant. As might be expected, Grant became outraged, telephoning Earl Wilson and other columnists to tell them, "I just can't believe that Sophia could exploit our friendship like this."

In rebuttal, Loren said, "When something as beautiful as that happens to two people, and a great deal of time has gone by, it shouldn't offend anyone."

A. E. Hotchner added a comment that wasn't in the book: "Sophia loved Cary the way she loved no one else. He was her romantic love. I think there may be ambivalence about her decision not to stay with him. Cary and Carlo Ponti are very different. Cary's urbane, not deep, and can make the person with him feel fantastic; but Carlo's somber, 100 percent involved in business, and leaves Sophia alone a lot."

On May 11, 1979, Cary Grant's second wife, Barbara Hutton, died of a heart attack at age sixty-six in her suite at the Beverly Wilshire Hotel, less than two miles from her ex-husband's home. While they hadn't seen each other in years, Grant and Hutton had frequently communicated by phone. Suffering numerous health problems and bordering on madness, she thought nothing of calling Grant in the middle of the night to complain that she was being kept prisoner by the lawyers and accountants who administered her dwindling fortune.

By the time of her death, Barbara Hutton had been married and divorced seven times. Despite a decade of reclusiveness, her obituary became front-page news all over the world. Cary Grant's only public comment was that "Barbara was really a very sweet girl. She could be very funny, and we had some wonderful times together." He did not attend the funeral, which was held in New York at Woodlawn Cemetery.

In August 1979, Grant did turn out for the funeral of Lord

Louis Mountbatten, who was assassinated by the Irish Republican Army. Grant's face looked tear-stained as he emerged from the hour-long service at Westminster Abbey in London.

While saying farewell to a longtime friend, Grant made a new one at a reception held afterward by the Royal Family. Mountbatten's nephew, the Duke of Edinburgh, introduced him to septuagenarian author Barbara Cartland, who told the septuagenarian movie star that she used Cary Grant as a model for some of the heroes in her romantic novels.

Cartland couldn't remember exactly which ones, since she'd written nearly two hundred overall. "She was all pink pearls and feathers," Grant said later. "I fell in love with her and we started a correspondence."

On a happier occasion, Grand attended Frank Sinatra's sixty-fifth birthday party at Caesars Palace in Las Vegas, held a year early in December 1979, so that NBC could videotape it for a special commemorating Sinatra's fortieth anniversary in show business. Seated at a stageside table, Grant found himself acting as stooge to impressionist Rich Little.

In the middle of his routine, Little marched over to Grant and in a perfect imitation of his voice said, "This man is too young to be Cary Grant. I don't believe it. But listen, if you really are Cary Grant—I'm a little skeptical—would you say something as Cary Grant for us?"

Grant asked, "What would you like me to say?"

Looking impressed, Rich Little said, "That was fair. Now could we hear your Burt Lancaster?" Grant's explosion of laughter could be heard in the farthest reaches of the room.

In 1980, Grant kept in the news via two controversies stemming from television, a medium he'd always avoided working in but one that an ex-wife said he spent too much time watching. As if he hadn't been annoyed enough by Sophia Loren's autobiography, he became incensed when he learned that NBC intended to make a three-hour TV adaptation of it.

Grant wanted to sue to stop the filming, or at least that portion including his involvement in Loren's life. The cooler head of his attorney prevailed, however, and they made an out-of-court settlement in which Grant reportedly received script approval plus $250,000 dollars for the right to use his name.

Publicly, however, Grant made it plain that he disapproved of the project. When asked whom he thought should portray him on the television screen, he snapped, "Who would want to?"

"Everyone would, Cary," Sophia Loren replied. "But in my book, no one can!" The part went to John Gavin, with Rip Torn as Carlo Ponti. Loren played herself except as a young woman, where Ritza Brown took her place.

In November 1980, Grant again blew his stack while watching Tom Snyder's late-hour NBC interview program "Tomorrow." When introducing that night's guest, Chevy Chase, Snyder compared him to other notable comedians of the past, including Cary Grant.

When Grant's name came up, Chevy Chase said, "He really was a great physical comic, and I understand he was a homo . . . What a gal!"

Needless to say, Cary Grant filed a ten-million-dollar suit for slander against Chevy Chase, claiming that his "masculine image" had been seriously damaged. The case was settled out of court after Chase apologized. He said that he only meant to parody people who used such words as "homo," but that the attempt went right over Grant's head.

"When I'm on something like the Snyder show," Chevy Chase said later, "I automatically fall into the way I like to be on TV—you know, rip it apart. That means break taboos, say things you feel, things that just happen to come out. But if people don't know you, don't know your style, then they wonder, 'Who the hell is this guy to say such things?'"

But that didn't end the controversy. In the wake of it, a homosexual magazine called *In Touch* facetiously named Cary Grant Heterosexual of the Month. Underneath a photograph of Grant and Randolph Scott breakfasting together during their roommate days, the magazine's editors noted how important a "masculine image" must be to a man who was an executive of a perfume company and had four failed marriages.

Not helping Grant's image, *In Touch* added, was a reference to him in a book called *Christianity, Social Tolerance and Homosexuality.* According to that tome, the first publicly recorded use of the word "gay" in a homosexual context was by Cary Grant in *Bringing Up Baby.* In a scene in the screwball comedy, Grant said "I've gone gay" to explain his running around in a woman's dress.

Apart from the slander suit itself, Grant never made any public comment about the Chevy Chase incident.

In November 1978, he seemed preoccupied with the presidential election and thrilled by the victory of his friend Ronald Reagan.

"He's going to make a fine President—if they let him," Grant said. "I think he'll bring back a sense of values, of decency, to America. That's what the people want."

Later that month, Grant and Barbara Harris went to England to visit her recently widowed mother. Talking to a reporter who cornered them at Heathrow Airport, Grant turned lightly defensive about his relationship with Harris, but without taking offense at the question.

"Will we marry?" he said. "I don't know. I haven't got a crystal ball. We're both unconventional people. So who knows?"

Grant touched momentarily on mortality. "It gets scary. All the stars I know are dying. There was Mae West. And George Raft. Steve McQueen. The other day Jimmy Stewart had to go into the hospital. I told him, 'Get out quick. I don't want you popping off.' Ah well, it happens to all of us. For whom the bell tolls," he said mock-pathetically.

"Not you," interrupted Barbara Harris. "You'll go on forever!"

20

The Show Must Go On

Cary Grant and Barbara Harris were married on April 15, 1981. A few months later, they filed a ten-million-dollar libel suit against the *National Enquirer* over an article which said that Harris forced Grant to marry her by threatening to leave him if he didn't. She allegedly became increasingly embarrassed by their live-in relationship, resenting the fact that they were the only unmarried couple among their circle of friends.

Grant himself told a different story. "I discovered that if you had been together for three years, you don't need a marriage license. You can be married by a judge and keep it very secret," he said. "I thought about it, and thought about it. Then I went to my daughter, Jennifer, who's now a lovely girl of fifteen and has grown very close to Barbara. I said to her, 'Look here, how would you feel if I asked Barbara to marry me? I'm getting on, I need her, and we get on so well together."

Noticing Jennifer's eyes turning misty, Grant thought, " 'Oh, my God, she's going to cry. She thinks I'm doing the wrong thing.' She did cry, but only because she thought it was marvelous. I said to her, 'For goodness' sake, don't you say anything to Barbara, because I might not have the courage to ask her.' "

When Grant eventually broached the subject with Harris, "We talked about my age, of course, and how it would affect our relationship," he said. "We talked over everything for days. We explored everything—what would come out of it, my probable demise before her, what effect it would have on her. All these matters were taken into consideration. I am absolutely delighted it was all my doing, all my idea, and of course, it has worked out marvelously well. Barbara is a lovely girl, very clever, confident. She knows exactly what she wants, and I like that in a woman."

His new wife bridged the age gap between Jennifer and himself, Grant said. "Barbara knows how Jennifer thinks, and she stops me worrying so much about how worrying it is to have a teenage daughter."

Cary Grant's fifth wedding took place in his Beverly Hills living room, with only Jennifer, Grant's lawyer and his wife, the judge and his wife, and two servants as witnesses. Mrs. Grant prepared the wedding breakfast of avocado soup, spinach salad, king crab, chocolate mousse pie and banana ice cream. "She's a marvelous cook," her husband said.

The wedding didn't become known to the public until ten days later, after the Grants attended a celebration in honor of the twenty-fifth anniversary of Prince Rainier and Princess Grace, which took up a full weekend at Frank Sinatra's closely guarded compound in Palm Springs. Someone among the scores of guests told a reporter about a party for the newlywed Cary Grants that took place within the larger celebration.

After the news broke, the Grants turned down interview requests from all over the world. "Everyone, for some strange reason, wants to talk to us about our marriage," Grant said. "I don't know why people bother with me. It's years since I was in a film. I'll never be in one again. I suppose I must remind them of their happy youth."

The nearest that reporters could get to the Grants was through his new mother-in-law in Devon, England, who revealed that her daughter ditched a local beau when she went to live with Grant in 1978.

"Barbara told me it was the best thing she'd ever done in her life," Lesley Harris said. "I know there's a vast difference in their ages, but Barbara was always impatient with the young men she used to go out with. She's always been attracted to older men. So when she told me she was in love with Cary, I wasn't surprised.

Mrs. Harris added that "Cary is an incredible man. He is a bundle of energy. They both are. I can't keep up with either of them. They are so obviously happy together. It wouldn't matter to her whether he was a dustman provided she loved him."

The seventy-seven-year-old "silver-haired epitome of elegance" was nearly a half-century older than his wife. The press put "Ageless Cary" in the May-and-December group that also included Fred Astaire and George Burns. The previous year, eighty-one-year-old Astaire had married thirty-eight-year-old jockey Robyn Smith. Widower Burns, eighty-five, frequently dated women sixty years his junior.

According to a noted British psychiatrist, such behavior was not unusual for men of advanced age. Dr. Bernard Camber said that cases of old men surrounding themselves with young women had been documented since the Old Testament. Dr. Camber, who was nearly seventy himself, discussed the condition humorously: "If an old man can run the London Marathon, he can easily cope with a young woman."

Grant seemed to be coping well. In an interview with the New York *Times* just two weeks before the wedding, he said: "I find I respond most to someone's trust. It's a commitment I understand. Currently, I've put my trust in quite a nice young woman. But I don't ever wish to be young again, even if my vocabulary is slowly diminishing.

"If I could wish for one thing, it would be to be sexually younger. But I can console you with one fact. As you age, the desire remains, but it's not as strong, nor is the emotion that goes with it. So you're free to do more useful things. You see there's one thing that can't ever be ignored. There is so little time. I just try to do the best I can. It may not be great in other people's eyes, but I think it's pretty good."

In May 1981, Grant confronted a tape recorder and gave a rare glimpse into his private world. With his new wife sitting beside him to fill in memory gaps and to curb his tendency to meander, he tried to describe a typical day in his seventy-seventh year.

"I suffer from insomnia," Grant said. "Always have. I usually wake around three and read for an hour or so. Never fiction. If it's not true, what's the point of it? I never was interested in the story lines of my movies—just the business interest. Even before I cut my own I always had a good percentage. Do you know I'm still getting a nice return on *To Catch a Thief*? Marvelous deal there.

"People still send me scripts," he continued, "but at the moment I'd rather read a book by Louis Nizer. Brilliant lawyer. It's a great comfort to read about some other sucker's cases since I'm always involved in law suits myself. I have also finally caught up with James Herriot. Wonderful storyteller.

"I probably drop off about four and I wake again between six-thirty and seven. I only take sleeping tablets if we've been traveling and I've got jet lag. My houseman leaves a tray outside our bedroom door with an orange, not peeled or depipped but sliced into four equal parts. I teeth off the flesh from the skin. Marvelous. And I drink a half demitasse of coffee. I probably drink eight half demitasses of coffee throughout the morning. Much as I like coffee, I can't drink too much at one time."

Grant said that "If my daughter Jennifer is staying with us, I have to get up and dress to drive her to school. We leave at 7:15, arrive at 7:45. When she's staying with her mother and if I'm not going any place, I probably spend the morning, if not the entire day, in pajamas and robe.

"I have a fireproof vault in my house which I use as an office. It contains all the important papers of my life. Correspondence about my daughter's school. Details of my marriages and divorces. Letters from many marvelous people I've been lucky enough to know. I'm not collecting papers for my autobiography. For one thing, I'm much keener on living now than writing about the past. For another, nobody is ever truthful about his own life. There are always ambiguities. Deeply unsatisfactory. I'd rather not be guilty of that."

Grant's male secretary arrived at nine and they went through the mail, "having to refuse a helluva lot of requests to open this or attend to that," he said. "I have a few letters about my business interests. I'm a director of Fabergé and MGM. And I'm connected with a museum and with a racecourse. I do most of my business on the phone. I go to board meetings, but I've no illusions about why I'm there. It's always for my public relations ability.

"I've never understood why people are surprised at an actor taking to business. If an actor can get three million bucks for ten weeks' work, he's no dope where business is concerned. Picasso was the greatest businessman I ever knew. Eight dollars worth of paint and a bit of canvas and if he said he'd let you have it for "$350,000, you said, 'Hold it right there while I run round to the bank."

Most mornings, Grant conferred with his attorney of forty years, Stanley Fox. "He sometimes comes out to the house and we might have lunch on the terrace," Grant said. "In the afternoon— oh, what do I *do* in the afternoon? Just more of the same, I guess. Certainly I don't crook a finger to keep fit. I take no exercise whatsoever. Barbara thinks I'm fit now because I started life as an acrobat."

The Grants lived a very quiet life. "We have a wonderful couple who look after us, the houseman and his wife. Both marvelous cooks, so we have meals at home. We watch television sometimes. More often we play cards. 'Spite and Malice.' Marvelous game. It's a great way of getting rid of all your hostilities. We have a few close friends. We see a lot of the Gregory Pecks—more of them than anybody else.

"We go to bed sometimes at eight, sometimes at twelve," Grant said. "In my view there's nothing worth doing once it's got dark. Who needs nightclubs? They're just full of sick people smoking, drinking. I can't stand cigarette smoke. Won't have anybody near me who smokes.

"I don't feel my age," he added. "Not often, anyway. I don't have a magic formula. I used to have a vodka before dinner, but I've given that up. I still have a glass of wine with a meal. If I have a secret at all, it's that I do just what I want. I think that stops the aging process as much as anything."

Late in 1981, Cary Grant fans rejoiced when *Variety* announced that he would make his first movie in fifteen years. Producers Howard Koch, Jr., and Gene Kirkwood were reported close to signing him to play the Russian police inspector in the film version of *Gorky Park,* with Dustin Hoffman as co-star.

The rumor became so widespread that Grant finally had to issue a denial: "It's not so. Gee, I can't even read a book on an airplane without some people jumping to conclusions. I'm perfectly happy with my business interests and have no desire to return to films." It turned out that a gossip monger had seen Koch's father presenting Grant with a copy of *Gorky Park* at Hollywood Park Race Track, where both men served on the board of directors!

Well on the way toward his eightieth birthday, Grant seemed content to remain just a husband, father and traveling business executive, but the world wouldn't let him. The prestigious Kennedy Center Honors for Achievement in the Performing Arts became the first of numerous tributes that went on for the rest of his life. Incredibly, except for that special Oscar in 1970, the peerless Hollywood star had never received a major award of any kind up to then!

Even for Cary Grant, that weekend of December 4, 1981, was extraordinary. On Friday, he and Barbara Grant flew to Washington for an intimate dinner at the White House with his longtime friends Ronald and Nancy Reagan.

On Saturday, the Grants were joined by fifteen-year-old Jennifer Grant, on weekend leave from her boarding school in Monterey, California. The presentation of the Kennedy Center medals, which also went to actress Helen Hayes, pianist Rudolf Serkin, choreographer Jerome Robbins and band leader Count Basie, took place that evening before members of the honorees' families at a private dinner in the Benjamin Franklin Room at the State Department.

At a White House reception hosted by President and Mrs. Reagan the following afternoon, Christmas wreaths festooned each window, fires crackled on the hearth and an enormous mistletoe ball hung in the grand foyer. The Kennedy Center honorees and scores of celebrities who traveled to Washington for the occasion nibbled on roast tenderloin of beef and king crab. Cary Grant and Audrey Hepburn turned all heads as they hugged and kissed in greeting.

President Reagan told the gathering: "We are here to honor five Americans. We honor them in our capital because they have done more than simply entertain us through a large part of the century—they have made us proud to be Americans. It is our spirit they captured when they danced—our hopes they played out on stage and screen. Because of their talent, our imaginations have been set free."

On Sunday evening, the weekend reached its zenith with a glittering two-hour extravaganza at Kennedy Center Opera House, which CBS-TV taped for a Christmas special. As Grant and the other honorees sat in box seats next to the President and First Lady—their medals hanging from their necks with garlands of red, white and blue ribbons—friends and colleagues saluted their lives and artistry with verbal and visual bouquets.

Introducing a segment of scenes from Grant's most memorable films, Rex Harrison said "The fact is, there is but one Cary Grant, the original, the supremely gifted man whom we honor tonight for a magnificent career on the screen."

Sitting next to Grant were his wife and daughter. Unofficially, it was Jennifer's public debut, since Grant had deliberately kept his only child out of the limelight since infancy as a safeguard against kidnapping. She had grown into a willowy, long-haired beauty, with her father's dark eyes and her mother's voluptuous mouth.

Early the next morning, Grant took Jennifer to Dulles Airport so that she could catch a flight back to California. Thanks to the three-hour time differential, she didn't miss a day of school, the condition that Dyan Cannon set down when she gave her consent for Jennifer to spend the weekend with her father. He was all too willing to comply, since he and his ex-wife shared a mutual concern for their daughter's welfare. Over the years, they had taken her out of several private schools after learning of drug-pushing and sexual promiscuity on campus.

The reason Grant didn't accompany Jennifer back to California himself was that he had travel plans in the opposite direction. Hours later, he and Barbara jetted from Washington to Monaco to visit with Prince Rainier and Princess Grace. Grant took it all in stride, for he'd been rubbing elbows with presidents and royalty for the better part of his life. But for his young wife it seemed like a fairy tale come true.

Amusingly, shortly after the Washington D.C. gala, the Hollywood Women's Press Club voted Grant its annual Louella Parsons Award for "presenting the best image of Hollywood to the world." While no one could say he didn't deserve it, Grant's lifetime loathing of gossip columnists—especially Louella Parsons and Hedda Hopper—made it seem rather inappropriate. Since the recipient happened to be in Monaco at the time, Phyllis Diller accepted in his behalf.

Hollywood soothsayers predicted that Grant would receive the highly coveted American Film Institute Award for lifetime achievement in 1982, but instead it went to one of his former directors, Frank Capra. Grant claimed later that he refused the award that year and on numerous other occasions because of the ninety-minute TV tribute that went along with it.

"It seemed to me like they wanted to use me to boost ratings and to attract advertisers. Also, I have an affiliation with Fabergé, and it would have been in bad taste for me to appear on a program that was likely to have commercials for its products or those of its competitors," Grant said.

In May 1982, the international show-business fraternity known as the Friars Club honored Cary Grant as Man of the Year, with a dinner gala in the Grand Ballroom of New York's Waldorf-Astoria Hotel that raised two hundred fifty thousand dollars for charities of Grant's designation. Unlike the dignified Kennedy Center affair, the evening stressed sentiment and lighthearted fun, but without the ribaldry of the famous Friars Club roasts. At Grant's request, there were no references to past marriages, Sophia Loren, Randolph Scott or LSD.

George Burns claimed to have been introduced to Grant by Abraham Lincoln's widow. Red Buttons remembered taking Grant and Ray Charles to a performance by Marcel Marceau. Rich Little did an imitation of dialogue between Grant and Sam Jaffe as the dying Gunga Din. Gregory Peck tried to be a comedian by cracking that "Cary is everyone's idea of what a man ought to be: talented, sophisticated and rich."

Peggy Lee, who hadn't worked in six years because of poor health, flew to New York especially to sing "Mr. Wonderful" to her longtime friend. Tony Bennett performed Grant's all-time favorite song, "It Amazes Me," written by Cy Coleman and Carolyn Leigh. Composer Coleman also sang and played his first big commercial hit, "Pass Me By," written for Grant's *Father Goose*.

Toastmaster Frank Sinatra kept calling Grant "this Cockney baby" and talked about his "international signature of style and charm." The highlight of the evening was Sinatra singing "The Most Fabulous Man in the World," a Sammy Cahn rewrite of Rodgers and Hart's "The Most Beautiful Girl in the World."

Sinatra's fervent performance got Cary Grant going: he couldn't stop crying. Wiping his eyes as he stepped to the speaker's podium, he said, "I tear up easily. I cry at great talent . . . art . . . music . . . even great baseball games. To indulge in one's emotions is a privilege allowed to the elderly."

Nineteen eighty-two also brought tears of sorrow. Within a few weeks of each other in August and September, Grant lost two of his favorite leading ladies, who also happened to be among his dearest friends. Ingrid Bergman's death at sixty-seven after a long battle with cancer came as no surprise, but Grant was inconsolable when he learned the news.

Upsetting him even more was the shocking and totally unexpected death of fifty-two-year-old Princess Grace of Monaco in an auto crash. Ironically, the accident occurred among the same twisting mountain roads of the Riviera where Grant and the ex-actress had filmed scenes for *To Catch a Thief* twenty-eight years earlier.

When Grant and his wife attended the funeral in Monaco on September 18, a French TV reporter rather cruelly pointed out that the American film star seemed younger than Prince Rainier, who was actually twenty years his junior. Stooped and white-haired, the bereaved monarch often stumbled as he walked in the funeral procession. Grant looked as robust as ever, but also deeply grieved. As he left the cathedral after the service, he gripped Barbara Grant's arm for support.

As a result of Princess Grace's death and the injuries of her daughter Stephanie, Grant became extremely concerned for his own sixteen-year-old Jennifer, who had just started to drive. For a time, he prohibited her from using the little Honda that he had given her as a birthday present. But his wife finally convinced him that he had no more cause to worry than other parents with children that age.

Grant's biggest problem concerning Jennifer—the constant battles with her mother—appeared to have ended. "I've been healed of all the hurts," Dyan Cannon said at the time. "I love him again. Now we're friends, thank God . . . It wasn't easy. Believe me, it took a tremendous effort, but we had to work something out for Jennifer's sake, so that she can grow up without feeling a continued animosity between the two people who love her the most.

"Both of us have seen so many instances of people separating and the child's being torn—the father coming into the house to visit and the mother hurriedly leaving the room. This isn't the kind of atmosphere in which we want our daughter to grow up."

Grant still resided in the hilltop house on Beverly Grove Drive that he bought after his divorce from Barbara Hutton in 1945. For years, including the time he lived elsewhere with Dyan Cannon and the baby, he kept it in a semifinished condition that resembled a railroad station waiting room. He drove Los Angeles realtors batty "auditioning" hundreds of possible replacements, never finding one that suited him or his wallet better.

But fatherhood and a fifth marriage finally caused him to remodel so that the house would be more compatible with the expensive and sumptuous residences that neighbored it.

"One day," Grant related, "the head carpenter came over to me. He hemmed and hawed around for the longest time. Finally, I asked him, 'What's on your mind?' 'Mr. Grant,' he said, 'I hope you will forgive me for saying this, and I don't want to sound impertinent, but I wanted you to know that all of us working on your house just feel that for a man of your age to be putting on additions shows one hell of a lot of courage.' "

The house itself became all white and modern, with natural woods predominating in the interior. One whole wing was reserved for Jennifer Grant, who got a luxurious apartment of her own for her visits with her father. Out beyond the swimming pool and sloping lawns, Barbara Grant tried to cultivate a typical English garden, despite frequent invasions by deer and other wildlife from the surrounding woods.

But Chez Grant's best feature remained unchanged except for time—a spectacular view over all Los Angeles from downtown to the Pacific Ocean. The Grants loved nothing better than to sit on their flagstone terrace in the late afternoon and watch the sun set.

Cary Grant might have spent the rest of his life as a contented homebody had it not been for a chance happening in October 1982. As a favor to a sick friend, comedian Steve Allen, Grant agreed to fill in for him one night as a celebrity lecturer at DeAnza Community College in Cupertino, about forty miles from San Francisco. Before a packed house of students, faculty and local residents, he spent two hours answering questions on the stage of the 2,500-seat Flint Center.

Grant told the audience that he had agreed to the atypical appearance because "I'm an inquisitive fellow and I wanted to see what it was like. My mind isn't as agile as it once was, and I've lost a lot of my vocabulary. But what the hell . . ."

Grant said he was "too happy living to write my memoirs. All people want to know is who did you ever sleep with and when." But the seventy-eight-year-old retired actor did plenty of verbal reminiscing about himself and his friends and colleagues.

When asked to name his favorite film, Grant balked. "What

the devil do you mean by favorite? Do you mean the one in which I had the best part? The one that did the best at the box office? The one in which I had the happiest time on the set? Or the one in which I most admired the writing, or my fellow performers, or my director?"

But Grant had no problem in naming his own least favorite performance. "It was in *Arsenic and Old Lace,* he said. "And you know, I *told* Frank Capra, 'I simply cannot do that kind of comedy.' And Frank said, 'Of course you can, old boy,' and I did it and I overplayed it terribly. Jimmy Stewart would have been wonderful in that part."

What, then, was the secret of playing comedy, a student wanted to know. "Doing it as naturally as you can, under the most unnatural circumstances," Grant said. "And film comedy is the most difficult of all. At least on the stage you know right away whether you are getting laughs or not. But making a movie, you have no way of knowing. So you try to time the thing for space and length and only hope that, when it plays in a movie house months later, you've done the timing right. It's difficult, and it takes experience."

Grant praised Grace Kelly as his favorite leading lady. "All of them were a delight to know and to work with," he said, "but Grace was not only astonishingly beautiful, but she also had that incredible serenity. That woman had total relaxation, absolute ease—she was totally *there.* Both she and Hitchcock were Jesuit trained, maybe that had something to do with it."

Of Mae West, he noted, "She wanted to be responsible for everything. She never told the truth in her life. She dealt in a fantasy world; the heavy makeup she wore was one sign of her insecurity. We were all very careful with her."

Grant described his distinctive manner of speaking as a combination of an English upbringing and then coming to America as a teenager. When John F. Kennedy was President, he recalled, JFK and brother Bobby often telephoned him, sometimes interrupting his lunch. "They would ask me to talk," he recalled. "They said they wanted to hear Cary Grant's voice."

About his long friendship with Howard Hughes, Grant said, "Howard was the most restful man I've ever been with. Sometimes we'd sit for two hours and never say a word to each other. We certainly weren't at all alike—maybe that's why we liked each other so much. I never saw him in his last years. Not too long before he died, we happened to be staying at the same hotel in London. One day I took the lift to his floor and waved hello at the TV camera that guarded the entrance to his suite. I hope he saw me on the monitor."

At the close of the evening, Grant received a tremendous standing ovation. That might have been the end of it except that a correspondent for *Variety* happened to be in the audience and filed a glowing account that landed on the front page of the so-called "Bible of Show Business." Within hours of publication, Grant was inundated with phone calls and telegrams inviting him to repeat the performance. Promoter Don King said he could get him one hundred thousand dollars a night at New York's Madison Square Garden and the Houston Astrodome.

But at seventy-eight, Cary Grant needed neither the money nor the glory. What he did need, however, was to prove to his much younger wife and teenage daughter that he wasn't ready for the Motion Picture Retirement Home.

"Cary dreaded growing old and decrepit in the eyes of Barbara and Jennifer," said a close friend. "He told me often, 'Jennifer needs a young father and Barbara needs a young husband. I'm not going to let them down by lying around the house like an old man. I'll keep active till I drop."

After a lot of thought and planning, he devised a ninety-minute one-man show called *A Conversation With Cary Grant,* which shrewdly protected him from his two main fears about such an endeavor. He would not appear in any big cities where the press might waylay him with embarrassing questions or "review" him unkindly. To prove that he wasn't doing it for the money, all proceeds, except for his traveling expenses, would go to the college or charitable organization sponsoring his appearance.

Aided by his wife, who took care of booking arrangements and public relations, Grant worked out a program that started with clips from his most notable films, including *Bringing Up Baby, The Philadelphia Story, Suspicion, Notorious* and *To Catch a Thief.* The montage concluded with a scene of Frank Sinatra presenting Grant with his honorary Oscar. At that point, a spotlight hit stage right and the real-life Cary Grant strolled out, looking not much different than he had in 1970.

It was an entrance calculated to cause a standing ovation, and it always did. While the cheering went on, Grant proceeded to perch himself comfortably on a plain wooden kitchen stool and announced that he would be happy to answer general questions. "Ah, General Questions, I knew him well," he would sigh, grinning and cocking an eyebrow.

Since Grant permitted no advertising or promotion beyond ten miles of each appearance, only he and Mrs. Grant knew the exact number he made, but all were in places like Texarkana, Texas; Joliet, Illinois; Red Bank, New Jersey; and Sarasota, Florida. In light of Grant's long retirement from acting and his basic shyness, many were puzzled by his sudden decision to "go public." Bob Hope believed "it satisfied the ham in him; he wanted to do something." Gregory Peck said "It was a return to his roots. He'd played many of the same towns and theatres when he was Archie Leach."

Longtime friend Henry Gris claimed that Grant "loved the intimacy of the smaller setting, the rapport with his audience. It was a formula that was very satisfying to him. If someone asked a question that was more personal than he cared to answer, Cary knew how to get out of it charmingly. He was a master of turning the tables. He would say 'Well, how would you feel if I were to ask you that question?' "

In 1984, Cary Grant turned eighty. It was the year that his daughter entered Stanford University and also the time of his first serious illness since that near-fatal attack of hepatitis thirty-five years earlier.

In October, following a week of dizzy spells and frequent headaches, Grant checked himself into Cedars–Sinai Medical Center in West Hollywood. The outcome of tests: a mild stroke. Doctors advised him to give up his hectic schedule of personal appearances and business directorships.

Grant refused to heed the warning. As soon as he started feeling better, he picked up where he had left off. Besides touring the lecture circuit, Grant and his wife turned up at all the big functions. They attended a gala for President Reagan at the Century Plaza Hotel in Los Angeles, flew to Dallas for a charity benefit for the Princess Grace Foundation, and to Monaco for the Red Cross Ball. They were regulars at the Hollywood Park Race Track and Dodgers baseball games.

"I know I'm overdoing it, going out night after night and

traveling the country," Grant told Henry Gris. "It totally drains me at times, but I'm not going to stop. I have to show Barbara and Jennifer I'm still young at heart."

In April 1986, Grant and his wife celebrated their fifth wedding anniversary by renewing their marriage vows. "Cary was far fitter at eighty-two than most sixty-year-olds, but at his age they both knew he could die anytime," said mother-in-law Lesley Harris. "Cary wanted to show Barbara how much he loved her."

Six months later came that fateful trip to Davenport, Iowa. At 2:45 A.M. on November 30, the heartbroken widow accompanied Grant's body back to Los Angeles on a private Learjet sent by his friend, Kirk Kerkorian.

Within hours, the news media responded so overwhelmingly that veteran show-business columnist Radie Harris said "I can't ever remember when an entire world was so grief-stricken as over the sudden death of Cary Grant. I have never seen so much coverage or in so many different languages."

President Ronald Reagan expressed his regret in a statement issued on Air Force One as he flew back to Washington from a stay at his California ranch. "Nancy and I are very saddened by the death of our very dear and longtime friend Cary Grant," Reagan said. "He was one of the brightest stars in Hollywood and his elegance, wit and charm will endure forever on film and in our hearts. We will always cherish the memory of his warmth, his loyalty and his friendship, and we will miss him deeply."

Tributes poured forth from friends and former co-workers. "Cary was one of the greats, in the same league with Gable and Tracy," said George Burns. "He was a consummate actor and a complete professional," James Stewart added.

"What Cary did, he did better than anyone ever has or, perhaps ever will," said Charlton Heston. "The only comfort we can take is we still have him on film. He was surely as unique as any film star and as important as anyone since Charlie Chaplin."

Loretta Young described Grant as *the* elegant man." Alexis Smith considered him the best movie actor that ever was: "There's a term 'romance with the camera,' and I doubt anybody had as great a romance with the camera as Cary did." Eva Marie Saint called him "the most handsome, witty, and stylish leading man both on and off the screen." Polly Bergen said "We have just lost the man who showed Hollywood and the world what the word 'class' really means. He was the one star that even other stars were in awe of."

The New York *Times,* which rarely devotes editorials to Hollywood personalities, made an exception in his case: "Cary Grant was not supposed to die. Sure, we all knew he was getting on—he had the silver hair to prove it—and that his last movie was 20 years behind him. But die? Never. Cary Grant was supposed to stick around, our perpetual touchstone of charm and elegance and romance and youth . . .

"Like Humphrey Bogart and James Cagney, his great contemporaries, he is easy to imitate and impossible to replace. He also was—is—easy to love. Yes, the haircut is perfect and so is the suit and that cleft in the chin is heaven's thumbmark. But they don't explain why three generations of women had crushes on him. Apart from being gorgeous, the adjective of many women's choice, he is also a friend. Cary Grant's promise is of more than one glorious night; it's of a lifetime of laughter."

Inevitably, medical second-guessing suggested that Grant might have survived if he had been hospitalized promptly. "Obviously, the earlier you start working with someone, the greater the chance of saving his life," said Dr. William Castelli, medical director of Harvard's Framingham Heart Study. "If Grant had high blood pressure—and 210 over 130 is very high—which was causing the stroke, and had he been brought into the hospital to have the blood pressure lowered, it could have saved his life.

"The sad thing about this is that here is a man who—regardless of his age—was doing very well and had a lot to live for, and he passed it up."

The day after Grant's death, police had to barricade the road leading to his Beverly Hills home to prevent the press and public from annoying the stream of celebrities who came to express condolences to the widow and daughter. Dyan Cannon was the first to arrive, followed by Frank Sinatra, Gregory Peck, Elizabeth Taylor, Irene Dunne, James Stewart, Jennifer Jones and numerous others. Robert Wagner looked the most grief-stricken, perhaps because of his awareness that Grant died on the fifth anniversary of Natalie Wood Wagner's accidental drowning.

In accordance with Grant's wishes, no funeral service of any kind—even for the family—was held. Following cremation of the body, the ashes were returned to Barbara Grant. What she did with them is unknown, but rumor has it they were scattered to the wind in the hills surrounding the Grant residence.

The probate of Cary Grant's will revealed that he bequeathed the bulk of his fortune to his wife and daughter. Although the document only described it as "in excess of $10,000," Hollywood insiders estimated it to be between forty and sixty million dollars.

The widow received their home and all its furnishings, artworks and automobiles. Grant also specified that half of what remained of the estate after taxes and miscellaneous bequests should be divided equally between Mrs. Grant and Jennifer Grant. Jennifer's half would be administered through a special trust fund, reportedly to make it difficult for Dyan Cannon to touch any of it.

Despite his tightwad reputation, Grant left $150,000 to trusted employees, $50,000 to the Motion Picture and Television Relief Fund and $25,000 to Variety Clubs International.

One of Grant's more unusual bequests was $10,000 to Dr. Mortimer Hartman, who introduced him to LSD. All of Grant's clothing, jewelry and personal effects went to longtime attorney Stanley Fox for distribution to family and friends, including Frank Sinatra and Kirk Kerkorian. Princess Caroline of Monaco received a trunk full of Grace Kelly memorabilia that Grant had collected over the years.

During his lifetime, Cary Grant often told interviewers that the epitaph on his tombstone would read "He was lucky, and he knew it." That turned out otherwise, since he has no final resting place except in the memories of those who love and admire him.

His monument will be his seventy-two movies, the best of which are all safely preserved for posterity. Somewhere, someplace, right at this very moment, Cary Grant is alive and well on some theatre or TV screen, kissing Ingrid Bergman and being kissed by Grace Kelly, conning Katharine Hepburn, laughing with Irene Dunne, razzing Rosalind Russell, succumbing to Mae West and living happily ever after with Deborah Kerr. Time and space and death are an illusion compared to that unfading reality.

ACKNOWLEDGMENTS

I am extremely grateful to the people who contributed information and a frame of reference for this biography. Listed alphabetically, they include George Barrie, Ralph Bellamy, Joan Bennett, Pandro S. Berman, Janet Blair, the late Frederick Brisson, Irving Caesar, Dane Clark, the late George Cukor, Tony Curtis, Jean Dalrymple, Doris Day, Stanley Donen, the late John Engstead, Eddie Fisher, Joan Fontaine, Truman Gaige, Stewart Granger, Audrey Hepburn, the late Alfred Hitchcock, the late Edith Head, the late June Hillman, Glenda Jackson, Garson Kanin, Deborah Kerr, Stanley Kramer, Peggy Lee, Leo Lerman, George Lloyd, Myrna Loy, Joseph L. Mankiewicz, the late David Niven, the late Walter Plunkett, Hal Roach, Adela Rogers St. Johns, the late Arthur Schwartz, Irene Selznick, Melville Shavelson, George Winslow, Fay Wray, Jerome Zerbe. Numerous others requested anonymity but know who they are.

Thanks also go to the staffs of the following research centers for their splendid assistance: the Performing Arts Library at Lincoln Center, New York; the Academy of Motion Picture Arts and Sciences Library, Los Angeles; the British Film Institute Library, London.

For their encouragement and good cheer, my thanks to George Bester, Jim Broaddus, Bob Christie, Barry Conley, Nick Cunningham, Roberta Harris Dana, Vladimir Drousz, Barbara and Norman Flicker, Eva Franklin, Lavinia Hallman, Wilbur Harris, Alan Hobbs, Hy Hollinger, Marilyn and Phil Isby, Edith and Dave Martorana, Barry McGoffin, Christina Munro Peters, Derek Pyper, Stevie Rawlings, Dr. Philip Richman, Rodger Robinson, Nen Roeterdink, Ron Samuels, Evelyn Seeff, Jerry Silverstein, Bill Smith, June Spickett, Ruth and Steve Spratt, Rick Tutoni, Bob Ullman, Carol Veprek, Jay Watnick, and Jerry, Yaffa and Christopher Weitzman. And, of course, Stella, Russell and Lisa Harris.

A special note of gratitude to my editor, Anne Sweeney, and to Owen Laster and Dan Strone of the William Morris Agency.

The Films of Cary Grant

1. **THIS IS THE NIGHT** (Paramount, 1932). Cast: Lily Damita, Charles Ruggles, Roland Young, Thelma Todd, Cary Grant, Irving Bacon, Claire Dodd. Director: Frank Tuttle. Screenplay: Avery Hopwood, from *Pouche* by René Peter and Henri Falk. 78 minutes.

2. **SINNERS IN THE SUN** (Paramount, 1932). Cast: Carole Lombard, Chester Morris, Adrienne Ames, Alison Skipworth, Walter Byron, Reginald Barlow, Zita Moulton, Cary Grant, Luke Cosgrove, Ida Lewis. Director: Alexander Hall. Screenplay: Vincent Lawrence, Waldemar Young and Samuel Hoffenstein, from a story by Mildred Cram. 70 minutes.

3. **MERRILY WE GO TO HELL** (Paramount, 1932). Cast: Sylvia Sidney, Fredric March, Adrianne Allen, Skeets Gallagher, Florence Britton, Esther Howard, George Irving, Kent Taylor, Charles Coleman, Leonard Carey, Cary Grant. Director: Dorothy Arzner. Screenplay: Edwin Justus Mayer, from "I, Jerry, Take Thee, Joan" by Cleo Lucas. 78 minutes.

4. **THE DEVIL AND THE DEEP** (Paramount, 1932). Cast: Tallulah Bankhead, Gary Cooper, Charles Laughton, Cary Grant, Gordon Wescott, Paul Porcasi, Juliette Compton, Arthur Hoyt, Dorothy Christy. Director: Marion Gering. Screenplay: Benn Levy and Harry Hervey. 78 minutes.

5. **BLONDE VENUS** (Paramount, 1932). Cast: Marlene Dietrich, Herbert Marshall, Cary Grant, Dickie Moore, Gene Morgan, Rita LaRoy, Sidney Toler, Cecil Cunningham. Director: Josef von Sternberg. Screenplay: Jules Furthman and S. K. Lauren, from a story by Josef von Sternberg. 80 minutes.

6. **HOT SATURDAY** (Paramount, 1932). Cast: Nancy Carroll, Cary Grant, Randolph Scott, Edward Woods, Lillian Bond, William Collier, Sr., Jane Darwell, Rita LaRoy, Grady Sutton. Director: William A. Seiter. Screenplay: Seton I. Miller, Josephine Lovett and Joseph Moncure March, from the novel by Harvey Ferguson. 75 minutes.

7. **MADAME BUTTERFLY** (Paramount, 1932). Cast: Sylvia Sidney, Cary Grant, Charles Ruggles, Sandor Kallay, Irving Pichel, Helen Jerome Eddy, Edmund Breese, Sheila Terry. Director: Marion Gering. Screenplay: Josephine Lovett and Joseph Moncure March, from a story by John Luther Long and the play by David Belasco. 86 minutes.

8. **SHE DONE HIM WRONG** (Paramount, 1933). Cast: Mae West, Cary Grant, Gilbert Roland, Noah Beery, Rafaela Ottiano, David Landau, Rochelle Hudson, Owen Moore, Fuzzy Knight, Louise Beavers, Dewey Robinson, Grace LaRue. Director: Lowell Sherman. Screenplay: Harvey Theu and John Bright, from *Diamond Lil* by Mae West. 66 minutes.

9. **THE WOMAN ACCUSED** (Paramount, 1933). Cast: Nancy Carroll, Cary Grant, John Halliday, Irving Pichel, Louis Calhern, Norma Mitchell, Jack LaRue, Frank Sheridan, John Lodge, Lona Andre. Director: Paul Sloane. Screenplay: Bayard Veiller, from a *Liberty* magazine serial co-authored by Rupert Hughes, Vicki Baum, Zane Grey, Vina Delmar, Irvin S. Cobb, Gertrude Atherton, J. P. McEvoy, Ursula Parrott, Polen Banks and Sophie Kerr. 70 minutes.

10. **THE EAGLE AND THE HAWK** (Paramount, 1933). Cast: Fredric March, Cary Grant, Jack Oakie, Carole Lombard, Sir Guy Standing, Forrester Harvey, Virginia Hammond. Director: Stuart Walker. Screenplay: Bogart Rogers and Seton I. Miller, from a story by John Monk Saunders. 68 minutes.

11. **GAMBLING SHIP** (Paramount, 1933). Cast: Cary Grant, Benita Hume, Roscoe Karns, Glenda Farrell, Jack LaRue, Arthur Vinton, Edward Gargan, Evelyn Silvie. Directors: Louis Gasnier and Max Marcin. Screenplay: Max Marcin, Seton I. Miller and Claude Binyon, from stories by Peter Ruric. 67 minutes.

12. **I'M NO ANGEL** (Paramount, 1933). Cast: Mae West, Cary Grant, Edward Arnold, Rolf Harolds, Russell Hopton, Gertrude Michael, Kent Taylor, Dorothy Peterson, Gregory Ratoff, Gertrude Howard, Nat Pendleton. Director: Wesley Ruggles. Screenplay: Mae West, Harlan Thompson and Lowell Brentano. 87 minutes.

13. **ALICE IN WONDERLAND** (Paramount, 1933). Cast: Charlotte Henry, Richard Arlen, Roscoe Ates, Gary Cooper, Leon Errol, Louise Fazenda, W. C. Fields, Skeets Gallagher, Cary Grant, Sterling Holloway, Edward Everett Horton, Roscoe Karns, Baby LeRoy, Mae Marsh, Polly Moran, Jack Oakie, Edna May Oliver, May Robson, Charles Ruggles, Alison Skipworth, Ned Sparks. Director: Norman McLeod. Screenplay: Joseph L. Mankiewicz and William Cameron Menzies, from the writings of Lewis Carroll. 90 minutes.

14. **THIRTY-DAY PRINCESS** (Paramount, 1934). Cast: Sylvia Sidney, Cary Grant, Edward Arnold, Henry Stephenson, Vince Barnett, Edgar Norton, Lucien Littlefield. Producer: B. P. Schulberg. Director: Marion Gering. Screenplay: Preston Sturges, Frank Partos, Sam Hellman and Edwin Justus Mayer, from a story by Clarence Buddington Kelland. 75 minutes.

15. **BORN TO BE BAD** (United Artists, 1934). Cast: Loretta Young, Cary Grant, Jackie Kelk, Henry Travers, Russell Hopton, Andrew Tombes, Marion Burns, Paul Harvey. Producer: Twentieth Century Pictures. Director: Lowell Sherman. Screenplay: Ralph Graves and Harrison Jacobs. 61 minutes.

16. **KISS AND MAKE UP** (Paramount, 1934). Cast: Cary Grant, Helen Mack, Genevieve Tobin, Edward Everett Horton, Lucien Littlefield, Mona Maris, Toby Wing, Clara Lou (later Ann) Sheridan. Producer: B. P. Schulberg. Director: Harlan Thompson. Screenplay: Harlan Thompson, George Marion, Jr., and Jane Hinton, from a story by Stephen Bekeffi. 78 minutes.

17. **LADIES SHOULD LISTEN** (Paramount, 1934). Cast: Cary Grant, Frances Drake, Edward Everett Horton, Rosita Moreno, George Barbier, Nydia Westman, Charles Ray, Clara Lou (later Ann) Sheridan. Producer: Douglas MacLean. Director: Frank Tuttle. Screenplay: Claude Binyon and Frank Butler, from a play by Alfred Savoir and Guy Bolton. 61 minutes.

18. **ENTER MADAME** (Paramount, 1935). Cast: Elissa Landi, Cary Grant, Lynne Overman, Sharon Lynne, Michelette Burani, Paul Forcasi, Adrian Rosley, Cecelia Parker, Frank Albertson, Diana Lewis. Producer: Benjamin Glaser. Director: Elliott Nugent. Screenplay: Charles Brackett and Gladys Lehman, from a play by Gilda Varesi Archibald and Dorothea Donn-Byrne. 83 minutes.

19. **WINGS IN THE DARK** (Paramount, 1935). Cast: Myrna Loy, Cary Grant, Roscoe Karns, Hobart Cavanaugh, Dean Jagger, Samuel S. Hinds, Bert Hanlon, Graham McNamee. Producer: Arthur Hornblow, Jr. Director: James Flood. Screenplay: Jack Kirkland, Frank Partos, Dale Van Every and E. H. Robinson, from a story by Nell Shipman and Philip Hurn. 75 minutes.

20. **THE LAST OUTPOST** (Paramount, 1935). Cast: Cary Grant, Claude Rains, Gertrude Michael, Kathleen Burke, Colin Tapley, Akim Tamiroff, Billy Bevan, Margaret Swope. Producer: E. Lloyd Sheldon. Directors: Charles Barton and Louis Gasnier. Screenplay: Philip Mac-Donald, Frank Partos and Charles Brackett, from a story by F. Britten Austin. 70 minutes.

21. **SYLVIA SCARLETT** (RKO Radio, 1935). Cast: Katharine Hepburn, Cary Grant, Brian Aherne, Edmund Gwenn, Natalie Paley, Dennie Moore, Lennox Pawle. Producer: Pandro S. Berman. Director: George Cukor. Screenplay: Gladys Unger, John Collier and Mortimer Affner, from the novel by Compton Mackenzie. 97 minutes.

22. **BIG BROWN EYES** (Paramount, 1936). Cast: Cary Grant, Joan Bennett, Walter Pidgeon, Lloyd Nolan, Alan Baxter, Marjorie Gateson, Isabel Jewell, Douglas Fowley. Producer: Walter Wanger. Director: Raoul Walsh. Screenplay: Raoul Walsh and Bert Hanlon, from a story by James Edward Grant. 77 minutes.

23. **SUZY** (MGM, 1936). Cast: Jean Harlow, Franchot Tone, Cary Grant, Lewis Stone, Benita Hume, Reginald Mason, Inez Courtney, Una O'Connor. Producer: Maurice Revnes. Director: George Fitzmaurice. Screenplay: Dorothy Parker, Alan Campbell, Horace Jackson and Lenore Coffee, from a novel by Herbert Gorman. 99 minutes.

24. **WEDDING PRESENT** (Paramount, 1936). Cast: Joan Bennett, Cary Grant, George Bancroft, Conrad Nagel, Gene Lockhart, William Demarest, Inez Courtney, Edward Brophy, Lois Wilson. Producer: B. P.

Schulberg. Director: Richard Wallace. Screenplay: Joseph Anthony, from a story by Paul Gallico. 80 minutes.

25. **WHEN YOU'RE IN LOVE** (Columbia, 1937). Cast: Grace Moore, Cary Grant, Aline MacMahon, Henry Stephenson, Thomas Mitchell, Catherine Doucet, Luis Alberni, Emma Dunn, Frank Puglia. Associate producer: Everett Riskin. Director: Robert Riskin. Screenplay: Robert Riskin, from a story by Ethel Hill and Cedric Worth. 110 minutes.

26. **ROMANCE AND RICHES** (Grand National, 1937). Cast: Cary Grant, Mary Brian, Peter Gawthorne, Henry Kendall, Iris Ashley, Leon M. Lion, John Turnbull. Producer-Director: Alfred Zeisler. Screenplay: John L. Balderston, from a short story, "The Amazing Quest of Ernest Bliss" by E. Phillips Oppenheim. 70 minutes.

27. **TOPPER** (MGM, 1937). Cast: Constance Bennett, Cary Grant, Roland Young, Billie Burke, Alan Mowbray, Eugene Pallette, Arthur Lake, Hedda Hopper, Virginia Sale, Hoagy Carmichael. Producer: Hal Roach. Director: Norman Z. McLeod. Screenplay: Jack Jerne, Eric Hatch and Eddie Moran, from "The Jovial Ghosts" by Thorne Smith. 98 minutes.

28. **THE TOAST OF NEW YORK** (RKO Radio, 1937). Cast: Edward Arnold, Cary Grant, Frances Farmer, Jack Oakie, Donald Meek, Thelma Leeds, Clarence Kolb, Billy Gilbert, George Irving, Oscar Apfel, Dewey Robinson, Gavin Gordon, Joyce Compton. Producer: Edward Small. Director; Rowland V. Lee. Screenplay: Dudley Nichols, John Twist and Joel Sayre, from *Book of Daniel Drew* by Bouck White and *Robber Barons* by Matthew Josephson. 109 minutes.

29. **THE AWFUL TRUTH** (Columbia, 1937). Cast: Irene Dunne, Cary Grant, Ralph Bellamy, Alexander D'Arcy, Cecil Cunningham, Marguerite Churchill, Esther Dale, Joyce Compton, Mary Forbes, Zita Moulton, Bess Flowers. Producer-Director: Leo McCarey. Screenplay: Vina Delmar, from a story by Arthur Richmond. 89 minutes.

30. **BRINGING UP BABY** (RKO Radio, 1938). Cast: Katharine Hepburn, Cary Grant, Charles Ruggles, Walter Catlett, Barry Fitzgerald, May Robson, Fritz Feld, Leona Roberts, George Irving, Tala Birell. Producer-Director: Howard Hawks. Screenplay: Dudley Nichols and Hagar Wilde. 102 minutes.

31. **HOLIDAY** (Columbia, 1938). Cast: Katharine Hepburn, Cary Grant, Doris Nolan, Lew Ayres, Edward Everett Horton, Henry Kolker, Binnie

Barnes, Jean Dixon, Henry Daniell. Producer: Everett Riskin. Director: George Cukor. Screenplay: Donald Ogden Stewart and Sidney Buchman, from the play by Philip Barry. 93 minutes.

32. **GUNGA DIN** (RKO Radio, 1939). Cast: Cary Grant, Victor McLaglen, Douglas Fairbanks, Jr., Sam Jaffe, Eduardo Ciannelli, Joan Fontaine, Montague Love, Robert Coote, Abner Biberman, Lumsden Hare, Ann Evers. Producer-Director: George Stevens. Screenplay: Ben Hecht, Charles MacArthur, Joel Sayre and Fred Guiol, inspired by the poem by Rudyard Kipling. 117 minutes.

33. **ONLY ANGELS HAVE WINGS** (Columbia, 1939). Cast: Cary Grant, Jean Arthur, Richard Barthelmess, Rita Hayworth, Thomas Mitchell, Sig Ruman, Victor Kilian, John Carroll, Allyn Joslyn, Donald Barry, Noah Beery, Jr., Melissa Sierra. Producer-Director: Howard Hawks. Screenplay: Jules Furthman, from a story by Howard Hawks. 121 minutes.

34. **IN NAME ONLY** (RKO Radio, 1939). Cast: Carole Lombard, Cary Grant, Kay Francis, Charles Coburn, Helen Vinson, Katharine Alexander, Jonathan Hale, Nella Walker, Peggy Ann Garner. Producer: George Haight. Director: John Cromwell. Screenplay: Richard Sherman, from the novel, *Memory of Love* by Bessie Breuer. 94 minutes.

35. **HIS GIRL FRIDAY** (Columbia, 1940). Cast: Cary Grant, Rosalind Russell, Ralph Bellamy, Gene Lockhart, Porter Hall, Ernest Truex, Cliff Edwards, Clarence Kolb, Roscoe Karns, Frank Jenks, Regis Toomey, Abner Biberman, Frank Orth, John Qualen, Helen Mack, Alma Kruger, Billy Gilbert, Pat West. Producer-Director: Howard Hawks. Screenplay: Charles Lederer, from *The Front Page* by Ben Hecht and Charles MacArthur. 92 minutes.

36. **MY FAVORITE WIFE** (RKO Radio, 1940). Cast: Irene Dunne, Cary Grant, Randolph Scott, Gail Patrick, Ann Shoemaker, Scotty Beckett, Mary Lou Harrington, Donald MacBride, Pedro de Cordoba. Producer: Leo McCarey. Director: Garson Kanin. Screenplay: Sam and Bella Spewack, from *Enoch Arden* by Alfred Tennyson. 88 minutes.

37. **THE HOWARDS OF VIRGINIA** (Columbia, 1940). Cast: Cary Grant, Martha Scott, Sir Cedric Hardwicke, Alan Marshall, Richard Carlson, Paul Kelly, Irving Bacon, Elizabeth Risdon, Anne Revere, Richard Gaines, George Houston. Producer-Director: Frank Lloyd. Screenplay: Sidney Buchman, from *The Tree of Liberty* by Elizabeth Page. 122 minutes.

38. **THE PHILADELPHIA STORY** (MGM, 1940). Cast: Cary Grant, Katharine Hepburn, James Stewart, Ruth Hussey, John Howard, Roland Young, John Halliday, Mary Nash, Virginia Weidler, Henry Daniell. Producer: Joseph L. Mankiewicz. Director: George Cukor. Screenplay: Donald Ogden Stewart, from the play by Philip Barry. 112 minutes.

39. **PENNY SERENADE** (Columbia, 1941). Cast: Irene Dunne, Cary Grant, Beulah Bondi, Edgar Buchanan, Ann Doran, Leonard Wiley, Wallis Clark, Walter Soderling, Producer-Director: George Stevens. Screenplay: Morrie Ryskind, from a story by Martha Cheavens. 125 minutes.

40. **SUSPICION** (RKO Radio, 1941). Cast: Cary Grant, Joan Fontaine, Sir Cedric Hardwicke, Nigel Bruce, Dame May Whitty, Isabel Jeans, Heather Angel, Leo G. Carroll. Producer-Director: Alfred Hitchcock. Screenplay: Samson Raphaelson, Joan Harrison and Alma Reville, from *Before the Fact* by Francis Iles. 99 minutes.

41. **THE TALK OF THE TOWN** (Columbia, 1942). Cast: Cary Grant, Jean Arthur, Ronald Colman, Edgar Buchanan, Glenda Farrell, Charles Dingle, Emma Dunn, Rex Ingram, Leonid Kinskey, Tom Tyler, Lloyd Bridges. Producer-Director: George Stevens. Screenplay: Irwin Shaw and Sidney Buchman, from a story by Sidney Buchman. 118 minutes.

42. **ONCE UPON A HONEYMOON** (RKO Radio, 1942). Cast: Ginger Rogers, Cary Grant, Walter Slezak, Albert Dekker, Albert Bassermann, Ferike Boros, Harry Shannon, Natasha Lytess, John Banner, Hans Conreid. Producer-Director: Leo McCarey. Screenplay: Sheridan Gibney, from a story by Leo McCarey. 117 minutes.

43. **MR. LUCKY** (RKO Radio, 1943). Cast: Cary Grant, Laraine Day, Charles Bickford, Gladys Cooper, Alan Carney, Henry Stephenson, Paul Stewart, Kay Johnson, Florence Bates. Producer: David Hempstead. Director: H. C. Potter. Screenplay: Milton Holmes and Adrian Scott, from *Bundles for Freedom* by Milton Holmes. 100 minutes.

44. **DESTINATION TOKYO** (Warner Brothers, 1944). Cast: Cary Grant, John Garfield, Alan Hale, John Ridgely, Dane Clark, Warner Anderson, William Prince, Robert Hutton, Faye Emerson, John Forsythe, Whit Bissell. Producer: Jerry Wald. Director: Delmer Daves. Screenplay: Delmer Daves and Albert Maltz, from a story by Steve Fisher. 135 minutes.

45. **ONCE UPON A TIME** (Columbia, 1944). Cast: Cary Grant, Janet Blair, James Gleason, Ted Donaldson, Howard Freeman, William Demarest. Producer: Louis Edelman. Director: Alexander Hall. Screenplay: Lewis Meltzer, Oscar Saul and Irving Fineman, from the radio play, *My Client Curly* by Norman Corwin and Lucille Fletcher. 89 minutes.

46. **NONE BUT THE LONELY HEART** (RKO Radio, 1944). Cast: Cary Grant, Ethel Barrymore, Jane Wyatt, June Duprez, Barry Fitzgerald, George Coulouris, Roman Bohnen, Konstantin Shayne, Dan Duryea, Rosalind Ivan, Joseph Vitale. Producer: David Hempstead. Director: Clifford Odets. Screenplay: Clifford Odets, from the novel by Richard Llewellyn. 113 minutes.

47. **ARSENIC AND OLD LACE** (Warner Brothers, 1944). Cast: Cary Grant, Raymond Massey, Priscilla Lane, Josephine Hull, Jean Adair, Jack Carson, Edward Everett Horton, Peter Lorre, James Gleason, John Alexander, Grant Mitchell. Producer-Director: Frank Capra. Screenplay: Julius J. Epstein and Philip G. Epstein, from the play by Joseph Kesselring. 118 minutes.

48. **NIGHT AND DAY** (Warner Brothers, 1946). Cast: Cary Grant, Alexis Smith, Monty Woolley, Ginny Simms, Jane Wyman, Eve Arden, Victor Francen, Alan Hale, Dorothy Malone, Tom D'Andrea, Selena Royle, Donald Woods, Henry Stephenson, Paul Cavanagh, Sig Ruman, Carlos Ramirez. Producer: Arthur Schwartz. Director: Michael Curtiz. Screenplay: Charles Hoffman, Leo Townsend and William Bowers, based on the career of Cole Porter. Technicolor. 128 minutes.

49. **NOTORIOUS** (RKO Radio, 1946). Cast: Cary Grant, Ingrid Bergman, Claude Rains, Louis Calhern, Madame Konstantin, Reinhold Schunzel, Moroni Olsen, Ivan Triesault, Alex Minotis, Wally Brown, Gavin Gordon, Sir Charles Mendl, Antonio Moreno. Producer-Director: Alfred Hitchcock. Screenplay: Ben Hecht, from an idea by Alfred Hitchcock. 101 minutes.

50. **THE BACHELOR AND THE BOBBY-SOXER** (RKO Radio, 1947). Cast: Cary Grant, Myrna Loy, Shirley Temple, Rudy Vallee, Ray Collins, Harry Davenport, Johnny Sands, Don Beddoe, Lillian Randolph, Veda Ann Borg, Irving Bacon. Producer: Dore Schary. Director: Irving Reis. Screenplay: Sidney Sheldon. 95 minutes.

51. **THE BISHOP'S WIFE** (RKO Radio, 1947). Cast: Cary Grant, Loretta Young, David Niven, Monty Woolley, James Gleason, Gladys

Cooper, Elsa Lanchester, Sara Haden, Karolyn Grimes, Almira Sessions. Producer: Samuel Goldwyn. Director: Henry Koster. Screenplay: Robert E. Sherwood and Leonardo Bercovici, from a novel by Robert Nathan. 108 minutes.

52. **MR. BLANDINGS BUILDS HIS DREAM HOUSE** (RKO Radio, 1948). Cast: Cary Grant, Myrna Loy, Melvyn Douglas, Reginald Denny, Sharyn Moffett, Connie Marshall, Louise Beavers, Ian Wolfe, Lurene Tuttle, Lex Barker, Jason Robards, Sr., Nestor Paiva. Producers: Norman Panama and Melvin Frank, in association with Dore Schary and Selznick Releasing Organization. Director: H. C. Potter. Screenplay: Norman Panama and Melvin Frank, from the novel by Eric Hodgins. 94 minutes.

53. **EVERY GIRL SHOULD BE MARRIED** (RKO Radio, 1948). Cast: Cary Grant, Betsy Drake, Franchot Tone, Diana Lynn, Alan Mowbray, Elizabeth Risdon, Leon Belasco, Chick Chandler, Richard Gaines, Anna Q. Nilsson. Producer-Director: Don Hartman. Screenplay: Stephen Morehouse Avery, from a story by Eleanor Harris. 84 minutes.

54. **I WAS A MALE WAR BRIDE** (20th Century–Fox, 1949). Cast: Cary Grant, Ann Sheridan, William Neff, Eugene Gericke, Marion Marshall, Randy Stuart, Ken Tobey, Robert Stevenson, Barbara Perry, Andre Charlot, Ben Pollock, Russ Conway, Harry Lauter. Producer: Sol C. Siegel. Director: Howard Hawks. Screenplay: Charles Lederer, Leonard Spigelgass and Hagar Wilde, from a story by Henri Rochard. 105 minutes.

55. **CRISIS** (MGM, 1950). Cast: Cary Grant, Jose Ferrer, Paula Raymond, Signe Hasso, Ramon Novarro, Gilbert Roland, Leon Ames, Antonio Moreno, Teresa Celli. Producer: Arthur Freed. Director: Richard Brooks. Screenplay: Richard Brooks, from the short story "The Doubters" by George Tabori. 95 minutes.

56. **PEOPLE WILL TALK** (20th Century–Fox, 1951). Cast: Cary Grant, Jeanne Crain, Finlay Currie, Hume Cronyn, Walter Slezak, Sidney Blackmer, Basil Ruysdael, Katherine Locke, Will Wright, Margaret Hamilton. Producer: Darryl F. Zanuck. Director: Joseph L. Mankiewicz. Screenplay: Joseph L. Mankiewicz, from *Dr. Praetorius* by Curt Goetz. 109 minutes.

57. **ROOM FOR ONE MORE** (Warner Brothers, 1952). Cast: Cary Grant, Betsy Drake, Lurene Tuttle, Randy Stuart, John Ridgely, Irving Bacon, Mary Lou Treen, Hayden Rorke, Iris Mann, George Winslow, Clifford Tatum, Jr., Gay Gordon, Malcolm Cassell, Larry Olson. Pro-

ducer: Henry Blanke. Director: Norman Taurog. Screenplay: Jack Rose and Melville Shavelson, from a book by Anna Perrott Rose. 97 minutes.

58. **MONKEY BUSINESS** (20th Century–Fox, 1952). Cast: Cary Grant, Ginger Rogers, Charles Coburn, Marilyn Monroe, Hugh Marlowe, Henri Letondal, Larry Keating, Esther Dale, George Winslow. Producer: Sol C. Siegel. Director: Howard Hawks. Screenplay: Ben Hecht, I. A. L. Diamond and Charles Lederer, from a story by Harry Segall. 97 minutes.

59. **DREAM WIFE** (MGM, 1953). Cast: Cary Grant, Deborah Kerr, Walter Pidgeon, Betta St. John, Eduard Franz, Buddy Baer, Les Tremayne, Donald Randolph, Bruce Bennett, Richard Anderson, Movita, Gloria Holden. Producer; Dore Schary. Director: Sidney Sheldon. Screenplay: Sidney Sheldon, Herbert Baker and Alfred Levitt, from a story by Alfred Levitt. 98 minutes.

60. **TO CATCH A THIEF** (Paramount, 1955). Cast: Cary Grant, Grace Kelly, Jessie Royce Landis, John Williams, Charles Vanel, Brigitte Auber, Jean Martinelli, Georgette Anys. Producer-Director: Alfred Hitchcock. Screenplay: John Michael Hayes, from a novel by David Dodge. In VistaVision and Technicolor. 103 minutes.

61. **THE PRIDE AND THE PASSION** (United Artists, 1957). Cast: Cary Grant, Frank Sinatra, Sophia Loren, Theodore Bikel, John Wengraf, Jay Novello, Jose Nieto, Carlos Larranaga, Philip Van Zandt. Producer-Director: Stanley Kramer. Screenplay: Edna and Edward Anhalt, from the novelette, *The Gun* by C. S. Forester. In VistaVision and Technicolor. 130 minutes.

62. **AN AFFAIR TO REMEMBER** (20th Century–Fox, 1957). Cast: Cary Grant, Deborah Kerr, Richard Denning, Neva Patterson, Cathleen Nesbitt, Robert Q. Lewis, Charles Watts, Fortunio Bonanova, Matt Moore, Louis Mercier. Producer: Jerry Wald. Director: Leo McCarey. Screenplay: Delmer Daves and Leo McCarey (updated version of the 1939 film, *Love Affair*). In CinemaScope and DeLuxe Color. 114 minutes.

63. **KISS THEM FOR ME** (20th Century–Fox, 1957). Cast: Cary Grant, Jayne Mansfield, Suzy Parker, Leif Erickson, Ray Walston, Larry Blyden, Nathaniel Frey, Werner Klemperer, Jack Mullaney, Harry Carey, Jr., Frank Nelson. Producer: Jerry Wald. Director: Stanley Donen. Screenplay: Julius Epstein, from the play by Luther Davis and *Shore Leave* by Frederic Wakeman. In CinemaScope and DeLuxe Color. 103 minutes.

64. **INDISCREET** (Warner Brothers, 1958). Cast: Cary Grant, Ingrid Bergman, Cecil Parker, Phyllis Calvert, David Kossoff, Megs Jenkins, Oliver Johnston, Middleton Woods. Producer-Director: Stanley Donen. Screenplay: Norman Krasna, from his play *Kind Sir.* Technicolor. 100 minutes.

65. **HOUSEBOAT** (Paramount, 1958). Cast: Cary Grant, Sophia Loren, Martha Hyer, Harry Guardino, Eduardo Ciannelli, Murray Hamilton, Mimi Gibson, Paul Petersen, Charles Herbert, Madge Kennedy, John Litel, Werner Klemperer, Kathleen Freeman. Producer: Jack Rose. Director: Melville Shavelson. Screenplay: Melville Shavelson and Jack Rose, from an idea by Betsy Drake. In VistaVision and Technicolor. 112 minutes.

66. **NORTH BY NORTHWEST** (MGM, 1959). Cast: Cary Grant, Eva Marie Saint, James Mason, Jessie Royce Landis, Leo G. Carroll, Philip Ober, Josephine Hutchinson, Martin Landau, Adam Williams, Edward Platt, Madge Kennedy, Carleton Young, Les Tremayne, Patrick McVey. Producer-Director: Alfred Hitchcock. Screenplay: Ernest Lehman. In VistaVision and Technicolor. 136 minutes.

67. **OPERATION PETTICOAT** (Universal-International, 1959). Cast: Cary Grant, Tony Curtis, Joan O'Brien, Dina Merrill, Gene Evans, Arthur O'Connell, Richard Sargent, Virginia Gregg, Robert F. Simon, Madlyn Rhue, Frankie Darro, Nicky Blair. Producer: Robert Arthur. Director: Blake Edwards. Screenplay: Stanley Shapiro and Maurice Richlin, from a story by Paul King and Joseph Stone. Eastman Color. 124 minutes.

68. **THE GRASS IS GREENER** (Universal-International, 1960). Cast: Cary Grant, Deborah Kerr, Robert Mitchum, Jean Simmons, Moray Watson. Producer-Director: Stanley Donen. Screenplay: Hugh and Margaret Williams, from their play of the same title. In Technirama and Technicolor. 105 minutes.

69. **THAT TOUCH OF MINK** (Universal-International, 1962). Cast: Cary Grant, Doris Day, Gig Young, Audrey Meadows, Alan Hewitt, John Astin, Richard Sargent, Joey Faye, Mickey Mantle, Roger Maris, Yogi Berra. Executive Producer: Robert Arthur. Producers: Stanley Shapiro and Martin Melcher. Director; Delbert Mann. Screenplay: Stanley Shapiro and Nate Monaster. In Panavision and Eastman Color. 99 minutes.

70. **CHARADE** (Universal-International, 1963). Cast: Cary Grant, Audrey Hepburn, Walter Matthau, James Coburn, George Kennedy, Ned

Glass, Jacques Marin, Paul Bonifas, Dominique Minot, Thomas Chelimsky. Producer-Director: Stanley Donen. Screenplay: Peter Stone, from the short story, "The Unsuspecting Wife" by Peter Stone and Marc Behm. Technicolor. 113 minutes.

71. **FATHER GOOSE** (Universal-International, 1964). Cast: Cary Grant, Leslie Caron, Trevor Howard, Jack Good, Verina Greenlaw, Pip Sparke, Jennifer Berrington, Stephanie Berrington, Lourelle Felsette, Nicole Felsette, Sharyl Locke, John Napier, Richard Lupino. Producer: Robert Arthur. Director: Ralph Nelson. Screenplay: Peter Stone and Frank Tarloff, from a story by S. H. Barnett. Technicolor. 115 minutes.

72. **WALK, DON'T RUN** (Columbia, 1966). Cast: Cary Grant, Samantha Eggar, Jim Hutton, John Standing, Miiko Taka, Ted Hartley, Ben Astar. Producer: Sol C. Siegel. Director: Charles Walters. Screenplay: Sol Saks, from a story by Robert Russell and Frank Ross (updated version of the 1943 film, *The More the Merrier*). In Panavision and Technicolor. 114 minutes.

(*Note:* Films 1 through 47, and 49 through 59 were made in black and white.)

Index